Gender, Society & Development

**Gender perspectives on property and inheritance
A global source book**

Gender, Society & Development

Gender perspectives on property and inheritance

A global source book

CRITICAL REVIEWS AND ANNOTATED

BIBLIOGRAPHIES SERIES

KIT (Royal Tropical Institute), The Netherlands

Oxfam GB

KIT (Royal Tropical Institute)
KIT Publishers
P.O. Box 95001
1090 HA AMSTERDAM
The Netherlands
E-mail: publishers@kit.nl
Website: www.kit.nl

Oxfam Publishing
274 Banbury Road
Oxford OX2 7DZ
United Kingdom
Telephone: +44 (0) 1865 311 311
Telefax: +44 (0) 1865 312 600
E-mail: publish@oxfam.org.uk
Website: www.oxfam.org.uk

© 2001 KIT Publishers (Royal Tropical Institute),
Amsterdam
First published by KIT Publishers and Oxfam GB 2001
Editors: Sarah Cummings, Henk van Dam, Angela
Khadar and Minke Valk
Information Services (IS) Department,
KIT (Royal Tropical Institute)
NUGI: 661

Design: Grafisch Ontwerpbureau Agaatsz BNO,
Meppel/ Nadamo Bos, Driebergen
Cover: Ad van Helmond, Amsterdam
Printing: Giethoorn Ten Brink, Meppel
ISBN 90 6832 714 3 (KIT Publishers edition) available
in the EU excluding UK and Ireland
ISBN 0 85598 461 9 (Oxfam GB edition) available in the
rest of the world
Printed and bound in The Netherlands

Gender perspectives on property and inheritance. A global source book
has been developed by KIT (Royal Tropical Institute) in The Netherlands. It is co-published with Oxfam GB to increase dissemination. KIT Publishers and the authors are responsible for its content.

Oxfam GB is a registered charity no. 202918, and is a member of Oxfam International.

Other titles in the *Gender, Society & Development* series:
- *Advancing women's status: women and men together?*
  M. de Bruyn (ed.)
- *Gender training. The source book.*
  S. Cummings, H. van Dam and M. Valk (eds.)
- *Women's information services and networks. A global source book.*
  S. Cummings, H. van Dam and M. Valk (eds.)
- *Institutionalizing gender equality. Commitment, policy and practice. A global source book.*
  H. van Dam, A. Khadar and M. Valk (eds.)

Contents

Acknowledgements   7

Preface   9

Acronyms   11

Introduction: women and property, women as property   13
Maitrayee Mukhopadhyay

1 Disjuncture in law and practice: women's inheritance of land in Latin America 19
Carmen Diana Deere and Magdalena León

2 Changing the meaning of marriage: women and family law in Côte d'Ivoire   33
Jeanne Maddox Toungara

**3 Family laws and gender discrimination: advocacy for legal reforms in the
Arab region**   51
Lina Abou-Habib

4 Women, tenure and land reform: the case of Namaqualand's Reserves   57
Fiona Archer and Shamim Meer

**5 Does land ownership make a difference? Women's roles in agriculture in Kerala,
India**   69
Shoba Arun

Annotated bibliography   79
Guide to the bibliography   80
Annotated bibliography   81
Author index   131
Geographical index   133

Web resources   135

About the authors   139

Acknowledgements

A major objective of this publication was to document various perspectives from the South with respect to gender, property rights and inheritance. The editorial team is delighted that it has been possible to realize this objective, and we would like to thank the authors for their important contribution to this book. It was a pleasure and privilege to be able to work with them. Special thanks go to Maitrayee Mukhopadhyay for the stimulating role she played in the conception of this book. We would also like to thank our colleagues in Information Services and KIT publishers for their valuable assistance.

Acknowledgements

Preface

The need for equality of inheritance rights between men and women is increasingly being recognized. In particular, the inequality in inheritance rights to land needs to be addressed. It has long been understood that control of the means of production is a source of economic and political power. Where men retain such control by exclusion of women from inheritance, inequitable inheritance rights perpetuate inequitable economic and political power within communities. This is particularly so in agricultural and rural communities, in which land furnishes the principal means of production.

Inheritance is, however, not the only issue: women who own land may still lack control over it. In most societies, women till the land and at the same time are the important caretakers of their households. Despite this, they usually lack control over resources such as land, cattle and housing. Matrilineal inheritance practices, which may offer women better access to resources, are slowly disappearing. Then, women's ownership of land and resources depends on testamentary inheritance, since customary succession in the absence of a last will and testament favours male succession, and is generally denied to women, whether widows, sisters or daughters.

Women's labour is characterized with a negative status, since their paid employment is often in menial tasks or devalued, and their work in the home is unpaid and often classified in economic reports as unemployment. Where social status and authority are determined by control of economic resources, women's exclusion from the economy renders them powerless. A person's status is often determined by the person's estate, the words 'status' and 'estate' having common linguistic origins. Men's larger control over wealth-generating property constitutes male authority. Women and girls are disadvantaged by customs that grant economic power to men. Even when constitutions enshrine women's equal rights, women's enjoyment of rights remains inferior to men's. The advance of social and economic equality requires that male and female children inherit land and other resources equally from their parents.

This book addresses women's unequal position in formal and customary laws. Many democratic countries have laws favourable to formal equality, but they are often unenforced in the absence of strong egalitarian institutions that penetrate down to the village level. In particular, rural and poor women have limited means of access to legal systems to challenge and end inequalities. Illiteracy and isolation may exclude women from practical enforcement of rights available to them in theory, and traditional attitudes of patriarchal society, which may be shared by male judges who see themselves as protectors of social tradition and stability, may hamper women's progress. Male village leaders may be ill informed on the law and official procedures that require women's equality, and they therefore maintain conventional or traditional resolutions of local disputes, unselfconscious of their self-interest in maintaining discriminatory practices against women, particularly when they are poor and vulnerable.

The 1995 Beijing Conference on Women helped focus attention on the inequity of discrimination against women with regard to land rights in general and inheritance rights in particular. Gender and human rights discourses are often viewed and treated as if they relate to completely different aspects of human interaction. Human rights issues are regarded as located in the arena where the interests of the state are in competition against those of the individual: the powerful against the powerless. Gender issues are regarded as located in the arena of sexual competition: the male versus the female. However, an analysis of gender interactions reveals the human rights competition between the powerful against the powerless. Inequitable power relationships perpetuate the stereotypical division of labour, where men's labour is valued and rewarded and women's labour is devalued or ignored, and maintain women's dependency and vulnerability. The inequity derives from and perpetuates unequal access to and control of resources, favouring men over women.

In this book, five reviews from Latin America, Côte d'Ivoire, South Africa, the Middle East and India focus on the contrast between the written law of equality, and discrimination in practice regarding women's property and land rights, inheritance, access to resources, marriage and employment. The papers show how important it is to the remedy of inequity that women should participate in decision-making forums and collaborate in or create political organizations for women's mobilization to redress gender discrimination regarding land and inheritance rights. Women's prospects of advancement of their fair interests can be promoted through women's activism and representation at all levels of decision-making, from community structures to international organizations and committees. Legal solutions in themselves will remain insufficient to remedy women's lack of access to jobs, land and authority.

The Universal Declaration of Human Rights, adopted by the UN General Assembly in 1948, specifically included sex as a prohibited ground of discrimination. Now, more than 50 years later, it is important to review the achievements toward sexual non-discrimination and consider what has yet to be done. The views and experiences collected in this book from different regions of the world, and the supporting detailed bibliography, offer perspectives on what has been achieved, and means to determine the urgent goals of women's equality, particularly concerning land and inheritance rights, that have still to be accomplished.

Rebecca J. Cook
Professor of Law, University of Toronto, Canada
August 2001

gender perspectives

Acronyms

AFI	Association des Femmes Ivoiriennes
AFLA	Africa Legal Aid
AFRA	Association for Rural Advancement, South Africa
AI	Amnesty International
AIDS	Acquired immune deficiency syndrome
APWLD	Asia Pacific Forum on Women, Law and Development
ANC	African National Congress
ATRCW	African Training Research Centre for Women
AVANCSO	Asociación para el Avance de las Ciencias Sociales en Guatemala
AWC	Arab Women Court
CALS	Centre for Applied Legal Studies, South Africa
CAP	Women's Commission of the Permanent Agrarian Council, Mexico
CBNRM	Community-based natural resources management
CCR	Centre for Conflict Research
CDR	Centre for Development Research, Denmark
CEDAW	Convention on the Elimination of All Forms of Discrimination Against Women
CGE	Commission on Gender Equality, South Africa
CNC	National Peasant Commission, Chile / Comisión Nacional Campesina, Chile
CNWS	Centre for Non-Western Studies, Netherlands
COHRE	Centre on Housing Rights and Evictions, Switzerland
CONTAG	Confederação Nacional dos Trabalhadores na Agricultura
CPA	Communal property association
CSD	(United Nations) Commission on Sustainable Development
CTA	Technical Centre for Agricultural and Rural Co-operation, Netherlands
ECA	(United Nations) Economic Commission for Africa
EZLN	Ejército Zapatista de Liberación Nacional
FAO	Food and Agriculture Organization
GDN	Global Development Network
GESP	Gender Equity Support Programme
GOK	Government of Kerala, India
GOU	Government of Uganda
GTZ	German Technical Co-operation
IDRC	International Development Research Centre, Canada
IFPRI	International Food Policy Research Institute
INTWORLSA	International Third World Legal Studies Association, USA
IPS	Inter Press Service
IRIN	Integrated Regional Information Network
IWRAW	International Women's Rights Action Watch

LACC	Legal Aid & Consultancy Centre, Nepal
LPN	Land Policy Network
MST	Movimento Sem Terra
NaSA	Nachrichtenstelle Südliches Afrika
NGO	Non-governmental organization
NLC	National Land Committee, South Africa
NWJC	National Women's Justice Coalition
NWF	Namaqualand Women's Forum
ODI	Overseas Development Institute, UK
PDCI	Partie Démocratique de Côte d'Ivoire
RDP	Reconstruction and Development Programme, South Africa
SAPES	Southern Africa Political Economy Series (Trust)
SARIPS	Southern African Regional Institute for Policy Studies
SDF	Social Development Foundation
SIGI	Sisterhood is Global Institute, USA
SIS	Sisters in Islam
SPP	Surplus People Project
THP	The Hunger Project, USA
TRAC	Transvaal Rural Action Committee
UN	United Nations
UNCHS	United Nations Centre for Human Settlements (Habitat), Kenya
UNESCO	United Nations Educational, Scientific and Cultural Organisation
UNICEF	United Nations Children's Fund
UNIFEM	United Nations Fund for Women
UNRISD	United Nations Research Institute for Social Development
URNG	Unidad Revolucionaria Nacional Guatemalteca
WCL	Washington College of Law
WEP	World Employment Programme
WILL	Women in Legislation League
WLEA-K	Women and Law in East Africa-Kenya
WLSA	Women and Law in Southern Africa

gender perspectives

Maitrayee Mukhopadhyay

Introduction: women and property, women as property[1]

Gender activism and the question of property

The first United Nations International Conference on Women (Mexico, 1975) and the declaration of the International Decade for Women, with the official themes of equality, development and peace, inaugurated three decades of greater visibility for the question of gender equality. Equality between the sexes has in the process been articulated as a development issue and as a human rights issue. Despite the many contestations in the international arena as to how best policy and programmes should address and aim to reduce gender inequality in development, the issue itself has remained firmly on the agenda.

Debates regarding gender equality have gained vitality in the last three decades through the three world conferences on women (Mexico, 1975; Nairobi, 1985; and Beijing 1995) and due to the international women's movements that have found ways of exploiting political spaces to get progressive policies onto the international agenda. This has entailed working through relevant international conventions (for example, the Convention on the Elimination of All Forms of Discrimination against Women – CEDAW) and pushing through resolutions in international forums (for example, the International Conference on Population and Development and the Beijing Women's Conference). It has enabled women's organizations and NGOs working in development to use the language of human rights to advocate for policies. Given this track record, it is difficult to comprehend why there has been such muted advocacy on behalf of women's right to hold and control property in their own right and not merely as wives, sisters, daughters or widows, or in other words, mediated by relationships with men (Mukhopadhyay, 1998).

Ownership and control over property signifies command over productive resources, which enables individuals to make choices regarding livelihoods, provides security against poverty and promotes autonomy. However, one of the most intractable issues in the debates over and programmes for gender equality has remained the unequal access and control that women as compared to men have over productive resources, especially property.

It is important to highlight that in most societies today it is men as a *gender* who largely control wealth-generating property, whether or not it is privately owned, including as managers in large corporations. Even property that is under state, community or clan ownership remains for the most part under the managerial control of selected men through their dominance in both traditional and modern institutions. Also, in most societies, it is men by and large who control the instruments through which property is regulated, such as the institutions that enact and implement laws and play an important role in shaping gender ideologies (Agarwal, 1994). Property relations above all signify authority relations, and men's larger control over wealth-generating property reproduces male authority. It is important to highlight this point as otherwise women's disadvantaged property rights can easily be rendered as a problem of underdevelopment, or as a characteristic of 'traditional societies' caught between custom/usage/tradition and modern state laws, which then draws attention away from the conceptual link between property and gender relations.

Women and men acquire property through inheritance, through marriage settlements and via public policies of redistribution. The option of acquiring property by buying it is not one that is open to most women because it would entail command over resources to be exchanged for the acquisition of other resources. Thus, for most women it is via social relations that first and foremost property is accessed.

The acquisition of property through redistributive public policies does not have the same effects for women and men. Let us take the issue of land rights. In many parts of the developing world, land has been and continues to be the most significant form of property in rural areas. Agriculture is still the most important source of livelihoods, and the ownership of land is the single most important source of security against poverty. It remains for many people a critical determinant of economic wellbeing, social status and political power. There is also evidence to suggest that economic resources under the control of male heads of households do not necessarily translate into wellbeing for women and children. Thus, independent ownership of such resources by women, especially land, can be critical in promoting the wellbeing of the family and the empowerment of women. And yet action by states to redress the class, caste and race imbalances in the control over land has rarely addressed the issue of gender imbalances. Thus land reforms in India and South Africa initiated by the state have virtually kept women out of the reckoning, and it is only through recent struggles to introduce a gender perspective in land redistribution that the issue of female control over land has been admitted in public policy forums (Agarwal, 1994; Meer, 1997). The contemporary political struggle that has erupted in Zimbabwe, for example, over the issue of land rights seeks to render the issue of confiscation of land from white farmers and its distribution to black farmers as a social justice issue and one that will right historical wrongs. No mention is made in this framework of women farmer's rights to land because the assumption is that women are part of families and that they will automatically gain from this redistribution.

Public policy and the female subject

In exploring why public policy has been so muted as regards equal property rights, it is necessary to examine the way in which gender relations, the role of the family/household, and the gender distribution of resources, has been construed in development discourse.

Economic theory and development policy has for long construed the household as a unit of congruent interests, an institution whose members share resources equitably irrespective of gender. In this framework, household members use scarce resources jointly and make joint decisions to allocate labour equitably in order to maximize family welfare goals. In practice, however, and through painstaking research into intrahousehold distribution patterns, it has been found that inequalities in the household, as for example between female and male children, reflected conflicting preferences and differential decision-making power between women and men (Kabeer,

gender perspectives

1994). The differential decision-making power arises from women's subordinate position within gender relations and their lack of effective command over resources and authority. Despite the empirical evidence to the contrary, the ideal of the unitary household has been very influential and a widely shared assumption among a whole range of development actors – governments, non-governmental groups, institutions and individuals. This has meant that women's economic needs are constantly elided with those of men and the family. Development planning to meet women's economic needs has typically been in the form of providing income-generating activities rather than on ensuring, for example, rights to land and other productive assets.

The elision of women's interests with that of the family/household and kinship and, therefore, the division of gender-specific interests that this elision obscures, is not specific only to liberal economic theory and development policy, it is pervasive as well in the language of rights. The discourse of rights assumes that we all possess a human core that comes prior to being of a particular gender, class, caste, community and race. Legal personhood is conferred on the basis of the 'human' core. The human subject thus produced, who is the bearer of rights, is then seen as the citizen-subject. What this conceptualization of the citizen-subject (the bearer of rights) does is, first, mask which kind of 'beings' in a given society are being taken as the norm for the definition of rights and thus which kind of persons are being excluded. Second, it assumes that everyone, irrespective of their gender, class and caste positioning has the same 'ability' to make claims (Tharu and Niranjana, 1994). With regard to property rights, this discourse of rights tends to treat property ownership as a relationship between people and things. However, if we take a closer look at the way in which property is accessed and controlled by gender, we find that property relations signify a relationship between people and people and that the relationship defines the ability or inability of persons to make claims (Whitehead, 1984).

This is best illustrated through empirical examples. In this present collection of essays, Jeanne Maddox Toungara interrogates the making of the 1964 family code in Côte d'Ivoire, which enshrined the role of the 'nuclear' family as the cornerstone of the edifice of the modern nation-state. She looks at the impact of these laws on women (whom these family laws were supposed to protect), women's activism to change the laws and finally the 1983 amendments to the family code. The 1964 family code sought to unite all Ivorians under one legal system and thereby diminish the importance and influence of the customary laws and Islamic law. The family code was to establish one idea of the family, i.e. the nuclear family, so as to eliminate the power of extended families to determine the future of women and girls. In other words, the 1964 family code was designed to achieve social change, especially in the status of women. However, as Toungara shows, the changed family laws did not have the desired effect of improving women's social position and not only because most women continued to operate under the customary laws, remaining, therefore, outside the ambit of the state sponsored family code. The nuclear family that the state sought to legislate into being was built on a very *specific notion of gender relations* within families. The husband remained the undisputed head of household, in charge of the community of property while both spouses were supposed to contribute to the household. In other words, this meant that women's dependent status was transferred from her lineage to that of her husband. A man's rights as husband and undisputed head of household to hold and control property became the '*norm*' on which the new rights were constructed. Inevitably, a wife's claims had less legitimacy than that of husbands.

Property and personhood

In my own research on Indian women's experiences of litigation in support of their rights to property under the personal laws, I found that laws regarding inheritance articulate notions of personhood constituted by forms of familial and kinship relations. This serves to hierarchize male claims to ancestral property over those of women's claims (Mukhopadhyay, 1998). A further empirical example will suffice to illustrate what I am saying. In India, personal law is that body of laws that in many other countries are referred to as family laws. Personal law has two salient features. First, it seeks to control and regulate social relations in the 'private' sphere of the family. Since it regulates marriage, divorce, guardianship of children and inheritance, it concerns women intimately. Second, personal law is specific to and separate for particular religious communities, namely, Hindu, Muslim, Christian and Parsi. Unlike in the case of other countries where customary law is adjudicated by traditional leaders, the personal laws in India are adjudicated in civil courts just like any other laws.

The Hindu Succession Act, 1956, gave women (Hindu women) the right to hold property as absolute owners and the status of co-heirs with brothers in the father's property, and made a daughter's share of inheritance equal to that of sons. It goes without saying that the Act did not give women the same share as their male kin in all kinds of property, but that is a different story and is a straightforward story of male bias. What I want to put forward is how the stated neutrality of the law regarding property and inheritance, where women and men are supposed to be equal, takes men's position in social relations as the norm on which women's claims are then judged.

One of the clauses of the Hindu Succession Act, 1956, states that when inherited property has to be divided between the heirs (brother, sister, wife/husband), a woman who is a sister cannot initiate partition of the property if there is a dwelling house on it. She will get an equal share of this property when the brothers ask for partition and she can ask for shelter in the dwelling house but she cannot initiate partition. What could be the rationale behind this and what effects does this have on real lives? The rationale behind this clause is that the partition of property, especially a house, threatens the break-up of the Hindu joint family of which men are the natural members. Women are not seen to be members of the natal family since they will inevitably get married and belong to another family and thus not be concerned about the welfare of their natal families.

I examined women-initiated litigation to demand a share of inherited property. I found that in large cities like Calcutta (in eastern India), women had brought these cases against their brothers at a point in their lives when all other resources were beyond their reach. Most of these women had little education, no jobs, were divorced and responsible for their children. The share of property they were claiming constituted a resource that could save them from poverty and dependence. The land, which constituted the property, was purchased by these women's fathers at a time when it was cheap. With the urban growth in the last two decades land in large cities has become very expensive. In most cases, the fathers had not been able to build a proper house on the land. The sons had sometimes continued to occupy the temporary houses that were built by their fathers, which in every case constitutes a very small part of the property. However, by declaring this property as one on which there is a dwelling house for the joint Hindu family (meaning brothers), men are able to fend

gender perspectives

off claims in court made by sisters. And there is everything to be gained by this construction of the Hindu joint family (which in reality does not exist). Land is so expensive that if the brothers can fend off the sisters' claims, they can then sell the land at high prices to property developers, thus excluding women. In the courts, the state subordinates the claim of women to that of their male kin by articulating notions of personhood constituted by forms of familial and kinship relations (women as strangers to the Hindu joint family and men as the 'natural' heirs of the family).

Dilemmas of gender activism

Women's activism, as I have stated earlier, has been muted as regards equal property rights for women and men. One of the reasons may be that it has been argued in the framework of liberal rights, which does not accommodate differences of positioning within social relations. It also does not provide a way out of the debates regarding the advantage and disadvantages of unified legal systems as opposed to legal pluralism that exist in most countries that were de-colonized in the twentieth century.

Activist demands for equality regarding property rights has been in many situations trapped in debates about legal systems. For example, in South Asia and especially in India (but also in Bangladesh) the discussion has been about scrapping the personal laws of religious communities (which govern family property and inheritance) in favour of a uniform civil code for all citizens, on the grounds that the maintenance of the personal laws does not give the same rights to all women as citizens. The inherent problem with this argument and activism is that uniformity of laws does not necessarily guarantee gender equality. In order to achieve gender equality in access to and control over property, especially family property, it has to be argued from the point of view of women's interests and not that of citizens or the family.

The ways forward

The ways forward to establish women as independent owners and controllers of property are complex, and diverse strategies are required, many of which are being deployed in different parts of the world.

Linking movements – Within the fold of the gender and development movement worldwide and locally there exist diverse concerns relating to gender equality. The common denominator of these movements is the establishment of gender equality as a basis for sustainable development. It is through the mobilization and linking of movements for gender equality that women's needs for and rights to property can be placed in the arena of public debate. As Deere and León suggest in their article in this book on women's inheritance rights in Latin America, the post-Beijing conference held in Peru became for diverse groups fighting for gender equality the forum for tabling their concerns. This forum has been successfully used by peasant women leaders to advocate for equal inheritance rights and to mobilize others to raise this demand. In this way the demand for equality of inheritance rights among men and women is beginning to enter the public discourse.

Bargaining with the state – Since in most situations the laws regarding property are gender inequitable, legal reforms remain an arena of struggle. However, bargaining with the state regarding equal property rights is not just a matter of legal struggles

introduction

17

but requires a multi-pronged strategy to establish women as independent beings requiring public policy initiatives. As Archer and Meer demonstrate in their article on land reform in South Africa, bargaining with the state requires the political organization and mobilization of women farmers, establishing women as a constituency in decision-making forums where demands on public policy can be made.

Increasing women's participation in decision-making forums – Whereas the mere presence of women in decision-making forums does not lead to gender-responsive programmes, there is enough empirical evidence to suggest that the presence of women in public decision-making forums alters the interests and concerns of such forums. The relative absence of women as compared to men in such forums has meant that not only are women's interests not adequately reflected in decisions but that development concerns and decisions raised are of a partial nature, from the perspective of men, and often elite men. The exercise of public power by a subordinated gender expands the political space within the private sphere of the household to bargain for gender equity.

Notes

1   The title is borrowed from Hirschon, R. (ed.), Women and Property: Women as Property (1984), which remains in my view the most remarkable collection of essays illuminating the connection between gender relations and property rights.

References

Agarwal, B., *A field of one's own: gender and land rights in south Asia*. Cambridge, Cambridge University Press, 1994.

Kabeer, N., *Reversed realities: gender hierarchies in development thought*. London, Verso, 1994.

Meer, S. (ed.), *Women, land and authority: perspectives from South Africa*. Oxford, Oxfam, 1997.

Mukhopadhyay, M., *Legally dispossessed: gender, identity and the process of law*. Calcutta, Stree, 1998.

Tharu, S. and T. Nirnajaana, 'Problems of a contemporary theory of gender'. *Social Scientist*, no. 250 and no. 251 (March-April 1994), p. 93-117.

Whitehead, A., 'Women and men, kinship and property: some general issues'. In: R. Hirschon (ed.), *Women and property: women as property*. London, Croom Helm, 1984.

Carmen Diana Deere and Magdalena León[1]

1 A disjuncture in law and practice: women's inheritance of land in Latin America

One of the striking aspects of Latin America compared to many other regions of the world is the legal tradition inherited from Iberian colonial rule whereby all legitimate children, irrespective of sex, inherit equally from both of their parents. This is still the default rule should the deceased die intestate in the 12 countries of Latin America reviewed here. The situation is more heterogeneous with respect to testamentary freedom. Four countries – Costa Rica, El Salvador, Guatemala and Mexico – allow full testamentary freedom, and two – Honduras and Nicaragua – allow near-testamentary freedom. The remaining six, all South American countries (Bolivia, Brazil, Chile, Colombia, Ecuador, Peru) place limits on the share of a person's estate that may be freely willed, in all cases requiring children of either sex to be forced heirs. The situation with respect to the inheritance rights of spouses is even more varied, but in general widows are in a less favourable position than are children.

Another striking aspect of Latin America is that the foundational myths of a number of the major pre-Columbian civilizations (the Incan and Mayan, particularly) were based on the notion of the complementarity of men and women. Complementarity has been associated by some with relatively gender egalitarian traditions and customs as well as bilateral or parallel inheritance systems. Bilateral inheritance is characterized by children inheriting from both parents; it thus assumes that women own and inherit property that they can pass on to their children. Parallel inheritance refers to sons inheriting through the male, and daughters through the female line. With such favourable norms, one might expect the distribution of land between men and women to be relatively equitable. Yet one of the salient features of Latin America today is that most land is owned by men, suggesting the discord that exists between women's legal inheritance rights and local practices (Deere and León, 2001).

Gender inequality in the inheritance of land in Latin America has been associated with a number of factors, among the most important being patrilineality, patrilocality (the residence of a young couple in the paternal home of the groom) or virilocality (residence on lands provided through the male line)[2] and what may be called the logic of peasant household reproduction. In peasant societies, inheritance of land is a fundamental condition of peasant household reproduction, for access to land is what guarantees the continuity of the unit of production and reproduction between generations (Deere, 1990). Where access to land is limited (by natural or socioeconomic conditions, such as the pattern of land tenure), inheritance has often constituted the primary means through which new units of production and reproduction are formed, and through which patrilineality is reproduced over time. The logic of patrilineality has been described as one in which the continuity of the community is maintained over time by the allocation of women to men through patri- and virilocal residency and of the conservation within the community of the lands within its domain. Inheritance systems that prioritize the eldest or youngest son and disinherit daughters from access to land are argued to have as their objective assuring the continuity of the family patrimony as well as guaranteeing security to elderly parents (Carneiro et al., 1998). [3] It is sometimes argued that if the rules of the Latin American civil codes were to be applied, this would lead to the rapid fragmentation of land and the end of viable peasant economies in several generations. That is, gender equality in inheritance of land might propitiate a process of depeasantization. Moreover, equal inheritance of land by all children might require selling off the family patrimony, leading to the end of the unit of production and reproduction and the demise of peasant communities. These conditions have thus been used to explain or justify male privilege as well as the custom of prioritizing one son in inheritance (Carneiro et al., 1998).

Another factor favouring male privilege in inheritance of land is gender socialization and stereotyping. Many Latin American countries are characterized by a gender division of labour that defines agriculture as a male occupation and women primarily as housewives irrespective of their contribution to family agriculture. Moreover, the right to inherit land is often considered an 'earned' right, following the principle of land belonging to those who work or earn it (Woortmann, 1995; Carneiro, 2000; Hamilton, 2000). Either women's lack of work in agriculture or the invisibility or lack of social recognition of this work may serve as mechanisms of exclusion of women from land rights. In many cases both factors – the locale of post-marital residency and gender stereotypes – combine to produce particularly strong systems of patrilineal land rights.

There is, however, abundant evidence that inheritance practices among the Latin American peasantry are neither uniform nor static. These practices have changed over time in response to a myriad of factors, and it is these changes – and whether inheritance is becoming more or less gender equitable – that is our primary interest. In the next section we consider inheritance of land by children, focusing on the six countries for which there is the most abundant data. Three of these are Andean countries with large indigenous populations and three are predominantly mestizo or ethnically mixed countries. Organizing our material in this fashion, it is evident that the Andean countries with large indigenous populations are characterized by more egalitarian land inheritance practices with respect to children than countries where the majority of the peasantry is white or mestizo. In the subsequent section, we consider inheritance of land by wives. Little empirical work has been carried out on this topic and we focus on the legal framework in the 12 countries and show that it tends to limit the possibility that widows remain in control of the family farm. The concluding section summarizes our main findings and highlights the demands of organized rural women's groups in the region for more equitable land inheritance practices.

Bilateral versus strong male bias in the inheritance of land by children

In general terms, the strongest evidence of bilateral inheritance practices – with both sons and daughters inheriting land and animals from both parents – comes from the Andean region of South America, from Ecuador, Peru and Bolivia. Nonetheless, bilateral inheritance practices do not necessarily result in the equality of inheritance among all children. In some communities different practices govern the inheritance of land as opposed to animals, with sons favoured with respect to land inheritance. In those where all children inherit some land, the youngest child or son is favoured with the largest parcel as well as by inheritance of the parent's home in return for the care he/she is expected to provide the elderly parents until their death. Moreover, where both sons and daughters inherit some land, sons generally inherit not only larger parcels, but land of better quality and location.

Bilateral inheritance

Ecuador

Drawing on a number of ethnographic studies of the indigenous, highland population, Sarah Hamilton (1998) states that 'women are likely to own, or control the usufruct of, land and animals independently from their husbands' and that this pattern is largely due to bilateral inheritance. She argues that the usual pattern is that upon marriage, both spouses each receive at least a part of the land that they will eventually inherit. These lands will be worked in a joint enterprise, but neither spouse can unilaterally control the holdings of the other. Moreover, husbands and wives do not inherit land from each other. Rather, land is held individually for the children, who inherit from both sides. By tradition, the youngest child, irrespective of sex, is expected to take care of the parents and will inherit the familial home and surrounding land.

Discussions with agrarian experts in Ecuador suggested the hypothesis that inheritance patterns in the highlands today largely depend on whether agricultural production is still a viable activity among smallholders.[4] Where land is still valuable, because agricultural production is still profitable, inheritance practices tend to favour sons. In contrast, in the southern, predominantly indigenous departments where soils are depleted and agriculture is a much less profitable activity and where there are high rates of male out-migration, bilateral inheritance practices appear to be the norm. In the opinion of one peasant women leader,[5] with such high rates of migration to the cities among both sons and daughters, the most important factor governing contemporary inheritance practices is which child is willing to stay on the land to farm it. Thus while there is strong evidence of the predominance of bilateral inheritance practices in the Ecuadorian highlands, it is difficult to disentangle the influence of indigenous customs and practices from the changing conditions of production and tenancy over the course of the twentieth century.

Peru

The consensus in contemporary Peru is that inheritance in the highlands tends to be bilateral with both sons and daughters inheriting land and animals from both parents (de la Cadena, 1995). Patri- or virilocal residence is the most common practice, favouring inheritance of land by sons. The locale of residency of a young couple nonetheless tends to be determined by which one's parents has more land, uxorilocal residency (with a woman's parents) not being uncommon (Lambert, 1977).

Data for the province of Cajamarca in northern Peru, a region characterized today by a predominantly mestizo peasantry, provides good evidence of bilateral inheritance and of men and women inheriting approximately equal shares of land. Although a 1976 survey of 105 households found that only one third of these households had been constituted as units of production primarily through inheritance, land purchases being the dominant form of acquiring land (Deere, 1990), nevertheless, of the 36 households where inheritance was the primary form, 42% corresponded to inheritance primarily by women and only 33% to inheritance by men; in 25% of the households, men and women inherited and brought into the household approximately equal shares of land. In the 1970s, it was common in this region for one sibling to purchase the inheritance shares of those who had migrated; women were just as likely as men to purchase land from the other heirs. It was also customary for the youngest child – son or daughter – to remain living at home, caring for the parents in their old age, and to inherit the parental home and surrounding land. This latter practice has been widely reported throughout highland Peru (Lambert, 1977). Susan Bourque and Kay Warren's (1981) study of two rural districts in the department of Lima also found that inheritance of land was bilateral. However, sons tended to inherit larger parcels than daughters and those that were better endowed.

Further south, in the largely indigenous Quechua district of Chuschi in the department of Ayacucho, parallel patterns of inheritance prevail, where sons inherit the property of their fathers and daughters that of their mothers (Isbell, 1978). There is also a predilection to favour the eldest, whether son or daughter, with a larger share in the distribution of property as well as the child, usually the youngest, who resides with the parents the longest and serves them the most.

Scholars have also reported a tendency toward greater gender equality in land inheritance in Peru over the course of the twentieth century (Bourque and Warren, 1981; Lambert, 1977). Among the factors that have encouraged more egalitarian inheritance practices, besides the growing lack of viability of peasant farming and increasing awareness of national laws (itself a product of rising literacy rates and internal migration), has been the growing number of female headed households in rural areas. In some regions of the highlands, it is socially acknowledged that female inheritance of land is one of the best insurance policies in maintaining a modicum level of security for women and their children in the case of their abandonment, an increasingly frequent phenomenon over the course of the twentieth century (Deere, 1990).

Bolivia
A recent survey of inheritance practices in Bolivia suggests considerable heterogeneity in inheritance patterns nationally, and different practices among different ethnic groups (Pacheco, 1999).[6] On the Bolivian Altiplano, where the indigenous Aymara population is concentrated, inheritance of land is reported to be primarily patrilineal. The most evidence in support of bilateral inheritance practices comes from the central Andean valleys, where the indigenous Quechua and mestizo peasantry are largely located. But even within one ethnic region, there may be wide variation in inheritance patterns reflecting, among other factors, different forms of insertion of indigenous communities to the regional economy and class relations. Balán and Dandler (in Paulson, 1996), for example, distinguish three different modalities in the Quechua region of Cochabamba:

- in the indigenous communities that operated relatively independently of colonial society and the hacienda system, inheritance was usually bilateral and work roles and rituals were organized around the principle of complementarity;
- in the indigenous communities that were enmeshed in the hacienda system, only male household heads generally received usufruct plots on the hacienda, with inheritance of these rights and obligations being patrilineal;
- in the independent indigenous communities integrated into commercial agriculture and in greater contact with mestizo cultural influences, notwithstanding the fact

that women often had more diversified economic roles (such as commerce), inheritance tended to be patrilineal.

Paulson (1996) argues that over time, through the agrarian reform, greater commercialization of agricultural production, and internal migration, these divisions in Cochabamba have become blurred. She suggests, nonetheless, that the general tendency has been in support of male inheritance of land.

It is difficult to disentangle traditional inheritance norms and practices from changes resulting from such factors as demographic pressure on a static land base and the growing commodification of land. It has been suggested that on the Bolivian Altiplano, for example, excessive land fragmentation may have led to a change from a system of bilateral or parallel inheritance in the past, to a system favouring either the oldest or youngest son during the twentieth century. In contrast, in other regions of Bolivia, it has been suggested that land scarcity and associated male migration as well as the decline of peasant agriculture and livestock production have favoured more gender equitable inheritance practices. There is also now a tendency for land inheritance in these regions to favour the youngest child, irrespective of sex, who remains at home caring for the elderly parents.[7]

Much more research is obviously required before one can safely generalize about inheritance practices in Bolivia in the past or today. Nonetheless, overall there is more evidence of the prevalence of patrilineal systems in Bolivia than in the Peruvian or Ecuadorian highlands where bilateral inheritance of land appears to be the norm. However, in all three countries bilateral inheritance practices do not necessarily result in equal inheritance of land by sons and daughters; rather, these often favour sons in terms of parcel size and quality.

Strong male bias

Mexico, Chile and Brazil are ethnically mixed countries, but largely mestizo in composition, and governed by different inheritance regimes. While Mexico is characterized by full testamentary freedom, Chile and Brazil are governed by civil codes that provide for egalitarian inheritance by children. Nevertheless, in all three countries there is a strong male preference in inheritance practices regarding land.

Mexico

In one of the few comprehensive national level reviews of land inheritance patterns, María de la Soledad González (1992) argues that in Mexico the general case is for only sons to inherit land. She describes the most common pattern across Mexico as that where the youngest son inherits the parent's home and sometimes the largest parcel of land in return for the care he is expected to provide to elderly parents. The division of farmland rarely takes place until the father's death or serious illness, although older sons may receive a small parcel of land upon which to build a house when they marry. She argues that this pattern serves to maintain the father's headship of the family and to assure that sons meet their obligations to the parents. Her review also suggests that the amount of land each son receives is closely related to his contribution to the parental household, be it in labour or cash. Daughters rarely inherit land from their fathers unless there are no male heirs. In contrast, if mothers own land independently, they tend to pass it on to their daughters (González, 1992).

Rocío Córdova Plaza (1999) argues that the main structural factor limiting women's access to land in Mexico has been patri- and virilocality. Since wives move to their husband's community, they lose all claim to land. If they receive something of their parent's patrimony, it is usually much less than what their brothers receive. Unmarried daughters, on the other hand, are more likely to inherit some land, and if they are the youngest child and there are no male heirs, they will inherit the parent's home and the primary land parcel. Another factor favouring patrilineality in Mexico has been the rules of *ejido* membership and inheritance, which specify that the *ejido* (communal landholding) parcel is indivisible and that land rights can only be transmitted to one person.

González (1992) also argues that inheritance practices are undergoing some change. Bilateral inheritance of land is becoming more common in regions where agriculture is no longer the primary household activity and which have witnessed some occupational diversification. She also finds bilateral inheritance to be increasing where there has been long-standing male and female out-migration, with sons and daughters inheriting land based on their contribution to maintaining the parental household through remittances. In this context it is also becoming more common for daughters to inherit the family home and to assume care for elderly parents. Moreover, it is reported that there is an increased interest by daughters in inheriting lands for the security this offers them and that they are beginning to contest land rights (Castañeda, 2000).

Chile
In Chile, the norm is for all children to inherit from their parents, but sons are privileged with respect to the inheritance of land. Ximena Valdés (1995) argues that rural women were generally the first migrants to urban centres as population pressure increased upon the land in the early twentieth century and that this pattern reinforced a tendency towards male inheritance of land. She considers rural women to be more likely than men to inherit houses rather than land, and for men to inherit the family farm, contributing towards the concentration of land in the hands of men.

Christopher Scott (1990), based on national-level field work in rural areas, reports that inheritance of land is formally considered to be bilateral, with all children having the right to inherit from fathers and mothers, but that in practice women find it difficult to actually claim a share of land. Female claimants seem particularly vulnerable to pressure from male siblings to renounce their legitimate rights of ownership. This pressure may take the form of physical intimidation or of an expressed expectation that female heirs will not exercise their entitlements, particularly after marriage. Thus, alternative income-generating opportunities and locale of residence are also important factors in influencing inheritance patterns.

Brazil
Researchers in Brazil have found considerable discontinuity between the norms of the civil code, which limit testamentary freedom and provide for equal inheritance of property among all children, and local inheritance practices. As summarized by Miriam Nobre (1998): 'In the countryside there is no law; what is relevant is custom. And the custom is not to give women land.' As in other countries, inheritance patterns in Brazil vary widely by region, ethnicity, race and class position, among other factors, but patrilineal inheritance is the dominant pattern. The region that has been

most studied in Brazil is the south, a region characterized by substantial immigration of German, Italian and Polish settlers during the late nineteenth and early twentieth century.[8] According to Maria José Carneiro (1998) the inheritance custom that these colonists brought with them to the New World was that of primogeniture, that is, where the oldest son inherited the family patrimony of land. Over time, however, this custom was transformed into an inheritance system favouring the youngest son (known as *minorato*). This change was the result of the initially favourable conditions that the colonists found in southern Brazil: an agricultural frontier that encouraged the formation of new settlements and allowed families to acquire additional land over time upon which to settle all sons who wanted to farm. As the older sons left the homestead, it was the youngest one who remained at home with the obligation to take care of the parents in their old age, maintaining the tradition of the indivisible family farm, but leading to the *minorato* system.

Most studies of the German colonies in the state of Rio Grande de Sul report that daughters were generally excluded from the inheritance of land. Inheritance of land was strongly associated with those who worked it directly and women were not considered to 'work' in agriculture. Moreover, it was expected that upon marriage they would move away, since patri- or virilocality was the usual practice, and that they would be supported by their husbands. While daughters were endowed with a dowry consisting of animals and household goods, the value of this dowry was generally less than what an equal land share would have been worth (Carneiro, 1998; Woortmann, 1995). Inheritance patterns among the Italian immigrants to Rio Grande Sul followed a similar pattern of patrilineal inheritance.

Woortmann (1995), whose work was among the German colonists in this state, notes a growing tendency in recent decades towards daughters inheriting land, although it is always a smaller parcel than that inherited by her brothers. Moreover, they are sometimes expected to sell this inheritance to the designated heir. When they do retain ownership of a land parcel, 'in practice, this land passed to the control of their husbands'. This had led to a contradictory situation, according to Woortmann, for when women only inherited animals it provided them with an independent economic activity – dairy processing activities – that allowed them to generate their own income. As inheritance of land by women became more common, inheritance of animals has diminished, and women have tended to lose the basis of their relative economic autonomy.

Recent changes associated with the modernization of agriculture, the rise in both male and female educational opportunities, and the expansion in the number of alternative income-generating opportunities, have brought about a number of changes in these southern colonies.[9] For one, inheritance shares have increasingly taken the form of family investments in education. Children with higher levels of education than their siblings who migrate to urban areas are expected to renounce any other claim to inheritance. This has allowed the more entrepreneurial son to consolidate the family holding and attempt to meet the challenges of commercial farming. Second, many families increasingly find themselves without any willing heir, or with only a single daughter remaining at home. Third, daughters are increasingly claiming their inheritance of land, a product of rising educational levels. Whereas in the past an unmarried daughter might have no choice but to become the live-in maid of her brother, this is no longer the case, as women become aware of their rights as well as the broader range of opportunities available to them.

Carneiro et al. (1998) argue the general point that as agriculture becomes less important as a source of peasant household reproduction, inheritance of land tends to become more equitable. In sum, while land inheritance has strongly favoured sons in Brazil, Chile and Mexico for most of the twentieth century, there is evidence of a trend towards more egalitarian inheritance practices in all three countries.

Inheritance of land by wives

Whether widows are legally able to maintain controlling ownership of the family farm upon the death of their husbands depends on a number of factors:[10]
- the marital regime under which a couple contracted marriage and the default regime governing in that country;
- whether or not the husband wrote a will, the share of his patrimony he may will freely and whether he wills that share to her;
- whether the civil codes provide for widows to automatically receive a share of their husband's estate, irrespective of the provisions of his will; and
- if the husband dies intestate, whether or not wives are included in the first order of succession, receiving an equal share with children, or only receive a 'marital share.'[11]

The possibility that a widow be able to retain controlling ownership of the family farm (with controlling ownership defined as more than a 50% share, so that she cannot be easily persuaded to sell the farm if she is not in favour of such a decision) is most likely in countries where the default regime is either *full common property or participation in profits* (since widows retain half of the common property of the union).

In the best of circumstances – marriage under the full *common property regime* – widows are guaranteed ownership of half of the family farm. However, if the husband dies intestate, only in those countries where women automatically form part of the first order of inheritance would they be guaranteed a controlling share of the property. Of the 12 countries reviewed here, the only one meeting these favourable conditions is El Salvador. Nonetheless, since full testamentary freedom prevails, if the husband makes out a will, there is no provision requiring that the widow inherit from his share of the estate, thus no guarantee that she will end up with the controlling share of the farm.

Under the *participation in profits* regime the likelihood of widows retaining control of the family farm is even more variable for it depends on:
- whether they themselves brought land to the marriage;
- the relative amount of land each spouse brought to the union; and
- the relative amount of land that was jointly purchased by the couple rather than acquired individually.

For simplicity, let us assume that all the land was jointly acquired and that the widow can prove joint ownership. In this case she is in the best position in Bolivia and Peru, for in both countries wives are in the first order of inheritance should the husband die intestate and they are protected if the husband left a will. In these countries she always inherits a share equal to that of one of the children, which, added to her half of the joint patrimony, would give her controlling ownership of the farm. In Brazil the widow is in a less favourable position, for if the husband dies intestate she inherits a fixed one quarter of his estate but only in usufruct and as long as she does not remarry. While this may give her sufficient bargaining power to dissuade children from breaking up and selling the family farm, it reduces her options as compared to the case of having full property rights over this inheritance. In practice, the lack of ownership rights over this inheritance has contributed toward the view that widows only temporarily 'hold' the farm for the children and lack effective land rights even over their half of the common property.

In the other countries with a favourable default marital regime (Chile, Colombia, Guatemala, and Mexico) widows are guaranteed a 'marital share' *(porción conjugal)* if their husband dies intestate, but the terms of this marital share vary. In Mexico, if a wife has no property of her own she inherits the same share as one child; otherwise she inherits the difference between the value of a child's share and that of her own estate. Under our assumptions (that the farm was jointly purchased, there being no other property) it means that it is unlikely that the widow will gain any more than her half of the farm. In Chile the marital portion is more generous in that it may equal up to twice the size of a child's share, but it is subject to even more limiting conditions. What we want to stress is that the marital share is primarily meant to take care of glaring inequalities in the value of each spouse's individual property.

What these examples illustrate is that the inheritance provisions of most Latin American civil codes are antithetical to the possibility of wives retaining control over the family farm in case of widowhood. They demonstrate that the marital share was primarily conceived to ensure that the widow not be left destitute in cases where there was great inequality between the spouses in terms of the property that each had brought to the union. The *porción conjugal* was not intended to provide women with economic autonomy, our primary concern. In most countries, whether widows are guaranteed a modicum of security in old age ultimately depends on social practices and the goodwill of judges, husbands and children. In those countries with testamentary or near-testamentary freedom, husbands could will their wives full control of the family farm; in the other countries, husbands could will their wives controlling ownership if they so chose.

Given the differing implications of different marital regimes, and the differing rules governing inheritance by wives, depending on whether or not the husband makes out a will, it should come as no surprise that, in practice, these rules are not at all very well understood. Moreover, there has been scant research on local practices regarding inheritance of land by widows. The data available suggests that there is a large gap between the legal norms protecting wives and local practices.[12]

Conclusion

This review of inheritance practices in Latin America, besides demonstrating their great heterogeneity, illustrates the disjuncture that exists between the egalitarian norms of most Latin American civil codes with regard to the inheritance rights of children and local practices governing the inheritance of land. Overall, inheritance of land in Latin America favours sons, even where bilateral inheritance practices are the norm. This pattern was supported, until recently, by patri- and virilocality marital residence, the logic of peasant household reproduction, and gender socialization and stereotyping that privileges men's work in agriculture, socially legitimizing inequality in land inheritance in favour of men. With regard to ethnicity, it is difficult to discern on the basis of the existing literature whether bilateral inheritance of land is any more closely associated with indigenous communities in comparison with those made up by the white and/or mestizo peasantry, although bilateral inheritance is more common in Peru and Ecuador than in Bolivia, Mexico, Chile or Brazil. Moreover, it is only in the Andean region where vestiges of parallel inheritance systems are found, alluding to a past where perhaps the distribution of land was more equitable between the sexes. In the Andean case bilateral inheritance of land is also supported by the greater visibility and social recognition of women's work in agriculture. Working against it have been patri- and virilocality,[13] and patriarchal forms of representation within indigenous communities that grant community membership and thus decisions over land rights only to male household heads. In Mexico, institutional factors (testamentary freedom combined with *ejido* regulations prohibiting partible inheritance) also strongly support patrilineal inheritance norms and, of the four countries with large indigenous populations, Mexico is the one most strongly characterized by patrilineal land inheritance.

It is difficult to disentangle ancestral inheritance practices from the many forces of change that have impacted for centuries upon indigenous communities and their practices. It is also difficult to discern the relative influence of gender equitable civil codes in fostering more equitable inheritance patterns over time, since other factors have also been at work, such as growing land scarcity, which may also alter the logic of peasant household reproduction. Nonetheless, such factors as growing schooling, internal migration and integration of local peasant economies into the national economy have fostered increased awareness of national legal norms, contributing towards the trend toward more equitable inheritance for all children.

Without doubt, one of the factors precipitating change has been relative land shortage, but the evidence suggests that this may work in two directions. Increasing land pressure over time may provoke a change from a system of equitable inheritance to concentration of land under the male line, as suggested in the case of the Aymara on the Bolivian Altiplano, as well as among the Chilean peasantry. At the same time, growing land scarcity may propitiate families to engage in multiple income-generating activities, relying less on farm activities. Data from Peru, Ecuador, Bolivia, Mexico and Brazil all support the proposition that as agriculture becomes less important as the primary source of peasant household reproduction, inheritance of land becomes more equitable.

With respect to the impact of migration, the evidence is mixed. Greater opportunities for female migration undoubtedly contribute to supporting inheritance of land by sons, as reported in Chile. On the other hand, the spread of schooling, growth of alternative employment opportunities and migration by both young men and women may reduce gender bias, with the most important factors in who inherits land being who wants to remain in the community and farm or who contributes the most through remittances to parents' security in old age. Similarly, demographic change in support of smaller rural families has reduced the number of potential heirs, a factor probably also contributing toward gender equality. Under these conditions it is more difficult to justify male privilege in land inheritance and the denial of the opportunity for women to accumulate capital or become agriculturalists. Where bilateral inheritance has predominated, growing land scarcity within peasant communities has also propitiated a change from patri- or virilocality to uxorilocal residency. This, in turn, has been associated with enhanced bargaining power for women (since wives are not under the direct or indirect control of their in-laws) and a subsequent tendency toward greater gender equality in inheritance of land. But these propositions require further research.

With regard to the inheritance rights of spouses, our review of legal norms suggests that it is only in special circumstances that widows may inherit the family patrimony of land, but this topic requires further study. Further empirical work is required on the relationship between different marital regimes and formal inheritance norms in fostering greater or lesser land ownership by widows and, particularly, their greater effective control over land. As Bina Agarwal (1994) argues, access to land is not the equivalent of control over land and in many situations women's inheritance of land simply serves as a vehicle for land to pass to brothers, husbands or sons.

Although rural women are often unaware of their inheritance rights, organized rural women throughout Latin America are increasingly becoming more cognizant of these rights and demanding them, be it as daughters or wives. Moreover, where civil codes are unfavourable to inheritance by wives, rural women's organizations are beginning to press for their reform. At the First National Meeting of Rural Women in Chile in 1986, organized by the Women's Department of the National Peasant Commission (CNC), among the main demands was reform of inheritance and property legislation (CNC, 1986; GIA, 1986). One of the main concerns in Mexico with regard to the changes in Article 27 of the Mexican Constitution regarding the *ejidos* was the abrogation of the inheritance provisions that protected wives. Since 1992 *ejidatarios* may freely choose their heir, with this choice not limited to wives or a child as was the case in the past, a change denounced by the Women's Commission of the Permanent Agrarian Council (CAP) (Flores, 1994), among other groups, such as at meetings of indigenous women in Chiapas. The Zapatista National Liberation Army (EZLN) has included the demand in its position papers: 'that women must be included in tenancy and inheritance of land' (Rojas, 1995; Stephen, 1998).

In the process leading up to the 1995 World Conference on Women in Beijing, rural women in regional meetings in Bolivia also voiced their discontent with the discrimination they faced with respect to inheritance. They denounced both the dispossession of widows from access to communal lands and the preference given to sons in inheritance: 'When it comes to inheritance of these territories from parents and spouses, we want to have property rights over these' (Salguero, 1995). The Beijing Conference helped focus attention on women's land rights in general, and inheritance rights in particular, and in most countries, following Beijing, the Platform for Action adopted at that conference was widely distributed by the national women's offices, serving as the basis for post-conference activities organized primarily by NGOs. In Peru, for example, at a post-Beijing conference held in Cajamarca, one of the main demands of the peasant women leaders in attendance was compliance with Peru's legal codes, so that all children, male and female, inherit land equally from their parents (De Jong, 1997). In this fashion, the demand for equality of inheritance rights among men and women is beginning to enter the public discourse.

Notes

1   This paper is drawn from their book (Deere and León, 2001). See Chapter 8 for more detailed empirical evidence of the arguments presented here.
2   Both are often associated with exogamy, where women marry outside their community of origin. The locale of post-marital residency is one of the strongest factors associated with different

inheritance systems cross-culturally. In Agarwal's (1994a) exhaustive study of inheritance systems in South Asia, for example, she found women's land inheritance rights in matrilineal and bilateral systems closely associated with women marrying and living within their natal villages.

3   As Carneiro (2000) argues, land has more than economic value in peasant societies, and inheritance systems also need to be studied from the point of view of their symbolic value in reproducing the family patrimony. She suggests that only in this way can the hierarchies and unequal relations within the family be fully understood as well as the way that individual interests are subsumed to the collective interests of the family.

4   Interview with researcher Mercedes Prieto, 22 July 1997, Quito, and discussion at the Seminar on Women's Land Rights organized for the authors by CEPAM, 24 July 1997, Quito.

5   Interview with Rosita Cabrera, former women's leader of ECUARUNARI, 22 July 1997, 'O la Toglla, Quito province.

6   Other evidence of the existence of parallel inheritance systems in Peru comes from Jane Collins' study of the Aymara in the Department of Puno (cited in Hamilton, 2000)

7   This survey of community inheritance practices was carried out by local-level NGOs in sixteen municipalities of seven departments of Bolivia. The study was based on a questionnaire filled out by community leaders, and is only indicative of general trends at the local level.

8   Relatively little research has been carried out on inheritance patterns in the northeast of Brazil, the least prosperous region of this vast country and the one characterized by the greatest racial diversity.

9   Interview with researcher Maria José Carneiro, Centro para el Desarrollo Agrícola, Federal Rural University of Rio de Janeiro, 19 June 1998, Rio de Janeiro; also see Carneiro (2000).

10 The same inheritance rules apply whether the deceased spouse is the husband or wife. Given the growing disparity in male and female lifespans in Latin America – five to six years in most countries – we will assume that the husband is the deceased in order to focus on the obstacles faced by wives in inheriting majority control over the family farm.

11 See Deere and León (2001) for a detailed discussion of the evolution of marital regimes in Latin America. A 'marital share' of a spouse's patrimony refers to a provision made by some civil codes for wives not to be left destitute; it usually depends on the relative value of each spouse's patrimony and can never exceed one quarter of the patrimony of the deceased.

12 See Deere and León (2001).

13 It would seem that locale of marital residence would have less of an impact in constraining gender equitable inheritance practices in the Andes than in other regions, since geography has imposed land use patterns involving access to parcels at different elevations and thus locales. That is, family farms rarely consist of contiguous land parcels.

References

Agarwal, B., *A field of one's own: gender and land rights in South Asia*. Cambridge, Cambridge University Press, 1994.

Bourque, S. and K. Warren, *Women of the Andes: patriarchy and social change in two Peruvian towns*. Ann Arbor, University of Michigan Press, 1981.

Carneiro, M.J., 'Memoria, esquecimento e etnicidade na transmissão do patrimonio familiar'. In: M.J. Carneiro, et. al. (eds.), *Campo aberto: o rural no estado do Rio de Janeiro*. Rio de Janeiro, Contra Capa Livreria, 1998. pp. 273-296.

Carneiro, M.J., 'Herança e identidade de gênero entre agricultores familiares Brasileiros'. Paper presented to the XXII International Congress of the Latin American Studies Association, March 2000, Miami.

gender perspectives

Carneiro, M.J., K. de Freitas and G. Guedes, 'Valor da terra e padrão de herança entre pequenos agricultores familiares'. Paper presented at the XXI Reunião da Associação Brasileira de Antropologia, April 1998, Vitoria, Salvador.

Castañeda S.M.P., 'Identidad femenina y herencia: aproximaciones a algunos cambios generacionales'. Paper presented to the XXII International Congress of the Latin American Studies Association, March 2000, Miami.

Comisión Nacional Campesina (CNC) and Comisión Femenina, 'La demanda de la mujer rural: el derecho a la tierra'. Folleto 11. Santiago, 1986.

Cordova Plaza, R., 'Mandiles y machetes: el acceso femenino a la tierra en una comunidad ejidál de Veracruz, México'. Paper presented at the workshop on Land in Latin America: new context, new claims, new concepts. CEDLA, CERES, WAU, Royal Tropical Institute, May 1999, Amsterdam.

Deere, C.D., *Household and class relations: peasants and landlords in northern Peru*. Berkeley, University of California Press, 1990.

Deere, C.D. and M. León, *Empowering women: land and property rights in Latin America*. Pittsburgh, University of Pittsburgh Press, 2001.

De Jong, S., 'Del diagnóstico al acceso a la titulación de tierra'. In: *Avance: fortalecimiento institucional*. Cajamarca, CIPDER, 1997, pp. 4-5.

De la Cadena, M., 'Women are more Indian': ethnicity and gender in a community near Cuzco'. In: B. Larson and O. Harris (eds), *Ethnicity, markets and migration in the Andes: at the crossroads of history and anthropology*. Durham, N.C., Duke University Press, 1995, pp. 329-348.

Grupo de Investigación Agraria (GIA), 'La demanda de la mujer rural'. *Noticiero de la Realidad Agraria*, vol. 42 (1986), pp. 1-10.

Gonzalez Montes, M. de la Soledad, 'Familias campesinas mexicanas en el siglo XX'. Ph. D. dissertation. Universidad Complutense de Madrid, 1992.

Hamilton, S., *The two-headed household: gender and rural development in the Ecuadorean Andes*. Pittsburgh, University of Pittsburgh Press, 1998.

Hamilton, S., 'Blood, sweat, and tears: gender and entitlement to land in Ecuador, Guatemala, and Mexico'. Paper prepared for delivery at the 2000 Meeting of the Latin American Studies Association, March 16-18, 2000, Miami.

Isbell, B.J., 'To defend ourselves: ecology and ritual in an Andean village'. Austin, Institute of Latin American Studies, University of Texas at Austin. *Latin American Monographs*, no. 47 (1978).

Lambert, B., 'Bilaterality in the Andes'. In: R. Bolton and E. Mayer (eds), *Andean kinship and marriage*. Washington, DC, American Anthropological Association, 1977, pp. 1-27.

Lara Flores, S.M., 'Las mujeres: nuevos actores sociales en el campo?'. *Revista Mexicana de Sociología*, vol. 2 (1994), pp. 77-88.

Nobre, M., 'Gênero e agricultura familiar a partir de muitas vozes'. In: M. Nobre, E. Siliprandi, S. Quintela and R. Menasche (eds), *Gênero e agricultura familiar*. São Paulo, SOF, 1998.

Pacheco Balanza, D., 'Tierra del padre o del marido, da lo mismo? Usos y costumbres y criterios de equidad'. Draft report. La Paz, Fundación Tierra, 1999.

Paulson, S., 'Familias que no 'conyugan' e identidades que no conjugan: la vida en Mizque desafía nuestras categorías'. In: S. Rivera Cusicanqui (ed.), *Ser mujer indígena, chola o birlocha en la Bolivia postcolonial de los años 90*. La Paz, Subsecretaría de Asuntos de Género, Ministerio de Desarrollo Humano, 1996. pp. 85-162.

Rojas, R. (ed.), *Chiapas, y las mujeres qué*. Mexico City, Ediciones del Taller Editorial La Correa Feminista, 1995.

Salguero, E., 'Primer encuentro de mujeres indígenas, campesinas, y originarias, Cochabamba, Bolivia, del 24 al 26 de 1995'. La Paz, Federación Nacional de Mujeres Campesinas de Bolivia 'Bartolina

women's inheritance of land

Sisa', Coordinadora Nacional del Foro de ONG de Bolivia a la IV Conferencia Mundial sobre la Mujer, Educación en Población, UNFPA, 1995.

Scott, C., 'Land reform and property rights among small farmers in Chile, 1968-86'. In: D. Hojman (ed.), *Neo-liberal agriculture in rural Chile*. New York, St. Martin's Press, 1990. pp. 64-90.

Stephen, L., *Women and social movements in Latin America*. Austin, University of Texas Press, 1997.

Stephen, L., 'Gender and grassroots organizing: lessons from Chiapas'. In: V. Rodriguez (ed.), *Women's participation in Mexican political life*. Boulder, Westview Press, 1998. pp. 146-163.

Valdés, X., 'Cambios en la división sexual del trabajo y en las relaciones de género entre la hacienda y la empresa exportadora en Chile'. In: S. M.L. Flores (ed.), *El rostro femenino del mercado de trabajo rural en América Latina*. Caracas, Nueva Sociedad y UNRISD, 1995. pp. 61-71.

Woortman, E.F., *Hedeiros, parentes e compadres*. São Paulo, Hucitec, 1995.

Jeanne Maddox Toungara

2 Changing the meaning of marriage: women and family law in Côte d'Ivoire

Women in Côte d'Ivoire are attempting to mobilize their forces so that they can play a determining role in setting national laws that affect their status as wives. They have recognized that only through increased mobilization will they be able to register their opinions in the ongoing efforts for social change designed to modernize the country and remove vestiges of what many legislators consider outmoded ethnic gender and family practices. These efforts were initiated by former President Felix Houphouët-Boigny,[1] who was unmatched in his desire to create a modern polity by developing Ivorian society in the political, economic and social policy arenas. The goal of a unified legal system with one set of modern laws regulating women's marital status and their rights and privileges vis-à-vis their husbands has thus been a part of the national agenda since independence from France in 1960, but today women are questioning whether such a system will subject them to new limitations. Although 'elite'(western-educated) women have been most vocal in registering their views, for a large number of non-elite women who still operate as members of ethnic and rural communities, the contradictions and implications of a unified family code are enormous.

The controversy over women's status under marital law has thus spurred a debate about the desirability of a 'unified legal system' versus 'legal pluralism' for African women. Leaders of newly independent African states, looking back on precolonial ethnic diversity and the subsequent colonial manipulation of ethnic pluralism through 'divide and conquer' approaches, initially saw pluralism as a potential source of conflict within the modern nation state. Côte d'Ivoire is itself an ethnically diverse area, with seven major indigenous ethnic groups, none of which account for more than 20% of the population. However, many Africanist scholars have seen new legal systems as an alternative to the use of force and as a mechanism for guaranteeing rights, fundamental change and social evolution where it is most needed (Kuper and Kuper, 1965). Other scholars have maintained that cultural pluralism persists (Hooker, 1975), even beneath the cloak of unified laws, because most Africans prefer customary practices, especially regarding family law[2]. Therefore, despite the existence of the civil code, which was implemented in 1964 and judged by Ivorian jurists and some social scientists as a successful experiment (Levasseur, 1976), most Ivorians have remained outside the law. The question, then, is whether the goal should be to integrate the two systems and, through recognition of African practices, to radically transform or 'revolutionize the legal heritage of African states' or to mediate the competing cultural tensions between ethnic communities by using the law to shape, lead and provide transitional integration as states move toward social self-realization (Deng, 1971).

Whether the law should be used to achieve social change is still being debated, particularly among Ivorian women. They are increasingly aware of the inadequacies of the 1964 family code with respect to women, as well as the need for women to use the formal legal sector to protect their rights and their families' ability to achieve progress. The debate itself has created the appearance of a division between elite women, who have accepted the civil code, and ordinary (often rural) women, most of whom follow cultural practices. However, Ivorian women have begun to realize, as have women around the world, the need for a progressive legal system (Schuler, 1986). The existence of many non-articulated legal systems that merely reflect the status quo is not enough because they reinforce existing oppression. The experiences of Ivorian women appear to suggest that legal pluralism may not lend itself to social change for women, and that the challenge is to shape national laws in ways that do.

Ivorian women under custom, colonialism and the civil code

The status of Ivorian women has been affected by:
- their membership in traditional families and ethnic groups;
- their position as French colonial subjects until 1960; and
- their subordinate position in families regulated by the civil code since 1964.

The next section reviews women's position before and during colonialism. I then examine how women were affected by independence and the civil code of 1964. Women's response to the civil code, the resulting amendments to it in 1983 and the various repercussions of these changes are the focus of subsequent sections.

Custom versus colonialism

It was not unusual under colonialism for Ivorians to be subjected to radical transformations of their traditional social systems in the interest of the state. Colonial rule both recognized and subordinated African customary law to the French system, thus interfering with the normal evolutionary process of African traditional legal practice. One of the first and most dramatic changes occurred in 1903 with the official liberation of slaves and captives throughout francophone Africa. This act affected millions of people and had a direct and definitive impact on African social systems by eliminating the slave owner as a major obstacle to full French colonial domination of subject peoples. However, direct French influence on women's status did not occur until well after colonialism was established.

Within the colony of Ivory Coast, a body of basic French law was applied by decree and modified by decisions made in the metropolis or, at the local level, through a series of laws and decrees promulgated by the lieutenant governor (Salacuse, 1969). The major characteristic of the French legal system in the colonies was the existence of dual or 'plural' regimes. Once French colonial policymakers resolved the issue of assimilating colonial subjects by adopting a policy of *association* (Skinner, 1975), they could control the numbers of Africans gaining access to French rights through citizenship. Most Africans in French colonies remained 'subjects' without full access to French law, which was available only to French citizens and educated Africans who qualified for *statut civil francais*; customary law was applied to all other colonial subjects, who were defined as having *statut coutumier*.

Under customary law, Ivorian women were under the control of their extended families and communities. This was especially true in patrilineal communities where women lived most of their lives among their husbands' relatives and worked on behalf of their husbands' kin groups.[3] In matrilineal communities women retained central positions in their families of origin and incurred obligations to control resources on behalf of their relatives and offspring that belonged to their matrilineages (Etienne and Etienne, 1967). However, customary law was open to interpretation by French administrators in local courts who evaluated the practices of each ethnic group, with special scrutiny regarding French prohibitions against slavery, human sacrifice and murder. The French did not begin to focus on the extended family and customary marital practices until several decades later.

Generally, whether in patrilineal or matrilineal groups, traditional marriages were arranged by elder members of the extended family and involved the transfer of women from their families of birth in exchange for the bride price, which compensated for the loss of women's work and reproductive value to their original families. The bride price was of significant monetary value among patrilineal groups, but less so among matrilineal ones. This exchange, which benefited families, did not necessarily require a woman's consent, and child betrothal was common.

Due in part to pressures from progressive political groups, as well as from religious missions, the French gradually passed new laws governing marriage and the family to curb what they defined as an abusive exploitation of women. The *Mandel Decree* of 1939 and the *Jacquinot Decree* of 1951 had a lasting effect on the evolution of civil law with respect to marriage.

The Mandel Decree
This decree fixed the minimum age of marriage for women at 14 and for men at 16, and required mutual consent. In addition, the decree invalidated all marriages involving children under the minimum age requirement (whether they had consented or not) and all marriages to women who had not given their consent. As a result, widows and other dependent persons could defy the levirate (customary law obliging a man to marry his brother's widow) and other customary laws by appealing to colonial legislation.

The Jacquinot Decree
Much to the concern of many African men, the Jacquinot Decree of 1951 went even further and liberated women over 21 by refusing to acknowledge that extended families had any claims to the bride price. The major effect of this law was to encourage African women in unsatisfactory relationships to exercise their option to divorce. The decree also sought to limit the maximum amount of the bride price based on locality, and authorized a tribunal to pass judgement on exaggerated claims. In addition, marriages could be registered without parental consent. Upon registration, however, the husband had to agree 'not to take another wife as long as the present marriage had not been officially dissolved'. In other words, monogamy became the only form of marriage recognized by the state. The above measures could be reinforced with sanctions under the French penal code, and any infraction could lead to five years in prison.

As one would expect, not all officials in French African colonies agreed with these decrees, especially in rural areas where the decrees appeared quite impractical. Consequently, there was a high degree of non-compliance among non-urban Ivorians.

Nevertheless, the implementation of the decrees did affect African societies both in theory and in practice. For example, the authority of lineages over marriage was diminished, and women's right to choose marital partners was protected. On the other hand, the state did not assume the lineage's responsibilities for safeguarding a woman's welfare, and thus a woman who married without the traditional consent of her lineage could easily find herself without support if marital problems arose. Moreover, the decrees' transfer of authority to the state set a precedent for state interference in customary law regarding marriage. After legislation was enacted, the courts became responsible for interpreting the limits of customary law, thereby involving the judiciary in transforming traditional society (Lampue, 1974). Once this practice was adopted, governmental authorities found legislation a convenient means to challenge traditional practices.

Reports of women's responses to this new legislation are contradictory. Some studies give an impression of wholesale acceptance of the new legislation, leading to a massive upheaval of traditional family values. Indeed, there were many cases of women in conflict with their families over the choice of a spouse. Some women rejected traditional marital obligations and parental responsibilities, even refusing to cohabit with their husbands and simply abandoning their households. Some colonial administrators thought that women's new 'right to consent' would increase their mobility and lead to rural exodus and urban prostitution. However, although statistics do reflect a rising number of divorces and a corresponding inflation of the bride price (Dobkin, 1968), these studies contain exaggerated reactions to the decrees. In fact, for many families the strength of tradition and lineage pressure provided safeguards against any disastrous effects of the new legislation (Levasseur, 1971). Many women simply chose to continue customary practices by not registering marriages, and the customary bride price continued to be exchanged (Toungara, field notes, 1987).

Independence and the civil code

The colonial experience regarding marriage proved that legislation alone, without dynamic and conscientious application, could not lead to social change. Nevertheless, following independence, President Houphouët-Boigny used the state apparatus to make the conjugal family the only legitimate socioeconomic unit and the only marital regime for Côte d'Ivoire. His actions elicited criticism from a number of Africans and westerners, some of whom saw them as a policy of continuity with colonial practices. However, a deeper understanding of Houphouët-Boigny's national economic objectives suggests that he may have been seeking a means to gain the full participation of every adult in the development process. By emphasizing monogamy, the state hoped to make every married man a responsible head of household, thus liberating the conjugal unit from any dependency upon lineage. Consequently, the traditional 'family patriarch'– as lineage head, spokesman and representative of several households – would no longer be an obstacle to development because he would not be responsible for determining the distribution of labour and productivity of the larger unit. Instead, each head of household would be expected to work for the wellbeing of his wife and children. Thus men, as well as women, would be liberated from lineage constraints and given the capacity to increase the competitiveness of the nuclear-family unit. Houphouët-Boigny, having opted for capitalism, probably hoped that competition would lead to an increase in productivity, decidedly one of the objectives of economic development.

The impact of these changes on women was considered secondary. In fact, when the civil code was voted on by the president's assembly of handpicked deputies in 1964, the minister of justice, in his introductory remarks, made no reference to local responses and the often negative effects of French legislation regarding the family. On the contrary, he praised the contribution of French civil law to the evolution of custom, and he made it clear that the direction of change was not to be questioned, even though each society had its peculiarities. He announced that monogamy would be the only marital regime acceptable before the state and insisted that the old regime (polygyny) was in conflict with the new directives of the economy.

The minister also stated that the same principles of equality that applied to political rights would apply to personal rights, except for the issue of equality of the sexes. This, he stated, could not be absolute, especially where the maintenance of family unity was concerned. Further, indirectly invoking the supremacy of leadership in the one-party state, he suggested to the deputies that the president had already benefited women by announcing, during his 1961 speech to the Secretary-Generals of the national party – Parti Démocratique de Côte d'Ivoire (PDCI) – that the bride price was to be eliminated (Débats de l'Assemblée Nationale, 1964).[4] Accordingly, the objectives of the 1964 civil code were seen as establishing the primacy of the nuclear family and as relieving women of the inferior status associated with the negative interpretation of the bride price. Several government decisions supported these ends, but those pertaining to marriage and property, divorce and separation, paternity, and inheritance are the focus here. Five of the 1964 civil laws (Journal Officiel de la République de Côte d'Ivoire, 1964) regulated these aspects of women's status.

Loi no. 64-375: marriage

The minimum age of marriage was set at 18 years for women, and 20 for men. Mutual consent was maintained, but parental consent was mandatory for minors of less than 21 years of age. Only one marriage could be recognized by the state, and the dissolution of previous marriages was required. Under the guise of protection for the majority of women who were illiterate and would no longer benefit from the security provided through kinship relations (fathers and brothers), a single marital regime was proposed, 'the community', over which the husband, who was given the undisputed title of head of household, had sole authority. In other words, the state transferred the woman's dependent status from her lineage to her husband. Spouses were considered mutually obligated to one another, pledging fidelity, help and assistance in the interest of the family. The wife could even replace her husband as head of household in his absence or if he became incapacitated. Both spouses were expected to contribute to household expenses, each according to his or her means. The salaries and revenues acquired by either spouse belonged to the community, meaning that the administration of the wife's salary was completely left to the husband. Even the financial and professional possibilities of female spouses were legislated: a woman was allowed to open a bank account only with her husband's authorization, and to hold a job only with his permission. The husband also had the right to officially demand that an employer remit his spouse's salary directly to him. Only women who were self-employed in some kind of trade or related commercial activity were permitted to manage their businesses as their separate property without their husbands' interference. Although the separate and personal property of both spouses was recognized, the husband could manage, dispose of or mortgage his own property as he pleased and also manage his wife's property. His only restriction was in the sale or mortgage of his wife's personal property or the alienation of community property without remuneration, but only her verbal permission was required.

Although the law was intended to recognize the equal status of women, it actually denied them equal jurisdiction over their own property, not to mention participation in the administration of community property (Folquet, 1974). While on the surface the law appeared to create a well-unified conjugal unit that could act harmoniously in the best interests of the couple, the children and the state, in reality the law had a detrimental impact on women. It reduced their status to that of dependent persons in a 'stranger' community (Paulme, 1960) and abolished their freedom to produce and control wealth, ultimately resulting in a loss of power. This aspect of the law was the main source of contention among women and led to their eventual stand against its restraints.

Loi no. 64-376: divorce and separation
The simple repudiation of wives was forbidden; only judges were authorized to pronounce a legal separation or divorce following specified judicial procedures. The conditions that could lead to divorce were enumerated and included adultery, excessive abuse, desertion and condemnation for dishonourable conduct. (In the case of adultery, special consideration was accorded to men, who could only be accused if adultery was committed in the household and was officially documented.) The innocent party could collect alimony not to exceed one quarter of the revenue of his or her ex-spouse. According to the assembly debates, alimony was meant to protect women who had no other source of income outside the marriage.

Loi no. 64-377: paternity and filiation
The paternity of a married woman's child could be contested under certain circumstances, but the paternity of children born outside marriage – the products of adultery – was cause for great concern. These children, referred to as 'natural children,' were to be recognized and to enjoy the same rights as legitimate children.[5] Although the permission of the legitimate spouse was necessary before a husband could accept paternity of a child born outside the marriage, if a wife refused to give her permission, the judiciary could intercede to declare paternity based on any number of simple facts. For example, evidence of a husband's relationship with a concubine during the period in which the child could have been conceived was sufficient to acknowledge paternity.

Loi no. 64-379: inheritance
In the event of death, the law regarding equal distribution of community property between husband and wife was applied prior to the law determining the line of inheritance. After receiving his or her share of community property, the spouse was also eligible for supplementary benefits after the children, the brothers and sisters, the father, and then the mother of the deceased. Matrilineal inheritance practices were completely phased out. The only way for the matrilineage to benefit was through a last will and testament. However, only a portion of the inheritance (three fourths of the deceased's share of community property) could be willed to others outside of the line of inheritance cited above. Once again, the primacy of the conjugal unit over lineage was emphasized.

Loi no. 64-381: general dispositions
This law officially condemned the bride price, and all previous laws, rules and customs in conflict with the new laws were nullified.[6] The law offered a few concessions, considered to be transitional and temporary, to those under customary law, including the registration of polygynous marriages. Several procedures were outlined for the registration and dissolution of such marriages contracted prior to the new law, as well as the distribution of inheritance. Registration provided the protection of the state to all co-wives and children on an equal basis.

The 1964 laws had a greater impact than the Mandel and Jacquinot decrees under the colonial regime. Economic growth provided an incentive for the registration of marriages, since eligibility for family allocations and tax exemptions was determined upon presentation of the family record booklet, which could be obtained only on the day the couple was married by an official of the state at the city hall. For the most part, however, as during the colonial period, marriages were made outside the parameters of the law. For example, Akan families, whose matrilineal traditions discouraged daughters from becoming legally entangled with men from different lineages, feared that the new law would allow such men to gain formal access to all of their property, both personal and inherited (Rattray, 1923). Those from patrilineal traditions also rejected the new laws. Men had no interest in legalizing their relationships and incurring new obligations and problems. For Muslims in particular, legalizing a marriage meant favouring one wife over the others, whereas their religious tenets provided for the equal treatment of all wives. The levirate, for instance, was intended to ensure that all wives and children would be equally provided for by brothers following a husband's death.

In general, the new laws were viewed as introducing many complications and few advantages. Moreover, for a body of laws supposedly drafted to improve the status of women, women had little involvement in their conception and even less in their implementation. Several studies have shown that Ivorian women were often not even aware of the law, and yet they could only benefit from the state's protection through a legally registered marriage. Therefore, a woman's ability to gain access to the law often depended on her knowledge of it and her spouse's willingness to comply with it. Contrary to expectations (see, for example, Hooker, 1975), the civil code in Côte d'Ivoire (described by Ivorians as *legislation choc*[7] because of its lack of ethnic pluralism) has not drawn the various ethnic populations into the whirlpool of social change. Because of popular resistance to the civil code, legal pluralism, although not formally recognized by the state, continues.

Women's mobilization for legal change

Experience since independence in 1960 suggests that as Ivorian women increase their involvement in political and economic arenas, they will decrease their dependence on men to act as their spokespersons. Consequently, they will be better able to articulate their own needs and make their own demands. The important role of elite women in this endeavour should not be minimized (O'Barr, 1984). Knowledge of politics, the ability to mobilize women effectively and the capacity to convince others of the importance of women in national development will determine the pace of change in many Third World countries. Whatever social progress is achieved will reflect the

changing the meaning of marriage

degree of collaboration between elite and non-elite women in raising their level of activism, and Ivorian women now seem to agree that they must play a larger role in their own emancipation. Women's participation in the economic sector alone does not automatically lead to their emancipation: although African women perform most of the agricultural work, they are largely invisible (Boserup, 1970; Sanday, 1973), and despite their contributions to subsistence, craft production and the economic development of their communities, they have been left without authority or control and have little influence in decision-making (Etienne, 1980). However, political activism by Ivorian elite women has helped to initiate some strategic changes for women as evidenced by their responses to the civil code.

In 1963 the women's wing of the PDCI (the national party), l'Association des Femmes Ivoiriennes (AFI), was founded, led by Madame Jeanne Gervais, a staunch party activist and educator. Women had been active supporters of the PDCI and participants in the events leading to independence. Through the AFI, Gervais was able to organize women throughout the country and to take advantage of the wave of feminism sweeping the western world. Eze (1984) reports that the United Nations played a very important role by providing a forum for discussion and debate. By the time the United Nations Decade for Women (1976–1986) was declared, the AFI was already putting pressure on the president to complete the image of Côte d'Ivoire as an 'economic miracle' by creating a ministry to focus specifically on women's development issues.

The president subsequently established the Commission Nationale de la Promotion Féminine on January 24, 1977, and in her address at the opening session, Gervais announced that, based on the results of a nationwide survey of women, the commission would focus its attention on judicial equality, education and employment. She emphasized the importance of women's contributions to the economy, cited the marital status of women under the civil code, and pleaded for the reform of archaic laws that deprived women of any control over the product of their labour. These laws were seen as an impediment to economic progress because they discouraged women from full participation in development.

The changing social environment had left women disadvantaged. Illiteracy among women was still high (78.8%), and men had greater access to education than women. Female enrolment in primary school was 3%; in secondary school, 20%, and in university and professional institutions, 15%. At the same time, only about half of the girls eligible to attend schools had been admitted. Women's economic disadvantage was demonstrated by the fact that they represented only 16% of the modern sector of the economy. The majority of women still worked in the traditional sectors of agriculture, crafts, the marketing of fresh and cooked foods, and textiles.[8] Given women's importance to the growth of the nation's agriculture, the commission was able to persuade the government to reconsider women's marital status as a variable in assisting their economic status.

The commission appointed a committee of 10 women and 15 men to study Ivorian women's marital status, and the committee made the following suggestions regarding the 1964 law:
- women should be allowed to use their maiden names;
- the husband should continue to be the head of household;
- women should freely exercise the profession of their choice unless the husband could officially prove that it was not in the interests of the family;

- the regime of community property should be maintained for the protection of the majority of the nation's women who were unsalaried and illiterate;
- household duties should be considered a financial contribution to the domestic community;
- women should collaborate in the administration of community property;
- women should freely manage their personal property.

The suggestions did not deviate from the government's desire to encourage the nuclear family and to protect the masses of illiterate women from abandonment and desertion, but the commission took a more radical stance on women's household role as responsible adults managing their own personal incomes and capable of collaborating with their husbands in managing the family. They sought to increase women's status further by suggesting that housework be recognized for its remunerative worth, an issue that remains important for women in the West as well as in the Third World (Taub and Schneider, 1982; Sacks, 1982).

The committee's proposals were not considered by the legislature, however, until 1983. Despite the fact that Gervais kept these issues on the public agenda, she, the commission and other elite women in the AFI were severely criticized for their ineffectiveness in meeting the needs of most Ivorian women. Some accused them of merely creating a stage for wives of the upper cadres to gain public notice and of not providing a viable program for political mobilization of grass-roots women (Kouame, 1987). While this may have been true in some instances, it is also true that what little progress has been made is largely due to the efforts of educated elite women who have articulated the needs of the masses to the party leadership. The AFI's thrust was towards reform and its methods conciliatory; given the nature of the one-party political regime, a different approach was impractical. Nevertheless, there have been some tangible results, as I shall discuss in the next section.

Social change and political reform

Despite the sometimes countervailing pressures of social change and the persistent popularity of cultural traditions, Côte d'Ivoire is an example of how a strong state can influence the process of reshaping family legislation and women's roles within marital relationships. By the time the proposals for new legislation reached the floor of the National Assembly in 1983, the national profile and the socioeconomic position of women had visibly changed.[9] The population had more than doubled since independence to 9.3 million people, with 42.5% living in urban zones. Although men had benefited most from independence and modernization, education and social services had also offered new opportunities for women. Educational progress was evidenced by increased female enrolments, which rose to 41.1% for primary schools (although completion rates differed significantly), 28.5% for secondary schools, and 51.3% for technical schools. At the university, where total enrolment reached 11,000 in 1982, 17% were women. Economically, women made up 22% of the service sector and 21% of civil service employees in 1986, and they were represented in medicine (doctors and pharmacists), law (judges, attorneys and notaries), business and education. Pressure from these working women for more control over self-generated revenues helped to emphasize the need for reform.

changing the meaning of marriage

41

On the other hand, the continuity of traditional behaviour could be observed in the persistence of polygyny and in the young age of women at marriage. In 1979, 24.3% of married men over the age of 12 were polygynous. The highest percentage (37.1) was for men between the ages of 60 and 64, who on average had 2.5 wives; about 80% of polygynous men had only two wives. Nearly 48% of women were married by the time they reached 20 years of age, compared to only 3% of men. Since population statistics reveal a fairly even ratio of men to women, it is clear that marriage to younger women accounted for the uneven ratio of married men to married women. Among younger men, polygyny persisted in part due to the prestige associated with the traditional view that a man's success is judged by the number of women he controls. Also affecting the potential for change was the failure of educated elites to adopt the behaviour they had tried to legislate. When younger men observe community leaders doing one thing while saying another, they tend to ignore legislation and embrace tradition instead (Mundt, 1975).

Nonetheless, legislative developments created political space for broader participation and women's activism. When the president announced during the 7th Party Congress in 1980 that deputies would be elected based on regional representation and by direct suffrage, the popular support for new democratic procedures encouraged individuals to run for office as representatives of specific regional constituencies (Toungara, 1986). The increased involvement of Ivorian women led to the election of eight women (5%) among the 147 deputies chosen in 1980. The success of women candidates in gaining both male and female support encouraged the participation of AFI and rural women in national politics and in extended debates on the marital status of women in Côte d'Ivoire. Stimulated by female party activists, as well as women from professional and social organizations, these debates led to the introduction of new elements into the civil code regarding family law.

Although some of the proposals put forward by the Commission Nationale de la Promotion Féminine appear progressive to outsiders, in Côte d'Ivoire they were viewed either as a welcome return to traditional values or alternatively as another thoughtless attempt to further weaken the traditional authority of men over their households. The response to the proposed changes by local people illustrates the difficulty of achieving balance among diverse ethnic groups in a young African nation. When the proposals were considered in 1983, the minister of justice faced a different atmosphere than that of 1964. Although there was still one party, there was not only one voice. This time deputies questioned the principles behind the new legislation and also its utility as a tool for social change. Several deputies went on record to defend their regional traditions (e.g. polygyny and the levirate) and to debate the impact of new legislation on rural people, and they generally insisted that any deviation from tradition could cause various social ills such as increased delinquency, illegitimacy and teen pregnancy. Others accused the state of attacking its citizens' individual liberty, while a large number of deputies expressed resentment over women's new financial autonomy. Opponents of the legislation generally defended legal pluralism and expressed a desire for laws that reflected an African reality (Archives de l'Assemblée Nationale, 1983).

Because Côte d'Ivoire was a one-party state where most decisions were made at the top and dictated to the lower echelons, deputies had little chance of altering the marital legislation: many of the points were not debatable. The minister reiterated the party's support of monogamy and reminded the deputies that the goal was to create a single national identity, not several, based on diverse traditions and religions. In the end, the 1983 modifications to the civil code represented a compromise with the objectives of the state. Central to the decision to accept the modifications were long-standing concerns about the security of married women without independent revenues, the protection of orphaned children and the stability of the monogamous conjugal unit, all of which are still addressed in the code. Also retained is the concept of a single regime (the community), but spouses now have a choice between two financial options: *community property* and *separation of assets*. Although the community property option in the 1983 amendments is made far more palatable to women than it was under the 1964 civil code, the separation of assets option gives each party full control and forbids unauthorized interference from spouses (explained below). Women are also accorded some of the same legal privileges as men; the state was finally willing to acknowledge women's judicial maturity and legal equality.

Loi no. 83-800: marriage
This law still recognizes only a single regime – the community – but without the previous financial constraints. Women may now open and manage their own bank accounts without their spouses' approval, and are allowed to choose any profession and to earn, collect and freely dispose of any revenues that remain after household obligations are met. The 1983 law defines three types of property: *personal*, *community* and *reserved*.
   Personal property consists of:
- any possessions acquired before marriage;
- possessions acquired afterward as an inheritance or gift;
- possessions acquired during the marriage through the exchange or sale of personal property;
- clothing;
- payments derived from settlements, loans or pensions; and
- professional equipment.
Each spouse retains the right to dispose of his/her personal property as he or she sees fit. This restoration of control over personal wealth was an important victory for women.
   Community property is defined as property acquired during the marriage by the couple, as well as items willed to the couple.
   Reserve property, some of which might be community property, includes salaries from professional activities, and savings from income or profits made on personal property.
   Even though women are allowed to manage funds derived from their reserved and personal properties, any available cash or funds on deposit (derived from salaries, property rents and other sources) belongs to the community. Although the husband is allowed to continue in his role as head of household in charge of administering community property, his role in the household is better defined by the 1983 law. He now has to procure his spouse's permission to give away, sell or mortgage any part of community property, and any spouse who feels she has been denied the right to collaborate can request the nullification of any act within two years of her knowledge of it. The law's recognition of the wife's right to collaborate in administering

changing the meaning of marriage

community property, as well as its provision for legal recourse, surpassed the limits of customary law and gave women greater control over their households.

Regarding debts, payment may be pursued and collected on both community property and the personal property of either spouse – the husband's property first – if contracted by one or both spouses on household items. If the debt is in the husband's name alone and was not used for the household, only the community property (not including the wife's reserved property) and the husband's personal property can be pursued. If the debt is in the wife's name, her personal and reserved properties can be pursued if she did not have her husband's prior written or tacit approval. The law grants further protection from the husband's mismanagement of property by allowing the wife to receive court approval to manage her own revenues separately if her husband's financial status can be shown to jeopardize her rights.

Although the above provisions have helped to make the community property option more popular than separation of assets, full financial autonomy remains possible. If a couple opts for a separation of assets, each spouse is fully responsible for administering personal property and debts before and during the marriage. According to the law, any property for which ownership cannot be established belongs to each in equal portions. Measures are also included to allow the administration of a spouse's property with tacit or written approval. Any fraudulent actions or negligence must be pursued within five years. Inheritance does not have to be shared with the spouse, but is divided among descendants and those cited in the line of inheritance established by the 1964 law.

If the chosen option – community property or separation of assets – is later found to be unsuitable, couples can switch to the other by mutual agreement. According to the law, however, spouses must wait at least two years before presenting a written request to the appropriate judicial authorities.

The repercussions of the change in marital laws

Despite the appearance of benefits for Ivorian women, criticisms of the law have come from women, men and organized constituencies in Côte d'Ivoire. The first complaints came from the Chambre de Notaires, an organization of corporate lawyers whose members intervene in all property settlements, such as those following inheritance or divorce proceedings. Although pleased with legislators' efforts to grant women some authority in marriage, they felt that the law did not fully liberate both husband and wife. First, given the fact that most women are still categorized as housewives or 'without profession', they argued that the crucial need to recognize household duties as a contribution to the household had not been addressed. Second, the law requires mutual consent for any changes in the marital regime, yet the refusal of one spouse can prevent the other from fully controlling his/her property in the event of a transfer to a separation of assets. Third, and most important, the government proposed only one legal regime and did not allow couples the freedom to establish a marriage contract that could legalize traditional forms of marriage as well as non-traditional arrangements. The family codes of Mali and Senegal, for example, allow polygyny as an option. The organization's members were also concerned about the competent dissemination of information to the population and offered to work with the media to achieve this (Chambre de Notaires, 1984).

Advocates of social change point out that none of the attempts to stimulate widespread change through legislation has been effective. Observations in the field show the continuing coexistence of customary, Islamic and secular law; little has changed since the colonial period. The government has not issued any sanctions and appears reluctant to disturb the political stability for which this country is known by forcing compliance with these laws. Consequently, in cases where couples ignore secular law, disputes in which the state is asked to intervene must be settled under other sections of the law (for example, the penal code).

Perhaps most importantly, women have not been protected or liberated to the degree suggested by the legislation. The laws may suggest acceptable behaviour, but it is not uncommon for couples to begin their marital relationship under customary law and then legalize the marriage only after many children and several years of cohabitation (although the law does at least provide for the recognition of children in marriages not sanctioned by the state). Furthermore, despite the government's efforts to establish the conjugal unit and its community of interests, both husbands and wives astutely manipulate the regime to safeguard their personal interests.[10] The lack of control by administrative services allows this to occur. In many cases, married women have acquired property during the marriage but have alienated it from the community by putting it in their children's names. The woman's intent may be to protect the fruit of her labour from illegitimate children, who would have equal access to community wealth in inheritance proceedings. Another problem concerns women whose marriages have not been registered. Although they are considered concubines and have no rights under marital law, many Ivorian men maintain such women, providing them with housing, cars, jewellery and other forms of wealth. Payments for such items are usually in cash and difficult to trace. Debts incurred in the conjugal unit, possibly as a result of this alienation of funds to concubines, are charged to community revenues. Concubines are never pursued for payment of debts charged to the community. Legal wives retaliate by spending more of their husbands' resources on consumer items. The deputies themselves admit that the ambiguity of the law leaves room for deviation, misinterpretation and misbehaviour. The failure of the law to prevent concubinage is its most problematic aspect. In fact, in this cultural milieu, the unique regime of the community, with its insistence on monogamy, has encouraged a proliferation of concubines whose relationships are controlled neither by the state nor by tradition. For reasons already stated above, men continue in polygynous relationships. It is true that children of these relationships are protected, but the financial security of married women is jeopardized, not to mention that of concubines, who are in unstable, temporary relationships.

As mentioned earlier, community property continues to be the most acceptable option, although mostly by default. It was thought that the separation of assets option might respond to the needs of several categories of women, including those in business and those concerned about protecting wealth from a husband's matrilineage. For young husbands struggling to develop their own businesses, the separation of assets could provide a means to protect the patrimony in the name of the wife. Nevertheless, the separation of assets is not popular, and few couples choose this option on the day of the marriage. One reason for this option's lack of acceptance is that it has already been condemned as 'the regime of the selfish.' The minister of justice, in his presentation of the amendments to the National Assembly in 1983, said, 'The best regime is one that allows the man, as much as the woman, to thrive in [an atmosphere of] total confidence. If you opt for a separation of assets at the start, there is scheming and mistrust.' Public acceptance of this view is evidenced by the fact that audiences attending marriage ceremonies usually listen attentively to hear which option the couple has chosen, and several women have admitted fear and possible embarrassment if they opt for the separation of assets. Until the authorities attempt to remove the stigma, the separation of assets will remain an unlikely choice for young couples.

Clearly other options are needed if marital relationships are to benefit both women and men. One logical step in the evolution of Ivorian marital law could be the acceptance of a marriage contract in which men and women can openly and honestly collaborate. Another means of bringing the law within reach of more women might be to make the registration of marriages easier. It is worth considering the possibility of allowing women to register their marriages without the consent of their spouses, but with witnesses who can confirm the existence of a monogamous union. Spouses could challenge the registration within, for example, 15 days of official notification. Failure to do so would lend tacit approval to the registration and would imply a willingness to cooperate in case of adjudication. Such simplification of the registration process would allow more women to have access to the law.

Conclusions

The experiment in Côte d'Ivoire has tested the capacity of the government to determine the direction of social change and marital relationships, but it has been an experiment over which women's influence has been limited by culture, political structures and public opinion. By imposing new laws, the government hoped to persuade Ivorians to adopt a style of behaviour that they felt would he more conducive to rapid national development. This study has shown that although the government has been instrumental in determining the direction of social change, it has not been able to control the pace of change. Evolution in this area appears to depend more on education, economic development, the tenacity of tradition, and the ability of women to participate in the process than on the desires of a handful of legislators.

Neither the efforts made under colonialism nor those in the first years of independence to legislate social change in marital relationships have had a widespread effect. Nevertheless, as advances in education and employment are made, women are beginning to take more interest in political and economic developments at the national level. Intervention by elite women led to the 1983 amendments. Many of these elite women belonged to the salaried class and were willing to operate within the confines of the law, although their interests had been severely compromised by the earlier 1964 laws. These women have been frequently criticized for acting more in their own interests than on behalf of the majority whom the legal system is made to serve, but whatever their reasons, the contributions of elite women as party activists and intellectuals should also increase women's participation at the grass-roots level.[11]

Ironically, the provisions of the 1983 amendments are much closer to the idealized traditional rights of women to manage personal wealth, such as those found in certain matrilineal cultures. They also protect the lineage from the alienation of family wealth when daughters marry. Yet the direction of change, as established by the president in 1964, is still toward monogamous marriage and individual responsibility. The 1964 legislation, however, left far too many marriages outside state control, partially because it rejected traditional concepts of property management. The more inclusive 1983 revisions illustrate the impact that women can have on legislation leading to social change.

Further progress in changing women's roles within marriage will also depend on the willingness of party activists and professional groups to participate in organized efforts to increase women's awareness of the law. Legal administrators and legislators must make legal services available to the poor and illiterate, and must demonstrate the benefits they can obtain from the law. Until rural as well as urban husbands and wives are able to recognize that the state legal system offers freedom from the constraints of traditional extended-family control, change will be slow. Regardless of its pace, change toward greater freedom for women within marriage is irreversible, not simply because it is protected by state law but because modern social and economic reality make it necessary. Men, however, are unlikely to relinquish authority over their families easily, and unless the state makes it more practical for women to comply with the law, traditional marital practices will persist for some time, despite the state's plans for social change.

Notes

1 Former President Felix Houphouët-Boigny was elected upon independence in 1960 and presided over a one-party presidential regime. He was continually re-elected to consecutive five-year terms and served until his death in December 1993.

2 Snyder (1982) explains that 'customary law' was not always indigenous practice, but a modification of tradition as interpreted by French colonial courts within a broader framework of French concepts of justice. On the other hand, customary law contained features more harmonious with ethnic traditions than most modern national law. Roberts (1974) summarized the findings of a seminar on African family law, which emphasized that national legal systems need to acknowledge the reality that no single legal system is legitimate for everyone.

3 For the patrilineal Guro and Senufo, see Meillasoux (1974).

4 Salacuse (1969) offers a competing suggestion that the decision to eliminate the bride price was a result of excessive inflation stemming from the impact of a cash economy, and that the bride price had lost its traditional significance.

5 This is one of the areas singled out by Dumetz (1975) to illustrate the creativity of Ivorian legislators. The recognition of children born out of wedlock was not accorded in France until 1972.

6 The results of surveys in rural and urban areas show an extremely low level of compliance. See Ellovich (1985), Levasseur (1976), and Mundt (1975) on Côte d'Ivoire. See Bleek (1977) for similar results in Ghana.

7 *choc* translates as 'shock' and infers radical social engineering.

8 See also Lewis (1982).

9 See World Bank, World Development Reports, 1984 and 1990, Oxford University Press; United Nations Economic Commission for Africa, African Socio-Economic Indicators, New York, 1986; The World Fact Book, US Government Printing Office, Washington, D.C., 1986.

10 Kuper and Kuper (1965) cite deviant behaviour as a probable consequence of a hastily unified legal system.

11 See Carlene Dei, Chapter 8 of Women and Family Law in Côte d'Ivoire.

References

Archives de l'Assemblée Nationale
1964   Commission Elargie Procès Verbaux, nos. 1-10 (Septembre).
1983   Expose des motifs modifiant et complétant les lois du 7 octobre 1964.
1983   Débats: Sixième Législature.

Journal Officiel de la République de Côte d'Ivoire
27 Octobre 1964
6 Octobre 1983
13 Octobre 1983

Books and articles
Bleek, W., 'Marriage in Kwahu, Ghana'. In: S. Roberts (ed.), *Law and the family in Africa*. The Hague,
      Mouton, 1977.
Boserup, E., *Woman's role in economic development*. London, Allen & Unwin, 1970.
Chambre de Notaires, 'Les régimes matrimoniaux en Côte d'Ivoire'. Abidjan, 1984.
Dei, C., 'Women and grassroots politics in Abidjan, Côte d'Ivoire'. In: G Mikell (ed.), *African feminism:
      the politics of survival in Sub-saharan Africa*. Philadelphia, University of Pennsylvania Press, 1997.
Dobkin, M., 'Colonialism and the legal status of women in francophonic Africa'. *Cahiers d'Études
      Africaines*, vol. 8 (1968), pp. 390-405.
Dumetz, M., *Le droit du mariage en Côte d'Ivoire*. Paris, Librairie Général de Droit, 1975.
Ellovich, R., 'Law and Ivorian women'. *Anthropos*, vol. 80 (1985), pp. 185-97.
Etienne, M., 'Women, men, cloth and colonization: the transformation of production-distribution
      relations among the Baoule'. In: M. Etienne and E. Leacock, *Women and colonization*. New York,
      Praeger, 1980, pp. 214-228.
Etienne, P. and M. Etienne, 'Terminologie de la parenté et de l'alliance chez les Baoulé (Côte d'Ivoire)'.
      L'Homme, vol. 7 (1967), pp. 50-76.
Eze, O. C., *Human rights in Africa*. Lagos, Macmillan, 1984.
Folquet, L., 'La situation juridique de la femme mariée dans le nouveau droit de fa famille ivoirienne'.
      Revue Juridique et Politique, 4 (1974).
Hooker, M. B., *Legal pluralism: an introduction to colonial and neo-colonial laws*. Oxford, Clarendon, 1975.
Kouame, N., 'Femmes ivoiriennes: acquis et incertitudes'. *Présence Africaine* IT87, no. 141 (1987).
Kuper, H. and L. Kuper (eds.), *African law: adaptation and development*. Berkeley, University of
      California Press, 1965.
Lampue, P., 'Le role de la jurisprudence dans l'évolution de la condition de la femme en Afrique noire
      francophone'. *Revue Juridique et Politique*, vol. 4 (1974).
Levasseur, A.A., 'The modernization of law in Africa with particular reference to family law in the
      Ivory Coast. In: Foster and Zolberg (eds), *Ghana and the Ivory Coast*. Chicago, University of
      Chicago Press, 1971.
Levasseur, A.A., *The civil code of the Ivory Coast*. Charlottesville, Michie Co., 1976
Lewis, B., 'Fertility and employment: an assessment of role incompatibility among African urban
      women'. In: E. Bay (ed.), *Women and work in Africa*. Boulder, Co., Westview Press, 1982.
Meillasoux, C., *Anthropologie économique de Gouro de Côte d'Ivoire*. The Hague, Mouton, 1974.
Mundt, R., 'The internalization of law in a developing country: the Ivory Coast's civil code'. *African
      Law Studies* 12 (1975).
O'Barr, J., 'African women in politics'. In: Hay and Strichter (eds), *African women South of the Sahara*.
      New York, Longman, 1984.

Paulme, D. (ed), *Women of tropical Africa*. Berkeley, University of California Press, 1960.

Rattray, R. S., *Ashanti*. Oxford, Oxford University Press, 1923.

Rattray, R. S., *Religion and art in Ashanti*. Oxford, Oxford University Press, 1927.

Roberts, S. (ed.), *Law and the family in Africa*. The Hague, Mouton, 1974.

Sacks, K., *Sisters and wives*. Urbana, University of Illinois Press, 1982.

Salacuse, J.W., *Africa south of the Sahara*. Vol. 1 of *An introduction to law in French-speaking Africa*. Charlottesville, Michie Co., 1969.

Sanday, P., 'Toward a theory of the status of women'. *American Anthropologist*, vol. 75 (1973), pp. 1682-1700.

Schuler, M. (ed.), *Empowerment and the law*. Washington, DC., OEF International, 1986.

Skinner, E.P., *African urban life: the transformation of Ouagadougou*. Princeton, NJ., Princeton University Press, 1975.

Snyder, F., 'Colonialism and legal form: the creation of customary law in Senegal'. In: C. Sumner (ed.), *Crime, justice and understanding*. London, Heinemann, 1982.

Taub, N. and E. Schneider, 'Perspectives on women's subordination and the role of law.' In: D. Kairys, *The politics of law: a progressive critique*. New York, Pantheon, 1982.

Toungara, J.M, 'Political reform and economic change in Ivory Coast: an update'. *Journal of African Studies*, vol. 13, no. 3 (1986).

Lina Abou-Habib

3 Family laws and gender discrimination: advocacy for legal reforms in the Arab region

Tripoli, North Lebanon – October 1998: A poor, polygamous and unemployed man, father of many children, from the nearby rural area of Akkar 'sells' his two daughters (eight and nine years old) to two families in the city of Tripoli to work as housemaids. One month later, Fatima, one of his daughters, is brought to hospital suffering from severe burns, beatings and other hideous forms of torture. Repeated blows on the head were to cause her a serious brain haematoma, whilst continuous chaining and beating of her tiny feet caused gangrene, which later necessitated the amputation of seven of her toes. The case caused temporary public indignation in Lebanon and led to the mobilization of a number of non-governmental organizations (NGOs), notably the Lebanese League to Resist Violence Against Women. As a result, the government was to decree a law raising the legal age of employment of children from eight to thirteen years. Case closed.

Tripoli, North Lebanon – October 1998: A young man rapes his girlfriend, then pours gasoline over her and burns her to death. Hardly any reaction from the private or the public sector. As the woman was apparently known for having a sexual relationship with this man, it was felt that she had brought it upon herself.

Beirut – September 1998: One of the religious family courts finally rules in favour of a woman in a matter of child custody. Her husband, a priest suffering from mental illnesses, has abused his status and deprived his former wife of the custody of her child, who was one year old when they separated on the grounds of physical and psychological abuses committed by the husband. Once the court verdict was pronounced, the priest fled the country with his daughter in what looked like a violation of a court order and a flagrant act of kidnapping. No legal procedures were started against him.

These horrific stories are not isolated cases perpetrated by sick or perverted individuals within a particular and specific context or country. They are the tip of the iceberg and denote a consistent pattern of unfettered discrimination and abuse against women in the Arab region. For the majority of women suffering injustice at the hands of husbands, brothers, fathers or even uncles and cousins, resorting to the law offers little if any help.

Despite some improvement in the situation of women in the Arab region, notably at the level of access to education and health, women remain in a subordinate and dependent position, often treated as second class citizens. The dichotomy between the public and private spheres remains as strong as ever, thus blocking any concrete advance towards gender equality. Whilst 11 Arab countries have signed and ratified the Convention on the Elimination of All Forms of Discrimination against Women (CEDAW),[1] all have expressed reservations with regard to clauses relating to family laws, thus preventing any possible advancement in this very important area for gender equality at the national and official level.

Family laws as the root cause of discrimination against women

My husband was a drug addict and an alcoholic. He would beat me and my two small daughters. When my divorce case was finally heard in court, he showed up with a man he picked up from the street. The man testified that he was my lover. I had never seen him before. I later found out that my husband had paid him to do this. The judge believed him nevertheless and ruled against me.
Nadia, 34, on her experience of seeking divorce in 1992.

The ways in which current family laws reproduce gender inequality and gender discrimination, as well as encourage and perpetuate gender oppression and violence against women, have been widely researched and documented. Indeed, current family laws are based on the supremacy of the male members of households as well as on the subordination and dependency of women. Thus, in matters of marriage, divorce, child custody and legal guardianship, alimony and especially inheritance, women are all too often in situations where they have lesser rights and a compromised access to legal recourse. Indeed, and according to the testimonies of numerous women in contentious situations, the antipathy and antagonism towards them is not only expressed in legal texts and procedures but is also reflected in the attitudes, behaviour and decision-making patterns of law enforcers at various levels.

This has very much transpired into and inspired 'modern' and secular state laws. In most Arab countries, and even when women's equality and full rights are enshrined in the constitution, women's rights are lagging behind men's. Witness to this is the struggle for women's right to vote, which has only been secured in the past decades in most Arab countries and remains withheld in a few others up until today. Another flagrant example is that of citizenship and naturalization laws, which are undoubtedly amongst the most discriminatory laws: in most Arab countries, women married to non-nationals may not pass on their nationalities to their spouse or children. Last but not least are the laws that fall under the umbrella of what is disgracefully known as 'crimes of honour'. In such situations, male members of the extended household receive little if any punishment if they commit a crime whereby a female member of the household is murdered because of alleged extra-marital emotional or sexual relationships. The laxity vis-à-vis 'crimes of honour' has not only been responsible for a legally permitted reign of terror over women but has also allowed male members of households to get rid of unwanted wives or sisters/daughters-in-law, often obtaining 'financial' benefit with the expropriation of assets and land owned by the victim.

Family laws and their reforms have never been the subject of a serious and committed discussion at the national level. Quite the contrary, family laws have always been held hostage to political manoeuvring and often used by the state as either a reward or a threat in struggles to maintain political supremacy. Even where minor reforms in favour of women have been introduced (such as in the case of Tunisia, for example), these have to some extent failed to gain massive popular support and have remained very much 'reversible' and threatened by contextual changes and imperatives. Hence, addressing the structural and root causes of gender inequality and discrimination has never been on the agenda. This has meant that progress in the implementation of CEDAW, where signed and ratified, has been slow, patchy, superficial and of doubtful impact on the lives of ordinary women.

For development NGOs in the Arab region, work on family laws and gender inequality has also been very limited, as many have shied away from tackling what is perceived to be a highly sensitive and political issue. In addition, the artificial dichotomy between the 'private' and 'public' spheres has meant that development NGOs failed to intervene in what they considered to be 'pertaining to the private sphere', such as family laws. This has also been reflected in the reluctance of many NGOs to deal with 'household' matters such as domestic violence. Thus, the daily challenges and struggles of women have been very much ignored or at best addressed inefficiently, thus posing serious long-term obstacles to women's development and to gender equality.

Women and men challenging discriminatory family laws

For women's groups and women's/feminist networks in the region, the issue of family laws has been considered as primordial for gender equality and as a unique priority for action, which has so far been both inspiring and empowering. Whilst many international aid agencies and donors have declared that issues pertaining to family laws are both 'sensitive' and 'cultural' and thus too tricky to deal with, women and men in the region have challenged such notions and have demonstrated ways in which concerted and collaborative action can be efficient and helpful in challenging gender discriminatory family laws.

Rather than portraying the image of women as helpless victims, a number of women in the region have resorted to daring public action and mobilization, often amidst hostile contexts and circumstances. The main purpose of this short exposé is to shed some light on model initiatives that are currently ongoing in the Arab region. The common denominator amongst these is the fact that they recognize the extent to which current family laws are the root cause of gender inequality and thus a major area of concern. Many of these initiatives combine grassroots action with local, regional and even global advocacy, and they operate in the midst of growing conservatism and antagonism and a widespread call for the exclusion of women from the public sphere. However, where women have succeeded in breaking the silence and speaking out, action and progress have been possible. At the very least, the mere steadfastness of such groups and such initiatives is a constant reminder of what is important for gender equality and a call for more tangible commitment from states and the international community to making gender equality possible and achievable.

The Arab Women Court: advocacy for reforms of the family code

The Arab Women Court (AWC), a feminist network gathering women's organizations from the Middle East, Maghreb and Gulf countries, was formed in 1995. The main aim was to establish a collective and regional pressure group to lobby for law reforms aiming at bringing about gender equality and curbing the growing trend and practice of gender violence and oppression. Despite certain contextual differences in the nature and manifestations of discrimination and violence against women, the Court believes that the root causes of gender equality are very similar throughout the Arab

family laws and gender discrimination

region: the deep-rooted patriarchal system, which is replicated in the political and legal systems.

Since its inception, the Court has strived to break the wall of silence and make known to the public the various forms of discrimination that women are subjected to by laws. In March 1998, the Court organized a public hearing on violence in the religious family laws. Women from Syria, Iraq, Tunisia, Algeria, Jordan and Lebanon presented moving and unprecedented testimonies of personal experiences in dealing with the laws in matters of marriage, divorce, child custody and inheritance. Twelve women who did not know each other and came from different Arab countries and various socioeconomic backgrounds described consistent patterns of discrimination and oppression by men, reinforced by family laws that perpetrate, reproduce and encourage situations of injustice vis-à-vis women. Given the magnitude of the problems that women face with religious laws, the AWC decided to launch a campaign for the reform of the divorce laws from 1999 for a two-year period. Through media campaigns, lobbying, awareness raising and education targeting students, professionals, policymakers and the public, the AWC aims to bring about reforms that will lead to a more egalitarian divorce law where women's rights to ask for divorce, gain child custody, legal guardianship and alimony, and share in the marital household are safeguarded.

The campaign aims at mobilizing women and men across the region regarding the wrongs incurred by women seeking divorce and the urgent need to introduce long-awaited legal reforms. The work of the AWC relies on extensive networking and collaboration amongst its members, most of whom are involved in direct grassroots-oriented programmes targeting women victims of abuse and violence. The wealth of experience and information gathered through such work provides the basis for a more regional and global campaign for the reform of family laws. The individual testimonies of women have indicated that divorce and its implications are a major source of discrimination and indeed misery for women. It is through the current legal procedures of divorce that women in various countries of the region find themselves deprived of their rights, of their property, and of child custody and guardianship. Thus, fears of being stigmatized as 'divorcee' and losing their children, homes and livelihood because of unfair laws and legal procedures prohibit women from entering into endless court cases that promise from the outset to be in favour of men, even in cases of severe abuse by the male spouse. The AWC hopes to transform the reform of the divorce laws into a public issue rallying local and international support. Although it will definitely be a long-term and difficult process fraught with risks and challenges, the AWC is adamant in its pursuit of gender equality through law reforms and public mobilization.

Collectif Maghreb Egalité: 100 measures for an egalitarian family code

Created three years before the Fourth UN Conference on Women (Beijing, 1995), the Collectif is a network of women's organizations, feminist lawyers, academics and activists from the three Maghreb countries of Morocco, Algeria and Tunisia.

As part of its work for the Beijing conference, the Collectif developed an alternative and egalitarian family code composed of 100 measures covering the thorny areas of marriage, divorce, child custody and inheritance. The code was presented in a model parliament during the international conference where the issue of the current family code as an obstacle to the advancement of Arab women was debated. The Collectif's work on an alternative and egalitarian family code provides practical and demonstrable tools for legal reforms. Concurrently, the Collectif is conducting research at the regional level, whereby precious information is collected on regular practices that individual women and men have elaborated to circumvent legally and resourcefully the hurdles that women face whilst dealing with the family code. Through such research, the Collectif hopes to demonstrate the ways in which loopholes in the current family codes can be used to women's advantage. The Collectif also argues that rather than simply allowing such practices to take place in order to seek justice for women, the family code ought to be reformed in such a way as to reflect gender equality and fairness.

Hope for the future

The initiatives described above mainly serve to demonstrate that family laws are not set in stone and impermeable to change. As in the case of gender relations, family laws are embedded in various social, cultural, economic and political contexts, which are prone to change. In addition, women and women's organizations and networks throughout the region have demonstrated that any development initiative aiming at empowering women is futile if it does not recognize and address the core and structural causes of gender inequality and oppression. They maintain that so long as these are considered as untouchable taboos, no real progress can be achieved towards gender equality. But mostly, such initiatives have provided the much needed hope of change. They have kept the issue of family laws high on the agenda, they have mobilized women and men at all levels, raised general public awareness at the local and global level and, most importantly, they have provided tangible alternatives and tools for change.

Notes

1   Source: UNIFEM Amman Regional Office / UNICEF Regional Office – 1997

Fiona Archer and Shamim Meer

4 Women, tenure and land reform: the case of Namaqualand's Reserves[1]

This paper grew out of a series of participatory workshops, meetings and discussions with women in the Namaqualand Coloured Rural Reserves in South Africa during 1993 and 1994.[1] The interviews and workshops were spearheaded by the realization that women stood to lose their security of occupational rights to land as a result of a proposed law to convert existing occupational rights to ownership rights. Women realized that the only way to fight the threat posed by this law was to become organized. They met in workshops facilitated by Fiona Archer, research facilitator for the Surplus People Project (SPP). They talked about their concerns and began the process of forming the Namaqualand Women's Forum. The research process itself was thus action-oriented, and facilitated the establishment of an embryonic organization of women.

During the workshops women raised many concerns. In this paper, we focus on the discussions pertaining to women's roles, control of resources and access to authority, in the context of land tenure and land reform. Critical issues of concern in this regard are that women's access to land, jobs and livelihoods in Namaqualand is predominantly through men; that women have very little decision-making authority in their homes or communities; and that there is a need to ensure that legislation is gender sensitive if women are to reap any benefits and achieve greater control over their lives. In addition to highlighting the struggles of women in Namaqualand's Coloured Reserves, this paper also serves to highlight that it is through organization that women can begin to take their lives into their own hands and begin to redress gender inequities in resource access and control.

Four main observations arise from the interviews and discussions. The first of these is that a gendered perspective is crucial in policymaking, as it uncovers women's previously shrouded experiences, and underscores the point that communities are gendered entities. Nongovernmental organizations (NGOs) and other policymakers that do not adopt a gendered outlook tend to privilege a male perspective, which they take as being the community's perspective. This is precisely what happened in the initial community-directed investigations into the future of the Namaqualand Coloured Reserves. These investigations began in 1993 after members from various communities in the Reserves approached the SPP for assistance. However, it was the men from these communities who approached the SPP. Women were initially not involved in these investigations, and it was only when threatened by the impact of the General Law Amendment Act No. 108 of 1993 that women placed their concerns on the research agenda.

A second point that emerges from this study is that gender relations and meanings are not fixed; they have changed over time, and are constantly in a state of flux. The changing nature of gender relations can be seen when tracing the gender division of labour, and the status afforded women in Namaqualand through the course of history. The impacts of state formation and capital accumulation over time resulted in changes in gender roles and meanings. This suggests that there can be changes leading to a more egalitarian system of gender relations in the future.

Thirdly, gender roles are often contested within the household, state and economy. The contestation of gender roles and meanings is revealed in individual women's daily survival strategies and the demands being made by the embryonic Namaqualand Women's Forum.

What follows from this understanding of the construction of present-day gender inequities is that gender sensitivity in legislation alone will not alter women's present status. Gender sensitivity in the law will open up space for women. Whether women can take up the opportunities afforded by this space will depend upon the extent of their organization.

This brings us to our fourth point: in addition to legal changes, women's empowerment through their organization is critical. The experience of the women in this study indicates that the organization of women is a key to redressing existing gender imbalances in society. Women in Namaqualand believe that it is through their organization that they can begin to make their voices heard, to ensure that they are part of decision-making and can push policymakers and legislators to greater sensitivity of women's needs.

Methodology

The methodology used in this study was largely interactive and participatory. SPP research facilitator Fiona Archer conducted interviews and participatory appraisals with individuals and groups of women in various communities in the Namaqualand Coloured Reserves. In addition, secondary sources were consulted. Talks and interviews about the role and rights of women were held in Kuboes, Sanddrif, Lekkersing, Steinkopf and Nourivier. Women from these communities played a role in directing the approach of the study and in information gathering. All the women interviewed were from the Coloured Rural Reserves. Thus white and African women in Namaqualand were not included in the interviews,[2] nor were women from the better-serviced towns and villages of Namaqualand. Individual and group interviews were not structured, but followed issues the women raised. While this approach made each meeting unique, many common concerns emerged. In cases where more than 20 women were present, the women broke up into smaller groups to allow more women to express their opinions. At one workshop, more than 70 women gathered in a lively and enthusiastic meeting. At another meeting, eight stockfarming women gathered in a *matjieshuis* (reed-house) at a *veepos* (stock-post). From here they could keep an eye on the stock that had to be kept off the wheat fields, while they talked about their lives and struggles.

Dispossession, proletarianization and changes in the sexual division of labour

Namaqualand is in the northwestern part of the old Cape Province in South Africa and currently falls within the Northern Cape province. The total area covers 4,796,000 ha (47 961 km^2) and is sparsely populated, with a population of 62,500 (1.2 people per km^2). Much of the population is concentrated in the so-called Coloured Rural

Reserves. Most inhabitants today rely on employment in the mining sector for survival, with farming as a secondary activity.

Roughly 2,100 years ago pastoralists entered the region from the northwest (the area that is Namibia today). The pastoralists travelled vast distances across today's Namaqualand and adjacent areas in search of the best pastures. They hunted, gathered and fished for survival. Competition over resources was minimal, since the area was sparsely populated. From historical accounts it is presumed that pastoralists lived in groups under the leadership of 'captains'. It is commonly accepted that the understanding among captains was that available grazing, game and other resources would be shared by all. During the late 1600s, European travellers entered the region. Initially, travellers posed no threat to the resource base of the indigenous people and were dependent on the Khoi inhabitants for their supplies of meat and other foodstuffs. Around the middle 1700s, *trekboere* (colonial pastoralists) entered the Namaqualand region. The existing system of reciprocity amongst the indigenous people made it easy for the *trekboere* to gain grazing rights from the captains of the Nama-speaking Khoi. Despite this encroachment, the *trekboere* did not initially have an impact on the indigenous people's movements or access to resources.

Around the same time as the arrival of the *trekboere*, missionaries began to enter Namaqualand.While the travellers and *trekboere* had not initially disrupted social and economic relations dramatically, the missionaries did. Missionaries were responsible for altering the lifestyle of many of the indigenous people. They attempted to limit their nomadic lifestyle and they encouraged the cultivation of crops and the establishment of permanent settlements. Mission villages with surrounding occupation areas were established. Within these mission villages, Christian notions of a woman's role and her status in relation to her man and family shaped the form of settlements and framed women's role in agricultural enterprise.

Women's role and status in traditional Nama society

Women played a very important role in traditional Nama society. Historians emphasize women's central role in socioeconomic structures and the respect with which Nama women were treated by their men. Reports on the role of the eldest sister around the 1860s state that '...to her was left entirely the milking of the cows. This was in accordance with the respect shown to the female sex in general...' (Vedder, 1928). In addition it was said that 'the highest oath a man could take was to swear by his eldest sister, and if he should abuse her name, the sister will walk into his flock and take his finest cows and sheep, and no law could prevent her from doing so' (Hahn, 1878). Women generally enjoyed more favourable status than in the present. For example, it was said that 'the position of the women among the Nama is by no means that of the devoted servant of man ... When in need of something the man has to approach his wife entreating[ly] and imperiously' (Vedder, 1928). Women's status was no doubt linked to their control of and access to key economic resources including stock. 'The status of women was relatively high in the economic field, for not only did they have access to some private property, but they also controlled the milking of livestock and milk and its products' (Vedder, 1928). However, in the political domain, women were at a disadvantage and relied on men: 'Politically women held office very infrequently and are not reported to have been members of the popular Assembly ... it is not true to say that a wife occupies an inferior status in the elementary family, but it does not follow that a husband and wife are equal. Since each occupies a different status husbands and wives are complementary' (Carstens, 1966).

The impact of mining

While the traditional way of life began to be eroded as a result of the advent of the missionaries, the traditional economy was destroyed as a result of the discovery of the area's mineral wealth. Following the discovery of minerals in the 19th century, settlers began to claim and privatize large sections of land, thereby pushing the weaker Khoi further and further north. Copper was discovered in the region of Springbok, and the first significant copper mine was opened in 1852. Following the discovery of copper, the colonial government and mining capital ensured that all ownership of resource-rich land was removed from the Nama-speaking people. The colonial authorities ruled that neither the mission stations nor their inhabitants had any rights to mineral deposits in these territories. This ruling was later formalized in the 1909 Mission Stations and Communal Reserves Act.

The missionaries and the Namaqua called on the colonial authorities to protect them from increasing encroachment by the *trekboere*. In response to this, the British Crown issued Tickets of Occupation from the mid-1800s onwards, in respect of partially surveyed lands surrounding mission stations. These Tickets of Occupation typically stated that land should be held in trust for and on behalf of the local Nama inhabitants. They covered rights to occupation and grazing, but not rights to minerals. In accordance with Victorian Christian notions of a woman's place in the home, and of her subservient status, these Tickets of Occupation were issued to men.

The Nama people had sacrificed their autonomous power to the missionaries in order to secure their access to land. The captains and missionaries decided jointly how and when land was going to be used. This was the start of the Reserves. In addition to gender implications for ownership and control over land, the issuing of the Tickets was also linked to racial classification and processes of economic differentiation in Namaqualand. The Tickets specified that the inhabitants had to be aborigines or Basters (the progeny of Khoi-colonist liaisons), thereby establishing the principle of access to land on racial terms. Gender, race and class hence came together to determine control, access and authority.

The traditional economy, in which people relied on the indigenous fauna and flora for their existence, was severely eroded with the discovery of minerals. The Nama-speaking people lost access to resource-rich land, and, in some instances, the fencing-off of land prevented access to traditional pasture routes. In addition, mining capital's need for labour in the region pushed the Nama-speaking people into wage labour. People became increasingly reliant on cash incomes in order to secure livelihoods. Whilst the loss of land did not exclude the Nama from access to land for pasture, agriculture, and wild plants and herbs, it led to increasing poverty (Sharp, 1984).

The position of women within the changing economy was eroded, and women were increasingly disadvantaged in access to and control over resources, status and authority, compared with their men. The introduction of a cash economy resulted in processes of differentiation along the lines of income and gender. Women at every level were worse off by comparison with the men of their class. Even among the most severely marginalized, resources shifted into the hands of men, adversely affecting women's position in households as well as in the community.

Legislation to bolster colonial and apartheid control

The discovery of diamonds at the end of the nineteenth century exacerbated a situation in which rich land was removed from the Nama-speaking people. Large tracts of land, especially on the west coast, were fenced off and became security zones to which entry was forbidden. A series of laws further entrenched ownership and control of both land and labour in the interests of mining and agricultural capital.

The Mission Stations and Communal Reserves Act 29 of 1909 brought mission trust land under secular control. This Act had two objectives: to ensure control over the wealth of the area and to create a cheap labour supply. Under the terms of this Act, a register was drawn up of the male household heads who occupied land within the Reserves. The Act placed the management of the Reserves in the hands of a central office in Springbok. A local Advice Board that included elected community members could take decisions on grazing patterns. Communal tenure remained the prevalent form of tenure. Nama-speaking families continued to live on white farms in return for labour until the 1940s, however, when they were forced to move into the already overpopulated, overstocked Reserves. Hence access to grazing resources outside the Reserves was severely diminished by legislation, while the increased population and stock pressures degraded the resource base inside the Reserves.

The Land Settlement Act of 1940 provided grazing licences to white farmers, and these were eventually converted to ownership rights. Coloured farmers thus lost access to nonprivatized land. This Act also severely restricted the movement of pastoralists. The Group Areas Act of 1950 confined farming by indigenous people to within the boundaries of the Reserves. Through this Act, the apartheid state sought to set up separate areas for each of South Africa's race groups. However, the Act was both ideological and economic in intent, securing the resource-rich land in the interest of white capitalists and the state.

Over the years, the government's and capital's policies ensured the underdevelopment and impoverishment of the region through the outflow of resources, with few or no profits being returned to the region. The eight Coloured Reserves that fall within this region have been severely marginalized through legislation designed by a system of racial capitalism.

However, during the 1980s, the Coloured Reserves did receive some support from the apartheid government, which attempted, during this period of 'reform', to woo coloured South Africans through the tricameral system of government. This support, however, lasted only until the late 1980s, when these areas were once more marginalized in terms of state resources.

Women's deteriorating position over time

The action of the state and capital contributed to the breakdown of the traditional economy and to the increasing impoverishment of the indigenous community. Within this scenario, women's position worsened in relation to that of men of the same race and class. Over time, these changes resulted in changing relations within the family. With the erosion of the subsistence economy, gender roles underwent change. In the traditional economy, women played a central economic role. As survival became more and more dependent upon a cash economy, however, men were pushed into wage labour. They now had access to and control over the means of survival – jobs and incomes. The divide between productive and reproductive spheres became wider, with women becoming increasingly marginalized in reproductive roles. Reproductive labour was not seen as having value, and women's status in society declined. Women, by and large, came to be dependent upon men, as even their productive work relied on cash earnings brought in by the men. Alongside this greater economic reliance on men, and the concomitant loss of access to natural resources, went an erosion of women's status and worth in society. In terms of political authority, women had never enjoyed this in the past. However, never before had they been as dependent upon men as they now were, and in this context lack of access to political authority took on a new meaning.

Women's roles and access to resources and authority today

As a result of apartheid policy, Namaqualand is divided into the large mining villages on the one hand, and the rural Reserves on the other. Women, children and the elderly form the majority of the population in the Reserves. Women in the Reserves depend, by and large, on men's incomes for survival. Men work in the mining villages or in Cape Town, returning to the Reserves at weekends or at the end of the month. Migrant labour results in women having to take sole responsibility for the daily managing and maintenance of the household. This places pressures on women and on the whole family, resulting in social problems, particularly with the youth. Women today provide for the needs of their families through their roles in reproduction, production and aspects of community management. Yet women get very little or no recognition for the work they perform. They play very little part in the political decision-making arenas of community life in the Reserves, and they are disadvantaged in access to and control over the very resources they need to perform their roles adequately.

Women's reproductive labour includes activities such as cooking, cleaning, rearing of children, sewing and ironing. In addition, it involves responsibility for the physical and spiritual wellbeing of the family. Women have had to provide for families with diminishing access to vital resources and amenities.

In addition, women engage in productive activities, usually for the benefit of the household. However, the incomes women earn are usually controlled by their husbands. Women's productive work includes agriculture and stock farming while men are away. Often this is arduous work. In the summer months, for example, keeping the goats out of the wheat fields is a difficult task. During this time, water sources dry up and women have to walk long distances to find water. During the lambing season women live at the stock-posts to assist with the management of the herd. All this work, when not resulting in cash income, tends to be regarded as an extension of women's reproductive labour. This is so even when these activities secure a means of livelihood for the family, when men are retrenched from the mines and return to the Reserves. Although jobs are generally a resource largely in male hands, in some instances women do secure jobs. In these cases, women often have access only to the lowest-paid, least-sought-after jobs. Usually this is domestic work in other towns. Women in these jobs live and work away from home. They earn small salaries, barely enough to buy food. Some women are employed on farms in the fruit-packing season. This is very strenuous work with very little pay.

As an extension of their reproductive roles, women also fulfil a community management role. This includes the handling of crises when the wellbeing of the community and household is threatened. In one instance, women were required to manage the crisis of a threatened water supply. Women in two villages – Kuboes and Komaggas – called meetings and organized themselves to solve the water problem. In Kuboes, the women took action without the approval of many of the men. Similarly, women played an active role in the 'economic unit' struggle of the 1980s, when livelihoods were threatened as a result of the apartheid state's privatization of communal lands. Women's reproductive roles were threatened, as the privatization resulted in a loss to women of firewood, water and medicinal plants. Because of this, women attended meetings and spoke out, even though few women were committee members or decision-makers.

Women's managing role must be seen as distinct from community decision-making, in which arena women have little say. Women are not involved in the planning and management of resources. Management boards seldom allow women to make decisions about issues such as water shortages. Since men are not directly affected by such issues, they do not see these as urgent and do not prioritize them at meetings. Because women do not share in decision-making, issues affecting them are ignored, and priorities with regard to development are distorted in favour of men's interests.

'A women's work is only recognized when it is not done'

Although women struggle and work hard at running homes and securing livelihoods, their work is seen as inferior to men's and is taken for granted. This attitude was clearly illustrated during a ceremony in the Richtersveld during 1991, when men were remunerated for their fetching, carrying and other labour, while women were expected to do the cooking and serving without receiving payment. As one woman said, 'a women's work is only recognized when it is not done'. Many men see their wives as unemployed, despite the fact that they spend many hours every day keeping their houses in order, cleaning, cooking and attending to sick children and the elderly. However, as worth is linked to money today, when women's work earns money the attitude to it changes. And as the value increases, the asset often becomes appropriated by men.

An example of how women's work acquires a new meaning or worth is seen in the history of gathering firewood in Namaqualand. When firewood was a free resource, women were responsible for gathering it. However, when wood became scarce it increased in value, and men began to gather it in order to sell it. In addition to the task becoming men's work, the nature of the work also changed. While women walked to collect firewood, men now transported the wood with donkey wagons and vehicles. Soon there was no longer any wood around town for women to gather and they were forced to buy wood. In addition to the collecting becoming men's work, control over wood resources changed hands as these resources became scarce and hence more valuable.

Women's dependence on men

In discussions, women in the Reserves made it clear that they are almost completely dependent on men. Their access to resources and authority is mostly through men.

They have limited access to land in their own right and therefore little security of tenure. Officially and administratively, the rights of women in Namaqualand are undermined, because women only become registered occupiers of land on the death of their husbands. Even though a widow can take over her husband's rights, this does not always happen. In Kuboes, for example, there are more than 300 plots, but only three women have occupational rights. Most women in the Coloured Rural Reserves, therefore, do not have occupation rights in their own name. During the last 50 years, it was uncommon for any land in the Reserves to be sold, so women's security of tenure was reasonable. However, the Second General Law Amendment Act 108 of 1993, which allows for occupational rights to be transferred to ownership rights, threatens women's security of tenure. Women in the Reserves became aware that this Act would be detrimental to their interests, as they were not registered as occupants and taxpayers. Men, as the registered occupants and taxpayers, would benefit from this law. The realization of the discriminatory effect of the law provided the incentive for women to debate property issues, perhaps for the first time in the Namaqualand Reserves. In particular, women were concerned that the law could result in their loss of formerly secure occupational rights. Given the adverse economic situation in Namaqualand, many women feared the attachment of properties for repayment of the owners' (men's) debts. In the case of divorce, women stood to lose everything. Women's security of occupation thus lies largely with their husbands. Women believe that issues of access to and control over resources and decision-making need to be addressed to improve their position as women. It is this belief that spearheaded the organization of women in the Namaqualand Women's Forum.

The way forward: women organize

In discussions at the local and regional meetings, women saw clearly that their disadvantage in access to and control over resources was linked to their lack of political authority. The women decided to network as a region, and held their first regional workshop on 3 August 1994 to raise their concerns about issues relevant to them. This was the largest gathering ever held in Namaqualand to discuss women's concerns. The 140 women attending this workshop decided that it was of critical importance to formalize the organization of women. They therefore formed the Namaqualand Women's Forum (NWF) and elected an interim steering committee, whose members were mandated to set in motion a process of regional workshops in order to plan the way forward. Women at this meeting also undertook to establish local village-based branches of the Forum, and to sound out their members about the vision, objectives and aims of a forum. By October 1994, local branches of the NWF had been set up in at least eight of the villages in Namaqualand. In order to facilitate a process whereby women become more confident and informed, the NWF aims to bring women together in the region. The women are adopting a strategy of organizing women separately and, through this, aim to ensure their involvement in local government and civic structures. Women feel that their organization is imperative in order that they may make demands collectively to increase their participation in community decision-making structures, so that women's interests are addressed.

Women's mobilization today takes place in the context of broader community struggles to ensure the future development of Namaqualand, as the government continues with its Reconstruction and Development Programme (RDP). The changes in the country and the new political space for communities to achieve a better life are among the factors responsible for spearheading the organization of women. In addition, women's mobilization took place because of the perceived threat to their security of tenure. The realization that the community-led investigations on the future of the Reserves did not include their interests led women to act.

It is clear from discussions with women and men that women's rights of security of occupation were given very little consideration in the past. In the face of the threat to their security of occupational rights, several women felt it was imperative that they got together to discuss the implications of the legislation, as well as the implications of various other aspects of the transitional period in South Africa. A wide range of women took part in discussions, meetings and workshops. Debates on property rights led to further debates on the role and rights of women in Namaqualand. Women were particularly concerned about development in general, the local government and transition, the RDP, and the welfare of communities in the region. The process of the workshops, and the embryonic women's organization, have already resulted in previously shrouded issues becoming the subject of wider community debate and concern. However, there are obstacles that women must confront as they move on to strengthen their organization.

Obstacles to women's participation in community decision-making

Women identified a number of obstacles to their participation in decision-making structures within the community. These were linked most crucially to their own lack of information and the lack of confidence that prevents women from participating at meetings, and to the time-consuming domestic work that prevents them from attending meetings. As one woman said, 'The role of the women in the house pushes her out of the community.' Women also face a lack of support from both men and other women. Often women are blocked by other women, who oppose their initiatives to start projects. More often they are blocked by men, who do not see a place for women in community decision-making. Men discourage women from taking part in meetings with comments such as, 'Do you want to wear the trousers?' Often these comments are made when a woman is alone with her husband and without the support of other women and therefore in a weak position to challenge them. Men are usually disrespectful and accusing when it comes to women's participation in the public sector.

The women's organization is still too young to have made headway with women's participation in local government structures. However, it would seem that with correct strategizing, women will be able to win their demands for greater representation. The ongoing battle will be to ensure that those women who get onto the presently male-dominated structures maintain their links with and support from the women in the Reserves and are able to place women's interests on the agenda.

Conclusion

This paper has shown how the increasing awareness by women of their marginalization from community decision-making arenas resulted in an awakening that led to the establishment of the Namaqualand Women's Forum. There are, however, serious obstacles to women's ability to organize themselves and become involved in decision-making arenas in the community. These include lack of information, lack of confidence, lack of experience in organizing formal networks, and pressures on women's time that result from the existing division of labour, according to which women are responsible for childcare, housework and general household maintenance. These issues need to be addressed in order to ensure successful organization.

We have alluded in this paper to the link between economic production, control over economic resources, and status. At the start, women in Namaqualand were seen to be active economic agents, and this imbued their position in society with positive status. As the economy shifted to greater reliance on cash earnings, and as the means to acquire cash incomes were placed in male hands, women's increasing dependency left them with greater reproductive responsibility. The split between productive and reproductive work became more intense, and women's (generally unpaid) work was now imbued with negative status. As women lost access to and control of key economic resources, so too did they lose their former status and authority. However, this link between access to resources and authority should not be oversimplified. It should be borne in mind that although in the past women did have a higher status than at present, they did not have political authority. And, as present-day experiences elsewhere have shown, having ownership of land in itself has not necessarily meant an improved status for women. Thus, while we should not oversimplify this relation, it would seem that women's position will be markedly improved through greater access to productive resources and political authority. With greater economic independence from men, women will be in a better position to make demands to redress existing imbalances.

In suggesting a gendered perspective, we have implied a challenge to notions of 'community' as a homogeneous entity. We have highlighted that communities are made up of men and women, each having specific priorities and interests, based on their position in the gendered division of labour. However, we need to point out, in addition, that women themselves are not a homogeneous entity. Age, income level, race, kin role (mother, sister, wife, daughter), all intervene to create distinct experiences and interests among women. Some of these divisions were noted in the workshops with Namaqualand women, and these differing experiences need to be taken into account when organizing women and when identifying women's needs.

Finally, it is through organization in separate women's organizations, and through representation on community-wide structures, that women will be able to advance their interests. Legal solutions in themselves will be insufficient in challenging women's lack of access to jobs, land and authority.

Notes

1 This research was supervised by Lola Steyn at the Surplus People Project (SPP), an affiliate of the National Land Committee (NLC). It was carried out with funds from the IDRC (International Development Research Centre, Ottawa, Canada) and Interfund. Copyright © Surplus People Project 1995.
2 As a result of the policy of apartheid, which made it illegal for African people to live in most areas of Namaqualand, there are very few Africans in Namaqualand.

References

Carstens, W.P., *The social structure of a Cape Coloured Reserve*. Cape Town, Oxford, University Press, 1966.

Hahn, T., 'The graves of Heitsieibib: a paper on the prehistoric race'. *Cape Monthly Magazine*, vol. 16, no. 97 (1878).

Merchant, C., *The death of nature: women, ecology and the scientific revolution*. New York, Harper & Row, 1983.

Sharp, J., 'Rural development schemes and the struggle against impoverishment in the Namaqualand reserves'. Second Carnegie Inquiry into Poverty and Development in Southern Africa. Conference Paper, no. 9. Saldru, University of Cape Town, 1984.

Shiva, V., *Staying alive: women, ecology and development*. Atlantic Highlands, NJ, Zed Books, 1989.

Vedder, H., *The native tribes of South West Africa*. London, Frank Cass, 1928.

Walker, C., 'Report on Cornfields Gender and Land Research Project'. Unpublished paper commissioned by the Association for Rural Advancement, Pietermaritzburg, 1994.

Shoba Arun

5 Does land ownership make a difference? Women's roles in agriculture in Kerala, India

Since the 1980s, Kerala has received attention because of its combination of low economic growth with high social development, compared to the rest of India and to other developing countries. Gender and development researchers are well acquainted with its impressive statistics on women: for example, Kerala's female-male ratio is 1,036 females for every 1,000 males, compared to a ratio for India as a whole of only 927 females for every 1,000 males (GOK, 1997). Life expectancy at birth is 69 years for men and 72 years for women, compared to 60.6 for men and 61.7 for women in India as a whole. According to the 1991 census, Kerala's literacy rate was 89.81%, whereas India's average rate is 52.21%; female literacy was 86.17% in Kerala, compared to the national average of 39.29% (GOK, 1997). Kerala's achievements relating to quality of life, high life expectancy, high literacy and low infant mortality are due to various social, historical and political reasons, but three key factors can be identified (Sen, 1992). The first is the relative autonomy of the government in two of Kerala's three subregions during the colonial period, which enabled it to spend more on health and education, creating public awareness as well as infrastructure. Second, women have been able to get equal access to these services, due to the matrilineal system of descent in Kerala, which has had a great influence on social and cultural development in Kerala. It has contributed to changing social attitudes and created conditions in which women made real progress in health and education.[1] Third, a surge of social and religious reform movements in the 19th and 20th centuries allowed social benefits to spread down the caste hierarchy, and a high level of democratization. Since 1956, successive governments in Kerala have been instrumental in improving health and education, and have also introduced radical land reforms, relatively high minimum wages and a wide network of social security schemes (Panikar and Soman, 1984). Improving 'woman's agency', for example, by promoting female literacy, is seen as contributing much to Kerala's exemplary social development (Panikar and Soman, 1984).

However, Kerala currently faces a number of crises, including low economic growth, high unemployment and a mounting fiscal crisis. Economic liberalization policies introduced in 1991 have led to fluctuating prices of cash and food crops, and the agricultural sector is in decline. This article examines the impact of the economic changes brought about by liberalization on Kerala's farmers, who are mostly smallholders, and links this to the questions of women's participation in agricultural production and gender equity in Kerala. The invisibility of women in Kerala's public domain has drawn considerable attention during recent years. Indian women's need for land rights[2] has been argued for on grounds of family welfare, efficient national development, gender equity and women's empowerment, and the argument that female inheritance of land would lead to land fragmentation has been refuted

(Agarwal, 1994). From a welfare perspective, women's land rights are promoted in the belief that they will enable women to have direct access to productive resources, so enabling them to meet their households' basic needs. But I have found that lack of direct access to productive resources is common even in households where women own land – a significant factor in perpetuating not only household poverty and economic inequality between women and men, but also social and cultural inequalities, both inside and outside the household.

The research

The article draws on a 12-month period of research into women's role in agriculture and how this is determined by their socioeconomic and cultural context, looking at both matrilineal and patrilineal[3] households. The matrilineal households (35% of the total households included in the research) were *nairs* (upper Hindu castes). *Nair* women may inherit and own land and property. The *nair* system of marriage, residence, land holding and inheritance has had tremendous implications for the status of women. Yet *nair* women have had little control over managing property, because men are the official heads of households (Gough, 1973; Agarwal, 1994). In addition, in 1960, the Kerala Agrarian Relations Act conferred ownership rights to tenants of land, and limited the extent of surplus land held by large landowners, which led to much land being taken away from matrilineal households (Saradamoni, 1983). The patrilineal households were Syrian Christian (30% of households in the research), *ezhava* (lower Hindu caste) and Muslim (10% each), and scheduled castes[4] and other Christian communities (15%). The scheduled castes mostly owned only dwelling plots, although some households leased small plots of land, usually less than half an acre. In patrilineal households, women do not own or inherit land; instead, they are provided with a dowry upon marriage, which may take the form of land given to the bridegroom, gold or cash, according to the preference of the groom's family. The daughter's family may pay for the non-land portion of the dowry by selling land or property; this is clearly negotiated, usually before the marriage. In most cases, women do not actually have a claim to household property, such as land. This has implications for their access to critical farm inputs and services, and agricultural practices.

Ummanoor and Moorkanad

The research took place in two locations, Ummanoor and Moorkanad. The first has a large *nair* community, while the latter has a large proportion of Muslim households. Communities of Christians, *ezhavas* and *pulayas*[4] are found in both regions. The *panchayat*[5] of Ummanoor is in the midlands, where the soil and water resources enable farmers to grow a variety of crops, including rubber and rice (GOK, 1996a)[6]. Agriculture is the main source of income in this *panchayat*; however, I found many men from farm households employed in teaching and clerical jobs. In spite of the high literacy rates of both women and men, it is not usual for women to take up paid employment, and it is particularly rare after marriage, when the husband's family may take such decisions. In a small proportion (7%) of cases, I found women had taken up teaching, if the school was located nearby; most of them were getting support from their natal families to meet their household responsibilities. More than three-quarters of land holdings in Ummanoor are below half an acre[7] in size, while 19% are between 0.5–2 acres of land (GOK, 1996a). Only 4.4% of the holdings are larger than this. In addition to agriculture and formal employment, cashew nut processing is a major source of income (other activities of lesser importance include brick-making[8]). Owing to the general stagnation of the cashew industry, most factories have moved to other states, thus leading to large-scale displacement of labour.

The *panchayat* of Moorkanad is in northern Kerala, in Malappuram district. The topography of the region is very varied, and crops include cashew, rubber, banana, tapioca, vegetables, coconut and arecanut. Here, it can be seen that the much-acclaimed Kerala model of development has not fully distributed benefits to the lesser-developed regions in the state. Malappuram district has the lowest income per capita in Kerala: 24% of households are without houses or farmland, though some may own their dwelling plots (GOK, 1996b). Out of a total of 3,081 landholders, 82% own less than half an acre, 13% have between half and two acres, and 5% own more than two acres of land (GOK, 1996b). Moorkanad is an industrially underdeveloped area, and there are also inadequate education facilities for higher education. The major medical centre in the area provides primary health care[9]; it is in poor physical condition, lacking a proper water supply, an adequate supply of medicines, and transport facilities (GOK, 1996b). The region has high levels of unemployment, and there has been a significant level of male out-migration[10] for many years, as a large population of this district works in the Gulf. In 1992–3, an estimated 119,200 migrants left Kerala for various destinations around the world: 53% of these migrated to the Gulf (GOK, 1997).

Many women and men in both locations reported that farming is seen as less profitable than it used to be. Over the past two decades, the cultivation of labour intensive crops like rice has declined in Kerala, and tree crops like coconut or rubber are cultivated instead, since they command a higher market price and require less labour. However, my respondents reported a steady increase in prices of inputs like fertilizers, and declining and unstable crop prices. Within six months in 1996–7, the price of one coconut varied between ten and two rupees, and the prices of rubber fell from 48 rupees per kg to 25 rupees per kg, resulting in extreme income instability (GOK, 1997). For many households, income from agriculture is now seen as a source of additional income rather than a livelihood in itself. An increasing preference for men to find employment outside the household has important implications for farming and gender relations in both matrilineal and patrilineal households.

Social norms and the gender division of labour

Overall, 45% of households in the research had a man in paid employment in the formal sector, while 30% had a man engaging in informal sector work, for example as an artisan or driver, and 15% had a man in paid farm labour. Almost 48% of women were managing the family farm, because their husbands had paid employment, were migrants or absent for another reason. About 35% of women were involved in paid work, and 7% of women were engaged in paid employment in the formal sector, like teaching, but also undertook some of the farm supervision. In households where men migrate to the Gulf (47% in Moorkanad), women shoulder a particularly heavy workload. It is amazing to see women single-handedly taking on all the responsibilities of the financial and social organization of the farm household, combining productive and reproductive tasks. In both locations, and in matrilineal as well as patrilineal households, women's limited role in many agricultural activities and traditional, narrow understandings of women's work led to constraints on what women were able to do on the farms[11], and to a lack of recognition of women's contribution to the household: for example, many women who manage the farm considered themselves to be housewives. This lack of recognition affects women's control over how income is spent, and their authority to participate in decisions regarding the sale of land or transfer of control or ownership of land to other family members.

Changing relationships: women and land

Nair women's control of land

Bina Agarwal argues that, in South Asia, women's land rights can, over time, help women negotiate less restrictive norms and better treatment from husbands (Agarwal, 1997). Although, in *nair* households, matrilineal inheritance laws enable women to inherit property such as land or houses, ownership of land does not seem to translate into control over it, or the income from it, or improved power relationships in the household. In many of my sample of *nair* households, women stand to inherit a majority of the family property, including farmland and other resources, but their ability to continue farming is largely determined by factors such as post-marital residence and paid employment. In several *nair* households, I found that the husband had taken charge of the household and farm responsibilities after marrying and moving to his wife's home. *Nair* households used to be matrilocal[12] as well as matrilineal, but I found that this has changed for many households. Women who live with their husbands away from their natal homes may see their share of property sold if it proves inconvenient or unprofitable. In the current economic climate, selling land is an attractive option for many, and the income accrued is used to buy property or build elsewhere. This process is given legitimacy by ideas about male control of dowry: a woman may inherit some of the assets of her natal family like property or gold, but the husband may use it as capital for setting up business, buying more land, or building a house. Revathi, aged 36, who described herself as a housewife (in the sense that she had no formal paid employment), told me: 'Sthridhanam [dowry] is given to our husbands, not to us, so that he can look after us. He and his family have all the right over it, whether it is cash, gold or land.' Another woman considered farming as not so lucrative as other business. She told me: 'Women are brought up to support decisions which are best for the family... for instance, I feel sad to sell my family property, but for the sake of a better future for my children, I have to do it.' (personal conversations, 1996–7)

In other cases, *nair* women have moved away from their land to accommodate a husband's paid employment – either to his home or a third location – and the wife's natal family is controlling her share of property, although the husband also has customary rights in matters over his wife's property. In many cases, the husband or the natal family seem to have more control over the woman's share of property than the woman herself. These findings in Kerala echo a study from northwest India, where many women who inherited land had only minimal control over the land they officially owned (Sharma, 1980). Nevertheless, in the Kerala study, some *nair* women were able to retain control over land and property that they inherit. For example, in some households, where husbands fail to do their share in maintaining the household, or do not save for the future, women – often with the help of their natal families or close friends – save the income accrued from cultivation on their share of the property, including that from cash crops such as rubber.

Changes to agricultural practices

Social norms regarding women's work and women's need to combine caring work with agriculture have led to changes in agricultural practices. The fact that labour intensive crops such as rice and tapioca are being replaced by tree crops, which need less attention, is positive. However, as one woman stated, 'often social norms restrict my time and labour as I cannot engage in cultivation like a man'. Many women in my study were supervising the farm, but avoiding tasks that are considered 'men's work', such as harvesting rubber and coconut, and purchasing agricultural inputs. Men were hired to take on these tasks. When men are engaged in paid employment locally, both men and women can make decisions about the farm, although men are the primary decision-makers in most households. In contrast, in households where husbands are absent, women are left to make decisions themselves. Some told me they were unhappy with this big responsibility, especially with tasks like organizing labour. Some women had decided to reduce the extent of farming and concentrate on growing most crops in the homestead garden. Another solution is to seek the assistance of close male relatives for labour, but depending on them leads to their involvement in household responsibilities and decision-making. Wives do not retain income from the main crops – this usually goes to their husbands. However, women do usually keep the income from secondary crops, such as cashew and tamarind, and from garden crops. In some households, I found that income derived from garden crops was being used by women to buy household appliances, to save in chitty[13] (informal savings) as a contingency fund, or for purchasing gold for their daughters.

Accessing extension services

In this context, women's ability to function as independent farmers needs to be enhanced by policies that support them in gaining direct access to credit, production inputs, and information about agricultural practices, and which rectify the male-biased farming system. In both locations, the Kerala state government has developed agricultural programmes, administered by local farm offices in order to distribute improved seeds and plants, pest management systems, and assist in small-farm mechanization. But both male and female respondents in my research reported that they do not receive adequate and timely information that is critical for farm productivity. In my conversations with women, it was clear that women have a great deal of indigenous knowledge about farm activities and crop cultivation, and, in the absence of exposure to technical knowledge that could potentially be gained from extension services, they resort to traditional methods of farming. However, women feel that they are less able than men to access technical advice. For example, Ummanoor women told me that farm extension services in their area tend not to approach women, because it is assumed that 'farmers' are men. During my fieldwork in early 1996, the incidence of root wilt for coconut was widespread, because farm

does land ownership make a difference?

extension officers failed to approach the households' women to discuss the scientific management of the problem. Similarly, most of the Moorkanad women who are left alone to head households while their husbands are away told me that they never approached the local farm offices *(Krishi bhavan)* directly, owing to a combination of social inhibitions and their increased involvement in other household activities. From my own observation, the extension officers – who are after all assigned to disseminate knowledge – only visited the fields, rather than searching out women in their homes. Although the social impropriety of visiting women at home might be cited as a reason, it is often assumed that women have no significant role in farm activities. Many women listen to agricultural programmes on the radio and television, and read daily newspapers, in an effort to improve their agricultural practices. This not only proves women's awareness of the need to improve agricultural methods and inputs, but is also a telling example of the instrumental value of women's literacy as a potential tool to increase farm efficiency and to ensure women's participation in the development process.

An example of how women who farm are marginalized from essential information is the wilting disease, which, in 1995, afflicted a new high-yield pepper, Panniyur-1. In Moorkanad, the disease destroyed almost all pepper cultivation. Women, who had little land, labour or money to hire labour, suffered most, since they had concentrated on growing garden crops, which do not need much labour and attention. Most women I spoke to had attributed the disease to natural causes, and did not receive timely information about the disease or alternative varieties; to a large extent, they had to rely on secondary information on agriculture gained through family networks and other local farmers. They had also not known at the time that they could have claimed for compensation (personal communication, 1996–7). This type of exclusion affects farm productivity and income: the prices of pepper had increased over 99% between 1991–97, especially after the introduction of economic reforms (GOK, 1997).

Accessing banking and markets

In Moorkanad, women also complained of lack of access to banking and credit facilities. In several households, women wanted to expand the farm or install pumps for irrigation, but said that they had been refused a loan because they could not provide any collateral security. There are only two banks in this region, and informal lending for high interest, or pawning of gold and other assets, are the main ways in which women borrow money; because they lack collateral in the form of land or production equipment, most are unable to borrow from formal institutions like banks, which could give them better rates of interest. Lack of access to credit also means that women have little flexibility in choosing income-earning activities to embark on without the help of male household members, who own the assets that could be used for collateral security. Moorkanad's marketing facilities are also inadequate (GOK, 1996b): for instance, despite increased production of coconut over the past 20 years, the oil mills in the region can only extract coconut oil for household purposes, lacking the capacity to meet the demands of commercial production. Farmers who cannot afford to transport unprocessed coconuts to markets out of the area, or who are unable to travel in order to do so, must sell them to local agents for a lower price, which creates a crisis for producers due to the decline in prices mentioned above. In this, as in other situations, women have to face the reality of the market's discrimination against them (Harriss-White, 1995). In the words of one woman farmer in my study: 'I cannot bargain with men in the market; I have to oblige with the social norms in our society'.

Decreasing opportunities in agricultural labour

In my sample, there were eight households across the two locations that were Latin Christians and belonged to the scheduled castes. Being engaged mostly in agricultural work, they were largely landless, although some owned their house plot. As noted earlier, women from Christian families do not inherit land, but bring a dowry in the form of land endowed on their husbands, cash or gold. In this category of household, women are disadvantaged at several levels. Agricultural wages have increased nearly nine times for men, and over eight times for women respectively over the past 16 years in Kerala (GOK, 1997), yet opportunities for paid work have decreased due to the transition from labour-intensive rice cultivation to less labour-intensive crops including rubber and coconut. Agricultural workers, especially from the lower castes like the *pulayas* and 'backward' Christian communities, usually cultivate crops like rice, tapioca and vegetables, which fetch lower prices compared to rubber and coconut. Since they work on very small land-holdings (whether of their own or leased), typically of about 0.2 acres in size, it is not practical for them to cultivate rubber, which takes a long time (about seven years) to grow. They thus continue to cultivate other, minor, crops, although they do not make a profit. Many male former agricultural workers have moved to take up artisanal jobs like carpentry, which provide more income and have a higher status than farm labour. One woman agricultural worker told me: 'I have to plead for higher wages to earn more so that I can feed my children'; this woman was also cultivating a small family farm.

Conclusion

As illustrated in the above examples, women may gain access to land in numerous ways – through inheritance, marriage or informal networks. However, none of these options guarantees effective command over it. Women's traditional rights to land have not been adequately recognized in Kerala: the gender gap in the ownership and control of property is the single most important contributor to the gender gap in women's economic wellbeing, social status and empowerment (Agarwal, 1994). It is disquieting to note that the current socioeconomic changes and crisis of confidence in agriculture as a main source of livelihood is leading to *nair* women's share of land being sold, with the proceeds going to men – thus reducing women's ownership of land to the status of male-controlled dowry.

Although legal provisions such as equal access to employment or land are important in recognizing women's rights to land, legal rulings alone can have limited impact on changing gendered power structures within societies, families or communities. The case of the Christian succession laws in Kerala is a case in point. In 1986, a group of pioneering women questioned the validity of the Travancore Succession Act of 1926, which gave property rights to sons rather than daughters. Although a favourable verdict was obtained from the Indian Supreme Court, this was strongly opposed by the church, state, and other institutions, and led to the ostracism of these women (George, 1994).

Land is the most basic resource of agricultural production. The recognition of women's differential access to property and their lack of command over its use – even if they own it – should be the starting point of a gender-sensitive agricultural policy. Since 1996, Kerala's government services have been undergoing a process of decentralization, with the aim of enabling more participation at the local level. However, women in agriculture have yet to be incorporated effectively at local level. Women involved in farming are hampered from gaining access to credit, extension and marketing, in addition to the purchase or lease of land. Women's role in farming in Kerala needs to be recognized, and institutional support must be increased, to enable women to gain access to agricultural inputs and technology, which would lead to better agricultural practices and a higher income from farming. Increasing male migration for work and diversification into paid employment means a growing number of de facto female-headed households, where women are wrongly perceived as dependent on men, despite their primary – and growing – responsibility for the daily financial management and organization of the household and the farm. It is important that women have direct access to critical farm inputs to enable them to maximize outputs, challenge ideas of 'women's work', and thence gain control over the other factors of production and change social norms. Most importantly, there should be a concerted effort to enable women to function as independent farmers who control their own land.

Notes

1 The matrilineal system of inheritance and family organization (practised by the *nairs*, the *ambalavasis* and by sections of the *ezhava* caste) involves property being inherited by and through women; a typical household consists of a male head, his sisters, and their children and grandchildren, while husbands have 'visiting rights'. Matrilineal, however, does not mean matriarchal: women do not dominate in household decision-making power. As this article will show, matriliny may have given women importance, but this has stopped far short of equality with men (Jeffrey, 1993).

2 Agarwal defines land rights as 'rights that are formally untied to male ownership or control, in other words, excluding joint titles with men. By effective rights in land I mean not just rights in law, but also their effective realization in practice' (Agarwal, 1994).

3 Patrilineal household: where inheritance is passed down the male line.

4 *Ezhavas* are the lower caste Hindus who along with Christians and the Muslim population used to be largely involved in trading occupations, while the *pulayas* and the *cherumas* are the scheduled castes who are largely the deprived classes as they were regarded as the 'untouchables' in society until the early 20th century.

5 Kerala is divided into 14 districts and 1,000 *panchayats*, which are the smallest unit of local administration.

6 According to the Agro-climatic Committee of 1974, Kerala has been conceptually divided into five agricultural zones based on the characteristics of rainfall, climate, soil, topography and elevation (NARP, 1982).

7 One acre is equal to 0.25 hectares.

8 Brick-making is a highly seasonal job, and dependent on weather conditions.

9 A primary health-care centre serves about 30,000 people and caters for the health needs of the local population, especially in family planning and immunization services. It is further supported by a community health centre, which covers a population of 100,000, and a sub-centre covering four to five villages.

10 Kerala contributes to nearly 50–60% of Indian workers in the Middle East (GOK, 1997). This outflow has increased since the beginning of the 1970s on account of the hike in oil prices and large-scale investment in all the oil-exporting Arab countries. Although a large number of skilled and educated persons regularly migrate to countries like the USA and the UK for work and education purposes, the pattern of migration to the Gulf is quite different. First, it is mostly temporary, as well as circulatory and repetitive. In addition, most of the migrants are unskilled and work as manual workers. There is a large predominance of males among these out-migrants, as most families cannot take their families on account of inadequate income and also owing to the constraints placed on women's migration by the Emigration Acts of India.

11 Each household organizes and manages agricultural activities and household responsibilities differently, depending on various factors, including norms about the division of labour between women and men. These norms may restrict women who manage the family farm from engaging in certain agricultural tasks – for example, women do not operate machinery such as tractors, tap the rubber trees or climb trees to harvest coconut and arecanut.

12 Matrilocal implies that on marriage, the husband moves to his wife's family home.

13 Chitty is a form of popular informal savings among households in southern India. On the initiative of one person, a group of individuals – say, five persons – pool equal sums of money – say, Rs 200 per month. On one day of every month, there will be a raffle where one person's name is drawn who receives the whole amount of money, i.e. Rs 1,000. In this way, every month one person is entitled to the total money.

References

Agarwal, B., *A field of one's own: gender and land rights in South Asia*. Cambridge, Cambridge University Press, 1994.

Arun, S., 'Gender, agriculture and development: the case of Kerala, Southwest India'. Unpublished Ph.D. Dissertation. Manchester, University of Manchester, 1999.

George, A., 'Kerala Syrian Christian women and subordination'. Trivandrum, AKG Centre, 1994.

Gough, K., 'Kinship and marriage in south-west India'. *Contributions to Indian Sociology*, no. 7 (1973).

GOK., 'Adhikaram janagalilekku'. Ummanoor Panchayat report. 1996a.

GOK., 'Adhikaram janagalilekku'. Moorkanad Panchayat report. 1996b.

GOK., 'Economic Review'. Trivandrum, State Planning Board, 1997.

Jeffrey, R., *Politics, women and wellbeing: how Kerala became a model*. New Delhi, Oxford University Press, 1993.

NARP., 'National Agricultural Research Project'. Kerala Agricultural University, 1982.

Paniker, P.G.K. and C.R. Soman, 'Health Status of Kerala'. Mimeo. Kerala, Center for Development Studies, 1984.

Saradamoni, K., 'Changing land relations and women: a case study of Palghat District, Kerala'. In V. Mazurndar (ed.), *Women and rural transformations*. New Delhi, Concept Publications, 1983.

Sen, G., 'Social needs and public accountability: the case of Kerala'. In: M. Wuyts, M. Mackintosh and T. Hewitt (eds.), *Development policy and public action*. London, Open University Press, 1992.

Sharma, U., *Women, work and property in north-west India*. London, Tavistock Publications, 1980.

Annotated bibliography and web resources

A guide to the bibliography: explanation of the records in the bibliography

The records in the annotated bibliography are listed alphabetically by author with both a subject and a geographical index, which give the record number within the bibliography. Each record is complemented by an abstract.

Photocopying services: libraries as well as individual users from any country in the world may request photocopies of articles and small books (up to 100 pages) included in the bibliography.
Photocopying services for users in developing countries are free-of-charge.
Charges for users in other countries are € 0.10 per page, plus postal costs.

Please state the Library code number in your photocopy request. Requests for photocopies should be sent to:

KIT Library
KIT (Royal Tropical Institute)
P.O. Box 95001
1090 HA Amsterdam, The Netherlands
Fax: +31 (0) 20 – 6654423
E-mail: library@kit.nl
URL: http://www.kit.nl/library/

An example of a typical record is shown below:

[1] **001**   [2] **AFRA confronts gender issues: the process of creating a gender strategy**
[3] BYDAWELL, MOYA. [4] *Gender and Development* 5(1997)1, p. 43-48 [5] 1 lit.ref. [6] ISSN 1355-2074
  The Association for Rural Advancement (AFRA) is an Independent rural land service organization in South Africa, affiliated to the National Land Committee. It works with communities to influence land reform and ensure the formulation of a just agrarian policy for South Africa. In 1990, the organization initiated a process of incorporating a gender strategy into its work with a one-day workshop on gender issues for AFRA staff. It is demonstrated that this and subsequent initiatives have not been without problems for AFRA. Issues of race and gender interact, causing conflict, tensions and misunderstanding. The way in which these difficulties have been addressed seems to have led to a more common understanding of gender as an aspect of social differentiation and as being concerned with the relationship between women and men rather than being a 'women's issue'.
KIT Library code: [7]429675

1) Record number.

2) Original title.

3) All authors are listed and entered in the Author Index, followed (where available) by the affiliation (professional address) of the first author.

4) The reference includes the journal title in full (in italics), the volume number, year of publication (in brackets), issue number, inclusive page numbers as stated in the original document. For monographs, the publisher, place, number of pages and year of publication are given.

5) Summaries, glossaries, indexes, illustrations and literature references are also noted.

6) The bibliographic data conclude with the ISSN or ISBN (if available) of the original document.

7) A unique Library code – of book, chapters or journal articles, available in the KIT Library – is given at the end of each record. Please state this number in your photocopy request. When it concerns an electronic document, the URL is provided, however, photocopies of these documents are also available at KIT Library.

Annotated bibliography

001 Rights-Uganda: women benefit from new land legislation

ACHIENG', JUDITH. *World News* Inter Press Service (IPS), <http://www.ips.org/> 3 p. September 1998

In July 1998 a Land Bill was passed by the Ugandan Parliament which stipulates that a woman has equal say to her husband in the family property. If a man dies without leaving a will, the Succession Act in the Bill automatically divides his property, 15% going to the widow, and 75% going to the children. The remainder can be shared by other dependants. The Land Bill was an initiative of Uganda's 52 women legislators who lobbied for support from their 152 male counterparts. The female legislators will soon be tabling a Domestic Relations Bill, which seeks to outlaw some traditionally accepted norms like polygamy and wife beating. Most African countries have little success in implementing laws that elevate women's status in relation to property and land ownership. In both South Africa and Zimbabwe, 80% of the land is in the hands of white farmers.

URL: http://www.oneworld.org/ips2/sept98/17_03_046.html

002 Working on land: livelihoods and land rights in Southern Africa

ADAMS, M. *Rural Policy and Environment Group Research Summaries* Overseas Development Institute (UK) <http://www.odi.uk> 2 p. 1999 Overseas Development Institute, Portland House, Stag Place, London SW1E 5DP, UK.

Land reform in Southern Africa is concerned with improving the security and availability of land rights. The complexity of the legislation and customary systems is exacerbated by the differing systems of property rights pertaining to private and communal land in many states. The legacy of colonial discriminatory land tenure needs to be replaced by a more equitable system but the process of reform remains a difficult one. This is an electronic summary of the 1999 paper 'Land tenure reform and rural livelihoods in southern Africa' *ODI Natural Resource Perspectives* No. 39.

URL: http://www.odi.uk/rpeg/adams. html

003 Did the constitution mean to legalise customary tenure or to lay foundation for the demise of customary tenure

ADOKO, JUDY Land rights in Africa at Oxfam, UK, <http://www.oxfam.org.uk/ landrights/> 4 p. November 1997

Published as a pamphlet by the Uganda Land Alliance, this paper focuses on customary tenure and its conversion into titled land and the relevant rules to be applied. It suggests that law makers lack interest in customary tenure. There is a basic contradiction in the Constitution of Uganda, which will make all customary owners insecure in their ownership and force them to apply for a title. Unfortunately, certificates and titles are expensive and difficult to acquire. The poor therefore run the risk of losing their land.

URL: http://www.oxfam.org.uk/landrights/ugacust.rtf

004 Protecting women's rights to land

ADOKO, JUDY. *Gender Newsletter – Links* Oxfam, UK, <http://www.oxfam. org/> 2 p. July 2 Programme Manager, Oxfam in Uganda

The 1998 Land Act in Uganda introduced individual ownership of land to encourage more productive use of land, based on the principles of economic liberalization. It converted customary ownership of land into formal ownership through the creation of written deeds. As a result of the Act, women have lost ownership of land and they are now doubly disadvantaged by the higher incidence of divorce and the fact that wives rarely inherit. Oxfam in Uganda worked with the Uganda Land Alliance to lobby the government to ensure that the Act protects the rights of women as much as possible.

URL: http://www.oxfam.org.uk/policy/gender/00jul/07 00protect.htm

005 Claiming our rights: a manual for women's human rights education in Muslim societies

AFKHAMI, MAHNAZ; VAZIRI, HALEH. Sisterhood is global institute, Bethesda, MD, 168 p. 1996. Includes lit.refs

This manual is designed to promote human rights awareness among women at the grassroots level in the South, and particularly in Muslim societies. The learning exercises provided aim to stimulate dialogue among women about themes related to women's rights in the private domain; their rights to education and employment; and their rights in the public domain. The themes correspond with the themes articulated during the 1995 Fourth World Conference on Women. The learning exercises offer a framework for Muslim women to discuss their realities and their rights. The annexes include sections of the Qur'an dealing with and referring to women; the Universal Declaration of Human Rights; and the text of the Convention on the Elimination of All Forms of Discrimination against Women (CEDAW).

KIT Library code: 224938

006   Tribal matriliny in transition: changing gender, production and property relations in North-East India: rural employment policy research programme

AGARWAL, BINA. World Employment Programme (WEP Research Working Papers) International Labour Organisation, Geneva, 77 p. 1990 ill., tabs. Includes lit.refs ISBN 92-2-107567-2

Over the past century, there has been a gradual erosion of traditional patterns of livelihood, of the communal basis of land access and control, and of the social and political norms and institutions governing tribal communities. This has led to the emergence of a much more class-differentiated and gender-hierarchical society that has worked especially to the detriment of women. These changes are particularly apparent in the context of matrilineal communities where, traditionally, women have been the main inheritors of property and have held a relatively privileged social and economic position. Three matrilineal communities of North-East India – the Garos, Khasis and Lalungs – are examined using historical accounts, in-depth village ethnographies and socioeconomic surveys of villages to trace the interlinkages between ecology, economy, technology, marriage norms and women's social and economic position, and how these affect women's land rights. Following an outline of the region, each of the three communities is discussed in detail and compared. The analysis clearly demonstrates that economic changes and the erosion of institutions on the one front can set off interlinked reactions on other fronts, including changes in social and family relations, leading to differential gender effects. State development interventions have seldom taken this into account and may have been eroding precisely those communal and social institutions that they should have strengthened. General directions are suggested for measures that may help strengthen the customary egalitarian aspects of gender relations in these communities and provide new bases for gender equality by promoting women's collective efforts as well as their greater participation in the local political spheres.
KIT Library code: 155810

007   Widows versus daughters or widows as daughters?: property, land, and economic security in rural India

AGARWAL, BINA. *Modern Asian Studies* 32(1998)1 p. 1-48 79 lit.refs ISSN 0026-749X

Independent command over land in India would reduce rural women's economic and social vulnerability and increase their livelihood choices, both as widows and daughters. The obstacles to the enforcement of women's claims clearly indicate that if women are to gain effective rights to land, these will have to be contested both within and outside the household and will have diverse legal, administrative, social and ideological aspects. The issues that warrant specific focus include not only establishing legal equality but also enhancing women's ability to claim and keep control of their rightful inheritance shares; reducing gender bias in the recording of women's shares in village land records; and increasing women's legal knowledge and literacy. Similarly, it is necessary to take measures to counter existing male bias both in the government's distribution of public land and in infrastructural support for farmers. Widows should not be seen as a category in themselves but as embodying a stage in most women's life cycle, a stage that is frequently coterminous with old age. Effective economic security in old age would therefore depend on securing women's property rights prior to the event, namely securing their claims as daughters in addition to their claims as widows. The lesser social opposition to daughters' claims in the southern states and the greater gender equality in property rights prevailing there suggest that these states could provide useful starting points.
KIT Library code: 422163

008   Disinherited peasants, disadvantaged workers: a gender perspective on land and livelihood

AGARWAL, BINA. *Man and Development* 20(1998)2 p. 1-32 83 lit.refs ISSN 0258-0438

The pace of agrarian transformation in India has not only left the vast majority of the population still dependent on land-based livelihoods, but has also created significant gender disparities in non-farm livelihood options. Although male workers are moving to non-agricultural work, women have remained substantially in agriculture, and their dependence on agriculture has increased in recent years. The prevailing male bias in access to land and in infrastructural support to farmers is undercutting the potential that exists for enhancing production through a more gender-egalitarian approach. To fully realize this potential, however, it will be necessary to look beyond the conventional approach of family-based farming and to experiment with and promote a range of alternative institutional arrangements, involving various degrees of joint investment and management by groups of women. To initiate such alternatives and the complex set of measures needed to reduce existing biases in women's access to land and livelihood, collective action by women is essential at many levels: the state, the market, the community and the household. Although class and caste differences between women could pose difficulties, it is argued that there are significant gender-linked commonalities of interests that would make cooperation among a broad spectrum of women possible on many counts.

KIT Library code: 426651

009   Women and social justice: some legal and social issues in contemporary Muslim society
AHMAD, ANIS. Institute of policy studies, Islamabad, 128 p. 1991 ill., tabs. Includes index. Bibliogr.: p. 107-120

Moral and legal issues that are being debated in contemporary Muslim society are examined, particularly in the context of the introduction of Islamic (hudud) laws in Pakistan. Two hundred and seven cases filed in the Federal Shri'at Court of Pakistan during 1985-88 with reference to hudud and family law ordinance are analysed. Islamic principles for human relations, social interaction and behaviour are outlined, and ethics, society and law in an Islamic framework are discussed. Implications of the family laws and the hudud ordinances are considered with reference to injustice to women, orphaned children, divorce and maintenance, and polygamy. Economic issues such as economic development and women, economic independence, labour force participation, and social conditioning are also examined. Other sociocultural issues discussed include inheritance, single women, and women and political participation. It is stated that there is presently much misinformation about women's issues in Pakistan and elsewhere. Scholarly bodies, and research and policy institutes should take up the challenge and deal with these issues at a scientific level. Consultations and seminars are also needed to deal in-depth with the current situation of women, their problems and possible Islamic solutions. Education and health care for women are areas where the Islamic Movement in Pakistan can play an important role. Social and cultural issues and elimination of discrimination should also be major objectives of their work. Other actions that need to be taken include a review of relevant writings on women by Muslim and non-Muslim scholars; a comparative study of legal, social and economic problems of women; a revision of the present procedures for divorce, inheritance and wills, and maintenance of widows and divorced persons; and finally an open approach to different views, so that contemporary and other issues can be resolved successfully.

KIT Library code: 183854

010   Making progress – slowly: new attention to women's rights in natural resource law reform in Africa.
Presentation to the CTA/GOU Regional Conference on the Legal Rights of Women in Agricultural Production. Kampala, Uganda, 19-23 February 2001
ALDEN, WILY LIZ. World Bank
<http://worldbank.org> 31 p. 2001

Statutorily supported rights to land and other landed resources are accepted as crucial in agrarian society for both women and men. Critical shifts are currently affecting rural resource rights in Africa through widespread reform in land, forestry and other laws. These are reflected in a new provision for wives to hold family property as co-owners with their husbands, a provision that could play a major role in revitalizing smallholder agriculture in the continent. Recognition that equity in domestic land relations may ultimately be a prerequisite for the modernization of subsistence agriculture in agrarian economies is the thesis underlying analysis of legal texts in this paper. Improvement in women's resource rights is emerging through indirect changes in law and particularly those that alter the balance of authority over land and landed resources between state and people, with broadly democratizing effect. Important for women is greater accessibility to tenure administration, dispute resolution machinery and resource management functions occurring through devolution of centres of control from centre to periphery. Also important is the changing status of customary rights in land under new laws, coupled with clearer constitutional restrictions upon practices that discriminate against women's land rights and through which family and group tenure may in future be secured. Although these developments are still new in law and far from widespread in implementation, the 21st century opens with opportunities for rural women to secure tenure over local resources, opportunities that were not even hinted at a mere decade ago.

URL: http://wbln0018.worldbank.org/essd/essd.nsf/ gender/home

011   Muslim women rights, and the role of the United Nations
AL-HIBRI, AZIZAH Y. Karamah: Muslim Women Lawyers for Human Rights <http://karamah.org> 2 p. March 1999. The T.C. Williams School of Law, University of Richmond, Richmond, Virginia 23173, USA. <hibri@uofrlaw. richmond.edu>

Over 1400 years ago Muslim women were actively engaged in political life while some governments in Muslim countries today continue

to debate women's right to vote and to engage in political activity. Some governments have abandoned religious ideals and guarantees in favour of imposing their own views as informed by their own interests and false ideologies. For these reasons, it is important that the UN empower Muslim women, not only through its resolutions, conventions and recommendations but also through positive actions such as providing Muslim women with high profile positions at the UN and involving grassroots Muslim women in the discussion and drafting of legal instruments. These actions would support Muslim women in their efforts to develop authentic international and local leadership. This speech was made at an event to celebrate International Women's Day at UN Headquarters.
URL: http://karamah.org/karamah/ speeches/un-women.htm

012   Women's rights
ALLEN, JENNIFER; BEYDOUN, RANA; NADEAU, MARC; PHIPPS, NICOLE. *Women's Rights Group Paper* Human Rights and International Law homepage at Eckerd College, USA, at: <http://www.eckerd.edu/academics/bes/irga/human.rights/> Eckerd College, 4200 54th Avenue South, St. Petersburg, Florida 33711, USA. 16 p. 1998
   Women's rights are human rights. The fight for achieving them has been long and hard, and it is far from over. Conventions such as CEDAW have established a normative basis for women's rights across the globe. Countries need to be committed to the normative standards of rights established by the revolutionary conferences and conventions of the last 20 years. For countries to be committed to those rights, society and tradition will have to change. It is imperative to remember that treaties designed to bring women onto a more level playing field with men are not giving them special rights, even if they contain affirmative action measures that act to bolster their position in society.
URL: http://www.eckerd.edu/academics/bes/irga/human. rights/womenrights.html

013   More than a football field!: access to land among South African rural women
ANDREW, NANCY. *Afrique Politique* (1998) p. 87-106 lit.refs
   Obstacles to acquiring land rights for rural black women in South Africa today are reviewed based on interviews in 1996 and 1997. Rural African women's demand and need for land revolve primarily around improving their homestead and the production of food, particularly as a supplement to household

consumption. Although the women interviewed wanted more and better land, their immediate concern tended to be tenure security. Problems associated with women's access to land can be broadly divided into structural restrictions linked to the organization of society under settler rule, and the social and legal obstacles affecting women in particular that have added to the exclusion and oppression of women. The national land reform programme has formally identified many of the social problems associated with land access, including those facing women. The most significant measures being proposed include removing legal barriers that prevent women from participating in land reform, and specific mechanisms to provide security of tenure for women, including the registration of assets gained through land reform in the name of women as direct beneficiaries. Removing the legal restrictions on women's rights to land will not end discrimination against women. Although women are a particularly disadvantaged group with respect to accessing and holding land, land access and property rights are problems faced by the black majority as a whole in South Africa today.
KIT Library code: 429702

014   Struggling over scarce resources: women and maintenance in Southern Africa
ARMSTRONG, ALICE K. Regional report / Women and Law in Southern Africa Research Trust. University of Zimbabwe publ., Harare, 157 p. 1992 ill. Includes index. Includes lit.refs ISBN 0-908307-27-6
   The results are presented of a two-year research project undertaken in 1990 and 1991 on maintenance laws in six countries of Southern Africa: Botswana, Lesotho, Mozambique, Swaziland, Zambia and Zimbabwe. The research aims to determine the content of the state-enforced rules governing maintenance of women and children and the procedures for and effectiveness of the enforcement of those rules. In Southern Africa today, men have more than their fair share of economic resources – better access to jobs, education, land and other means of production. Women are therefore left with limited access to cash. The laws of maintenance allow women the power, unprecedented under traditional law, to obtain financial support from a man and thereby to acquire control over part of his income. This power is perceived by men, as well as some women, as being contrary to African traditions. The law has therefore become the focus of a fierce struggle between men and women over scarce resources as well as over power. Suggestions for legal, administrative and

policy changes both in the short- and long-term are highlighted, which will lead to increased family income levels and ensure that women and children get their share of the resources available. Although maintenance laws operate in the context of plural legal systems in Southern Africa, the customary and general laws on maintenance have fused to a great extent. However, principles of traditional law remain an influence on the way people think and the way trials are conducted.
KIT Library code: 169811

015   Crossing the barrier of time: the Asante woman in urban land development
ASIAMA, SETH OPUNI. *Africa* 52(1997)2 p. 212-236 ill. 32 lit.refs. With French and Italian summary ISSN 0001-9747

The status of women in the Asante ethnic group in central Ghana, is examined in relation to the institutions of chieftaincy, marriage, inheritance and some societal norms and practices. The land tenure system in the Asante culture is discussed in relation to its effect on women, focusing on urban land development. The Asante woman is not fettered by any institutional structures in her upward mobility. In the traditional regime, women were at an advantage and these sociocultural and political arrangements have endured to their benefit. In the modern system, women are free to participate in the urban land market. A woman can enter into business and own property without reference to her husband. Women's inability to participate fully is not due to any institutional constraints but rather to maladjustment to the new economic order prescribed by urbanization and its concomitants. Programmes to address this trend would need to address women's economic disabilities and should not be prescriptive. They should encourage women to do things for themselves within their own perceptions of their sociopolitical circumstances. External prescriptions stand a good chance of damaging marital relations and the interests of children, which are fundamental requirements for a stable society.
KIT Library code: 420120

016   She comes to take her rights: Indian women, property, and propriety
BASU, SRIMATI. State University of New York press, Albany, NY, 305 p. 1999 ill., tabs. Bibliogr.: p. 277-297. Includes index ISBN 0-7914-4096-6

This book focuses on the myths and practices surrounding property transmission in India – the material and ideological structures through which the current distribution of property is

maintained. It examines the ways in which cultural practices and particularly notions of gender ideology guide the workings of the law. Information is provided on property divisions within families; property exchanges surrounding marriage; the ideologies used to rationalize women's alienation from family property; the financial resources preferred by women; and the principal social problems experienced by them. Representations of women's entitlements in legal texts are also examined. Finally, some of the principal questions concerning the power of ideology in maintaining property relations are discussed, including family responsibilities and dowry; the ways in which dependence within marriage determines women's entitlements; the effect of social class on women's attitudes and options; and the importance of legal solutions for social change. The book demonstrates that it is not passivity, ignorance of the law, naiveté about wealth, or unthinking adherence to gender prescriptions that guide women's decisions, but rather an intricate negotiation and optimization of kinship, socioeconomic and emotional needs.
KIT Library code: 240376

017   Cutting to size: property and gendered identity in the Indian Higher Courts
BASU, SRIMATI. In: *Signposts: gender issues in post-independence India* ed. by Rajeswari Sunder Rajan. Kali for Women, New Delhi p. 248-291 1999 76 lit.refs

This article focuses on inheritance and succession within family law in India, highlighting the conflict between postcolonial legal change and the persistence of privileges. The cultural and judicial perception is that radical change was brought about through the Hindu Succession Act (1956) shortly after independence, yet after four decades, most women are either not given or themselves refuse shares in family property. This continual disenfranchisement is maintained not by legal barriers but by cultural constructions of gendered entitlements on the part of both male and female heirs as well as on the part of judges. The realm of inheritance is therefore particularly appropriate for examining how cultural constructions of gender, family, religion and nation saturate the allegedly impartial and progressive milieu of legal decision-making in India. The cases provided here replicate common rationales and strategies privately used in families to circumvent the rights of female heirs and deter women from pursuing claims. These property cases also reveal the atypical resistances of women who publicly persist with their legal claims, despite the time and expense of court cases and the distinct possibility of family wrath. The history of jurisprudence in the new Indian nation, as well as the profile of contemporary property cases provided here, show that women are far from being treated with universal favour and leniency in the courts. While the impact of changes in property law is unlikely to be widespread in the absence of changes in the labour market and constructions of kinship, post-Independence reform has opened up spaces of possibility.

KIT Library code: 427135

018   Women and property inheritance: scant and slippery footholds

BASU, SRIMATI In: She comes to take her rights: Indian women, property, and propriety Srimati Basu. State University of New York Press, Albany, NY p. 41-77 1999

The significance of women's property in India is examined, focusing on how much property Indian women own and how actual ownership of land or housing corresponds with the legal possibilities envisaged for women. Based on interviews with household members, a map of property ownership is constructed revealing the relationships between gender and class, and between property and cultural entitlements. Women's rates of property ownership are shown to be better than the 1% world average cited in UN statistics. However, while property ownership appears to be a source of security for women of all classes, they have few opportunities to profit from it. The relationship between urban and rural wealth and differential access to prime resources in the capitalist economy play a significant role, and women among the urban poor are particularly cut off from rural family wealth enjoyed by males. Most property divisions are supposedly in the spirit of customary law and ignore changes. Within this scenario, women's role is always to have access to property mediated through marriage, and to experience property through the gendered codes of protection and vulnerability, rather than in terms of acquisition of power and wealth.

KIT Library code: 429882

019   Protecting property: gendered identity in the Indian Higher Courts

BASU, SRIMATI In: She comes to take her rights: Indian women, property, and propriety Srimati Basu. State University of New York Press, Albany, NY p. 191-219 1999

Women's recent encounters with the law relating to property are examined, focusing on questions of class, women's entitlements to property under customary law and the efficacy

of legal solutions. An overview is provided of the ways in which gender has been inscribed within Indian law in recent history, showing how women's rights signify both cultural heritage and emancipatory progress. A brief account of wins and losses by women in cases dealing with property is provided, alongside detailed analysis of recurrent judicial tropes. In general, substantial resources are required to persevere in the legal arena, explaining the widespread disinclination of families to engage in litigation. The cases discussed reveal that the law has sometimes been able to function as a strategic ally; while the impact of changes in property law is unlikely to be widespread in the absence of changes in the labour market and constructions of kinship, post-independence reform has opened up spaces of possibility. Despite the formidable tasks of maintaining surveillance over legal rhetoric, it is important to use the law as a potential mode of change and site of negotiation with dominant ideologies.

KIT Library code: 429883

020   Rights of women to the natural resources land and water

BENDA-BECKMANN, KEEBET VON. Women and Development (1997)2 Ministry of Foreign Affairs. Development Cooperation Information Department, The Hague 59 p. 1997. Includes lit.refs ISBN 90-5328-150-9

The increasing scarcity of the natural resources of land and water is having a severe impact on individuals and households whose rights to these resources are being eroded. A literature study is provided, exploring the problems surrounding women's rights to these resources. The belief that women should share these rights on an equal footing with men is now gaining widespread international acceptance. The legal aspects of women's rights to natural resources are examined and the links between these legal aspects and their socioeconomic and political context are illustrated. A number of key legal terms are identified, defined and explained and a legal analysis framework is compiled. Ways of strengthening women's rights to natural resources are suggested; these strategies may require statutory amendments but may equally involve a review of local or religious law. Key points which could be included in a specific strategy to strengthen the legal status of women are: support for local institutions; launching a sociolegal study; support for activities aimed at legislative amendments; promoting knowledge of the law among women, government bodies and credit institutions; encouraging awareness and social acceptance; working towards communal rights for women; and encouraging the formation of women's organizations.

KIT Library code: 223604

021 Land right, marriage left; women's management of insecurity in North Cameroon

BERG, ADRI VAN DEN. *CNWS publications* (1997)54 Leiden University. Research school CNWS, 349 p. 1997 ill., graphs, tabs. Also doctoral diss. Leiden. Bibliogr.: p. 321-340. Includes index. With French summary ISSN 0925-3084 ISBN 90-73782-81-3

The mounting insecurity of Giziga women in the region of Mindif, North Cameroon, is discussed, and the strategies they have developed to manage their situation, as well as the constraints they encounter in their struggle against insecurity, are examined. Three factors make their situation particularly urgent. Firstly, while marriage is the only way for women to acquire access to resources, more than 60% of women dissolve their marriages, thereby losing those resources. Secondly, the sociopolitical situation in Mindif, recently aggravated by the scarcity of natural resources, contributes to their insecurity. Thirdly, strong male control over female labour leaves women with little autonomy and control over resources. Women follow various strategies to manage their insecurity. Two types of strategies are presented: strategies used by women who farm their own plots and seek economic independence, and strategies used by women who seek security through their husbands' material resources. None of the strategies prevent a woman from losing access to her resources after divorce. Although access to land is important in their daily struggle against insecurity, Giziga women often give priority to the freedom to divorce. A requirement for the negotiation of improved land security is that Giziga women claim more recognition and control over their labour. They must also try to negotiate better rights through individual exercise of power, group organization or political pressure, and legal actions. These changes demand a transformation in the habits and ideas relating to gender labour relations and land tenure systems, as well as willingness to take measures to overcome such gender biases. More field research is necessary to examine the suitability and the consequences of flexible, temporary land security.

KIT Library code: 211014

022 Family law and customary practices of Muslims in Southern Kerala

BHASKAR, MANU. *Eastern Anthropologist* 49(1996)1 p. 1-26 ill., tabs 10 lit.refs. With glossary ISSN 0012-8686

Muslims are the second largest religious group in Kerala State, India, constituting 21% of the state population in 1981. Data were collected through in-depth interviews with Muslim women in Thiruvananthapuram District. The major issues confronting women are illiteracy, early marriage, polygamy, lack of resources, lack of an adequate support system, and lack of motivation and awareness of their social, political and legal rights. Economic dependency, religious orthodoxy and subjugation result in the suppression of women. Even where they take up employment, women remain in low paid and unskilled jobs. The Muslim Women's Welfare Society has been unable to address this situation due to lack of participation by the women themselves. Interviews with legal personalities reveal that the number of Muslim women litigants has increased, as has their legal awareness. Women are generally seeking legal redress for cruelty, adultery and abandonment. Repeated misinterpretations of the Muslim Personal Law have resulted in making the laws regressive.

KIT Library code: 422993

023 Women, land, and labor: negotiating clientele and kinship in a Minangkabau peasant community

BLACKWOOD, E. *Ethnology* 36(1997)4 p. 277-293 ill., tabs 41 lit.refs

One of the central dynamics shaping agrarian change, and one seldom highlighted, is the structure and ideology of kinship and clientage in peasant communities. The importance of kin ties in the maintenance of non-wage labour relationships in a wet rice farming community in West Sumatra, Indonesia is examined. In this village, patron-client ties are primarily organized on the basis of matrilineal kin ties through and between women. Elite women and their client kin are both bound to and have invested in a complex relationship with land, labour and obligations that supports the continued interdependence of landlord/tenant and helps keep agricultural wage labour from becoming the dominant relation of production in the village.

KIT Library code: 429817

024 Droit de la famille burkinabé: le code et ses pratiques à Ouagadougou

CAVIN, ANNE-CLAUDE. Sociétés Africaines et Diaspora. L'Harmattan, Paris 392 p. 1998 ill., graphs, tabs. Includes lit.refs ISBN 2-7384-7397-0

In French-speaking West Africa, the coexistence of two sources of family law – state norms stemming from colonialism alongside ancestral tradition – has long been problematic.

It has often been considered that these two types of law existed side by side without being influenced by each other. On examination, however, it appears that multiple responses have been found within the unitary organizational model envisioned by the state. This work aims to examine actual practice in the town of Ouagadougou in Burkina Faso. It draws on three typical conflicts in family law – inheritance problems; paternity disputes; and divorce – focusing on the fate of women in these conflicts and demonstrating the actual methods used to resolve conflict, as well as the development of new procedures that combine tradition and modern ideas. These new procedures may one day lead to the establishment of new laws capable of meeting the needs of the majority of Burkinabé citizens.

KIT Library code: 236449

025   The third Chimurenga
CAWTHORNE, MAYA In: *Reflections on gender issues in Africa* Keshia Nicole Abraham.et al. Southern African Regional Institute for Policy Studies (SARIPS gender series. SAPES, Harare p. 55-83 1999 52 lit.refs

The independent government of Zimbabwe appears committed to removing the obstacles that faced African women during the colonial period. However, whilst there have been certain legislative changes, particularly in customary and family law, little has happened in the 17 years since independence, and women do not appear to be benefiting from such legislation. A literature review is presented and a methodology constructed to explore the difference between theory and reality for black Zimbabwean women. Before colonization, women were subjected to patriarchal control, but appeared to have some rights in informal areas. Colonization drastically changed African economy, social relations, gender relations and labour. For women especially, whatever power and prestige they had was taken away. Although the focus of the research is Zimbabwe, the regional context of Southern Africa is also examined (Botswana, Lesotho, Mozambique, Swaziland and Zambia). As colonies or protectorates, all of these countries developed plural legal systems. As they gained their independence, they opted to keep the system of legal pluralism. Since independence, family laws have been changing. In Zimbabwe, the changes include allowing unmarried mothers to apply for maintenance; granting majority status to African women; outlawing sex discrimination in employment and in relation to immovable property rights; giving equal pay for equal work; and independent taxation for women.

In comparison with women in the rest of Southern Africa, women in Zimbabwe are doing extremely well under the law. However, there are still many problematic issues in the relationship between women and law in Zimbabwe and the author concludes that the government has not fulfilled its commitment to women's advancement and empowerment and is not truly committed to women's rights.

KIT Library code: 429078

026   Women, the law, and the family in Tunisia
CHEKIR, HAFIDHA. *Gender and Development* 4(1996)2 p. 43-46 ISSN 1355-2074

The article considers the links between civil law, the family, and religious custom in Tunisia. It assesses the status of women in the Tunisian family, suggesting ways in which family life could be democratized to enable women to achieve equal status to men.

KIT Library code: 416043

027   Widows in India: social neglect and public action
CHEN, MARTHA ALTER. Sage, New Delhi 455 p. 1998 ill., graphs, tabs. Includes index. Includes lit.refs ISBN 81-7036-703-4

A conference on widows in India was held in 1994 in Bangalore, India. The conference aimed to achieve a better understanding of the social and economic conditions of widows, focus attention on widowhood as a social problem and promote public action and policies in support of widows in India. The contributions are grouped in sections, exploring: the dominant ideological construction of widowhood in India, as well as variations in local customary norms regarding widowhood; the demographics of widowhood; and widows and property rights, social security, employment, poverty and social identity. Short case studies are provided on actual practice, as well as illustrative case histories of individual widows. Conference participants offered recommendations for future action, policy and research, and a Charter of Demands from widows who had attended an earlier workshop. The demands put forward by the widows during the closing session were for stable property rights; personal security and security for their children; and pensions for those who cannot secure property rights or gainful employment. Widows experience special difficulties and deprivation connected with the restrictions that are imposed on their lifestyle and the persistence of negative social attitudes towards them. Within the context of social science research, it is important to pay attention to widowhood as a cause of deprivation, as well as to organize and

support them in their specific demands. There are intimate links between the predicament of Indian widows and a wide range of patriarchal institutions such as patrilineal inheritance, patrilocal residence and the gender division of labour. The cause of widows must be seen as an integral part of the broader battle against gender inequalities.
KIT Library code: 229124

028   Listening to widows in rural India
CHEN, MARTHA ALTER In: *Independent India* ed. Anita Roy – Women: a cultural review vol. 8, no. 3. Oxford University press, Oxford p. 311-318 1997 9 lit.refs ISSN 0957-4042

A cross-section of 550 rural widows in nine states of India were interviewed during a field study in 1994, in addition to 25 widows who participated in a workshop. The first two sections of the paper draw heavily on an earlier article co-authored with Jean Drèze, which also appears in this bibliography. The first section contrasts the dominant images of widows with the everyday realities of widowhood. Although the status of widows varies a great deal across different regions, social groups and age groups, some basic factors account for the disadvantages and insecurity faced by many Indian widows: patrilocality; patrilineal inheritance; restrictions on employment; social neglect; and social isolation. The second section presents the expressed needs and demands of the widows interviewed, which include having a house or land in their own name; a secure job, source of livelihood or maintenance; education for their children; and a positive social image. The concluding section calls for the transformation of widowhood. There is a need to create more opportunities for widows to come together and redefine their image as women with dignity and rights. It is also necessary to create more opportunities for the society as a whole, as well as policymakers, to listen to widows and hear their demands.
KIT Library code: 424108

029   Die Umsiedlung hat mein Leben verandert: die Landrechte der Frauen in Zimbabwe
CHENAUX-REPOND, M. In: *Land und Macht: die Landfrage im Südlichen Afrika* Josette Cole et al. Nachrichtenstelle Südliches Afrika (NaSA), Basel p. 93-115 1996 ill., photogr., tabs

A two-year field study was carried out to assess women farmers' access to land in resettlement schemes in Mashonaland, Zimbabwe. The gender bias in resettlements is illustrated with the case studies of three women. Of an agricultural population of 5.7 million, about 0.4 million live in resettlement schemes, where farm families are given five ha each by the government. The status of women from the perspective of government is compared with traditional gender roles and access to land. Because Zimbabwe has signed the United Nations Convention on the Elimination of All Forms of Discrimination against Women (CEDAW), it is argued that the government must improve the land rights of women in the government-run resettlement schemes. Currently, only men and unmarried women have so-called settlement permits and divorced women lose their right to stay in the scheme. About 70-90% of the women are in favour of settlement permits for women.
KIT Library code: 429789

030   Choice, complexity, and change: gendered livelihoods and the management of water
CLEAVER, FRANCES. *Agriculture and Human Values* 15(1998)4. Kluwer, Dordrecht 114 p. ill., graphs, maps, tabs. Includes lit.refs ISSN 0889-048X

Gender is increasingly identified as a prime concern in policy documents regarding water resource management. There are key thematic similarities between current approaches to the management of water in both the irrigation and the domestic water sub-sectors. The papers in this special issue argue in favour of improved gender analysis of water resource management. Topics covered include: gender aspects of new irrigation management policies; gender, irrigation and environment; women's land rights in Gambian irrigated rice schemes; gendered participation in water management; incentives and informal institutions in the management of water; reform and counter-reform in Latin America; and water rights, gender and poverty alleviation in public irrigation infrastructure development. Existing mainstream policies relating to water resource management are critiqued for the inadequacy of their social and gender analysis. If development projects and programmes related to water are to be truly gendered, there are substantial implications for the ways in which such projects are planned and implemented. A framework is needed for gender analysis of water resource management. This framework should encompass issues of social relationships and infrastructural provision; account for both collective and individual actions; and recognize complexity, diversity and change at a number of levels. The papers included highlight the interactions of individual agency and collective action with social structure, and the critical role of formal and informal institutions in shaping public and private actions.

031   Land und Macht: die Landfrage im Südlichen Afrika
COLE, JOSETTE. Nachrichtenstelle Südliches Afrika (NaSA), Basel 184 p. 1996 ill., tabs. Includes lit.refs

Finding a solution to the land question is one of the greatest challenges for the governments of Southern Africa. Owners of large amounts of land have economic power and determine the fate of millions of people. The future of the large majority of the population will therefore be decided by land distribution. In Latin America, the land question was resolved in favour of a numerically small but powerful upper class. Southern Africa appears to be on the verge of this ominous development. Contributions from various authors from South Africa, Zimbabwe, Mozambique, Germany and Switzerland provide an insight into the land problem in Southern Africa, including its historical dimension and the current cultural, political and economic situation. The book is divided into three sections covering 1) apartheid and the African National Congress in South Africa; 2) women's land rights in Zimbabwe and the role of women in the land question and; and 3) socialism and the market economy in Mozambique, focusing on land development policy in Mozambique and Tanzania, the history of land policy in Mozambique, and small farmers' struggle for survival. The demand for land reform is currently an important issue in Southern Africa. After decades of freedom struggles coupled with regional destabilization due to the apartheid regime, competitive struggles for land have maintained an intensity that goes beyond temporary economic processes.

032   Positive state duties to protect women from violence: recent South African developments
COMBRINCK, HELÉNE. *Human Rights Quarterly* 20(1998)3 p. 666-690 lit.refs in notes ISSN 0275-0392

The combined influence of the South African constitution and recent developments in the sphere of international human rights on state obligations to address violence against women is considered. The nature of state rights created by human rights generally is first examined. The role of international law in the interpretation of the South African Bill of Rights is analysed, together with the obligations created under a number of international human rights'

instruments. This analysis is then used as a basis for examining the effect of the adoption of section 12(1)(c) in the 1996 Constitution, which entrenches the right 'to be free from all forms of violence from public or private sources'. It is concluded that the duties resting on the South African state extend beyond responsibility for the failure of police and other state actors to take protective action. Pervasive legislation and other measures are needed to alleviate current shortcomings in South African law. These duties affect state action on both micro and macro levels, ranging from obligations to develop national plans of action that promote the protection of women from violence to effective intervention in individual cases. One area in which the law is currently deficient is in its duty to punish violations. There is strong evidence that the cautionary rule (namely that the court is permitted to exercise an excessive level of discretion in deciding whether to believe women who allege that they have been raped) in sexual offence cases seriously undermines the successful prosecution and punishment of offenders in rape cases.

033   Comparative study of national laws on the rights and status of women in Africa
UN. ECA. ATRCW, Addis Ababa 38 p. 1990. Includes lit.refs

Considerable differences exist in the legal status of women in the various countries, tribes and communities of Africa, as a result of economic, cultural, religious and political divergences. This study describes the legal status of African women in the light of the various constitutional provisions and legislation relating to civil law, particularly family law. A large number of African states provide for sexual equality, but constitutional rights are often abrogated by customary or religious laws and practices. Major problems arise with regard to equal rights for men and women in the context of family law. It is demonstrated that, despite the many laws that exist, African women are unable to enjoy their rights as equal citizens. Given the pluralism in the law, they are confronted with complicated legal systems, difficult access to the courts and many strong social and cultural pressures. The Convention on the Elimination of all forms of Discrimination Against Women (CEDAW) has led to some progressive changes in specific areas affecting women, but these changes have been piecemeal and uncoordinated. Despite the differences between the various countries, there are similarities in the reform needed. Among these are changes in civic law, family law, polygamy, property and inheritance rights, divorce, and alimony and child support. Recommendations are provided to facilitate change, including legal and political education for women, setting up legal aid schemes, seminars for legal and paralegal personnel and government staff, and research at national and international levels to determine and evaluate the position of women.

KIT Library code: 183948

034 Gender roles, inheritance patterns, and female access to land in an ejidal community in Veracruz, México

CÓRDOVA PLAZA, ROSÍO In: *Current land policy in Latin America: regulating land tenure under neo-liberalism* ed. Annelies Zoomers and Gemma v.d. Haar. Amsterdam: Royal Tropical Institute 2000, p. 161-173, ill., tabs, 27 lit.refs

For agrarian societies, land is not simply a means of production; it also symbolizes a set of social relationships involving ownership and position within a social structure. In this respect, one of the most recurrent factors for explaining the subordination of women based on gender in the Mexican rural environment is their exclusion from the possession and/or control of the means of production. Among the main mechanisms that support and justify this exclusion are, on the one hand, the concept of sexual labour division that prevails in the rural environment favouring agriculture as a male activity, and on the other, the kinship system, which minimizes female possibilities of access to resources, due to its patterns of residence, conjugality and inheritance. This study examines how the perception of sexual roles and the traditional rules of kinship do not necessarily result in denying women's access to land. On the contrary, given specific historical and cultural configurations and particular circumstances, such as those present in the Mexican agrarian community examined in Tuzamapan, Veracruz, they can favour and legitimate women's positions of authority. In the community under study, the recognition of female capacity in the field of agriculture allowed women access to land and control over means of production. Women came to be considered worthy of the right to inherit the family patrimony. The conclusion that the incorporation of rural women into hired labour transforms their condition of subordination by offering them greater autonomy, authority or power of decision cannot be generalized. However, it is important to identify the particular situations that favour the establishment of less hierarchical and oppressive relations for women.

KIT Library code: 430121

035 Women and tenure: marginality and the left-hand power

CROSS, CATHERINE; FRIEDMAN, MICHELLE. In: *Women, land and authority: perspectives from South Africa* ed. by Shamim Meer. Oxfam, Oxford p. 17-34 1997 lit.refs in notes

Sociocultural issues related to women and the prevailing forms of rural land tenure in South Africa are considered. The various forms of existing tenure are outlined (state land systems, communal or tribal tenure, freehold communities, informal land systems, and white farms) and the plight of women and families of women evicted from farms is described. The next section considers men's and women's concepts of land rights, discusses how various households may gain tenure, and explores gender priorities and male fears about giving land tenure to women. The chapter highlights how various households run by women experience a disadvantage that differs by degree for households composed of widows with grown children, younger widows with young children, single mothers with children, and married women with absent husbands. The chapter suggests that research is needed to determine 1) the assumptions about land tenure systems and various kinds of rights; 2) the range of variation in women's perceived land rights; 3) how class factors influence women's control of land; 4) how land is actually held and transferred; 5) how successfully women can defend their rights to land from challenges; 6) women's access to power structures and influence on power brokers; 7) the specific points of male/female conflict over land; 8) the extent to which violence impedes women's access to land; 9) the impact of women's increasing access to land rights; 10) the involvement of women in production; 11) how inheritance systems will affect legal changes; and 12) how to support women in the effective use of land.

KIT Library code: 429835

036 Women and land in the rural crisis

CROSS, CATHERINE. *Agenda* (1999)42 p. 12-27 ill., photogr. 47 lit.refs ISSN 1013-0950

In this article, the author argues that institutional barriers to women's positive use of land and deepening rural poverty in South Africa are leading to increasing migration. Although women are still attributed the role of farmers, their actual foothold on land is very slight. Their right to make agreements for access to land, to transfer or dispose of land, and to use land for entrepreneurial purposes is marginal and exists mainly in the narrowest local context of family relations. The article questions whether rural policy that promotes women's independence under the present conditions would alleviate poverty or contribute to the deterioration of family units. It considers land issues for women migrating from one place to another; women's farming activity in relation to their control of land; women's household roles and power; and their institutional access to land. Some possible interventions are offered in the light of the analysis. The author concludes that dealing with women's institutional risks will not by itself provide more land to families now trying desperately to live on too little; gender-effective land reform on a mass scale will also be needed. Interventions should ideally be those that help both men and women, rather than those that target women alone. Overall tenure security, greater security around economic land use, incentives for entrepreneurial activity, and general access to markets would be possible examples of objectives that could help women. Any set of options for promoting rural women's land utilization will also need to be tested against women's own perceptions, evaluated for possible effects on the wider institutional setting, and improved with women's views and ideas.

KIT Library code: 430515

037 Women's right to land and natural resources: some implications for a human rights-based approach

CROWLEY, EVE. Food and Agriculture Organization, Sustainable Development Department, <http://www.fao.org/sd/index_en.htm> 5 p. 1999

The approaches of governments around the world to gender equality in access to land and natural resources are highly variable. This presents a dilemma for UN Organizations, such as the Food and Agriculture Organization (FAO) that are by mandate driven by the needs and requests of member nations. In this paper, a case study is used to demonstrate some of the practical problems that rural women face in establishing and exercising their rights to land and natural resources, and some of the FAO's approaches are then outlined. The circumstances of rural women vary greatly; it is therefore not possible to use the same approach or the same solution for all tenure systems, even if gender equality of rights is a universal standard. The author states that the FAO's current paradigm for land reform combines market, property rights and reforms in a comprehensive supporting institutional framework to enshrine the rights and security of individuals. This paradigm combines several approaches that are used in different combinations in different countries, depending upon the specific problems and

institutions involved. For the most part, the approaches are aimed at improving the access of landless and poor farmers to land and natural resources. Very few of them target women specifically. The strategies include: imposed redistribution and land reform through restitution; market-led reform; land tenure reform/negotiated land reform. A brief description of these strategies is provided, highlighting their implications for a rights-based approach to gender equality, as well as the challenges facing such an approach.

URL: http://www.fao.org/sd/Ltdirect/Ltan0025.htm

038 Women and land rights in the Latin American neo-liberal counter-reforms

DEERE, CARMEN DIANA; LEÓN, MAGDALENA. *Working papers on women in international development* 264. Michigan State University, East Lansing, MI 81 p. 1997 ill., tabs. Bibliogr.: p. 68-81

Rural women did not fare well in the land reforms carried out in Latin America during the 'reformist' period of the 1960s and 1970s, with women being underrepresented among the beneficiaries. The extent to which women have gained or lost access to land during the 'counter-reforms' of the 1980s and 1990s is examined. Case studies are provided from Chile, Colombia, Costa Rica, El Salvador, Honduras, Mexico, Nicaragua and Peru. Under the neoliberal agenda, production cooperatives as well as communal access to land have largely been undermined by privatization and the break-up of collectives into individual parcels. Significant land titling efforts are also being carried out throughout the region to promote the development of a vigorous land market. Nonetheless, this latter period has also been characterized by the growth of the feminist movement throughout Latin America and a growing commitment by states to gender equality. The extent to which rural women's access to land has potentially been enhanced by recent changes in agrarian and legal codes is considered. Colombia and Costa Rica are found to be leaders in gender-equitable legislation. The Mexican neoliberal counter-reform is found to have had a retrograde impact on women's rights to land. It is concluded that during periods of state intervention in agriculture, feminist strategies must focus on assuring that both men and women are beneficiaries of agrarian reforms or counter-reforms, either through joint titling of land so that the family unit is the beneficiary in practice, or by demanding that men and women be titled to land individually.

KIT Library code: 232822

039   Gender, land, and water: from reform to counter-reform in Latin America
DEERE, CARMEN DIANA; LEÓN, MAGDALENA. *Agriculture and Human Values* 15(1998)4 p. 375-386 ill., tabs 59 lit.refs

Rural women did not fare very well in the land reforms carried out during the Latin American 'reformist period' of the 1960s and 1970s, with women being underrepresented among the beneficiaries. It is argued that women have been excluded from access to and control over water for reasons similar to those that excluded them from access to land during these reforms. The extent to which women have gained or lost access to land during the 'counter-reforms' of the 1980s and 1990s is also examined. Under the neoliberal agenda, production cooperatives as well as communal access to land have largely been undermined in favour of privatization and the individual parcelization of collectives. Significant land titling efforts are also being carried out throughout the region to promote the development of a vigorous land market. This latter period has also been characterized by the growth of the feminist movement throughout Latin America and a growing commitment by states to gender equity. The extent to which rural women's access to land and, thus, water has potentially been enhanced by recent changes in agrarian and legal codes is reviewed.
KIT Library code: 429780

040   Mujeres, derechos a la tierra y contrarreformas en America Latina
DEERE, CARMEN DIANA; LEÓN, MAGDALENA. Debate Agrario (1998)27 p. 129-153 ill., tabs 51 lit.refs

The land rights of women in Latin America during the current period of counter-reform and the preceding period of agrarian reform are evaluated, and the role of the state is analysed. The participation of women in the agrarian reforms of Chile, Colombia, Costa Rica, El Salvador, Honduras, Mexico, Nicaragua and Peru and the gender sensitiveness of the counter-reforms are examined. The neoliberal counter-reforms are characterized by restitution, the privatization of communal land, the end of land distribution by the state and the strengthening of individual land title. With the exception of Colombia, and to some extent Nicaragua and Honduras, women are not well represented at national level. It is argued that even where women have the right to own land, they are still at a disadvantage in relation to men. Issues such as land inheritance, land ownership, and access to other production factors still remain largely to be resolved and will depend on the representation of women in the national political arena.
KIT Library code: 429814

041   Mujer y tierra en Guatemala
DEERE, CARMEN DIANA; LEÓN, MAGDALENA Guatemala: Asociación para el Avance de las Ciencias Sociales en Guatemala (AVANCSO), 1999. 35 p. Includes lit.refs ISBN 99922-68-02-6

The history of Guatemala's agrarian reform since 1952 is elaborated. The land act of 1952 aimed to distribute land that had not been cultivated for the previous three years on farms larger than 200 ha. The issue of gender in this land distribution programme has only recently gained some attention after the 'Acuerdos de Paz' (Peace Treaties) between the state and the Unidad Revolucionaria Nacional Guatemalteca (URNG) at the beginning of the 1990s, in which land rights, indigenous rights and women's rights were specifically formulated. After the Beijing Conference (1995) and a Women's NGO forum consisting of 16 rural women's organizations, the issue of gender equality and land rights was recognized. It is recommended that rural women and women's groups be considered and consulted at every stage of land policy development.
KIT Library code: 501843

042   Towards a gendered analysis of the Brazilian agrarian reform
DEERE, CARMEN DIANA; LEÓN, MAGDALENA. *Occasional papers / Latin American studies consortium of New England* no. 16. University of Connecticut. Center for Latin American & Caribbean studies, Storrs, CT 56 p. 1999 ill., tabs. Includes lit.refs

Brazil is one of the few Latin American countries where, in the 1990s, agrarian reform was still on the agenda. In 1988, a new constitution was adopted that reaffirmed that land could be expropriated for social purposes. While implementing legislation is weak in terms of allowing any fundamental redistribution of landed property, the rise of an organized movement of the landless in the 1980s, the Movimento Sem Terra (MST), has kept the need for agrarian reform before the public eye. In addition, Brazil was the first country to establish in its constitution that under the agrarian reform, women have the same right as men to have land titled in their own names or jointly with their spouses or partners. Nonetheless, rural women have not fared much better than those in other Latin American countries with respect to land rights. This paper considers why this has been the case. After an overview of Brazilian land

reform efforts from 1964 to 1994, the paper examines 1) the manner in which rural women were excluded from being beneficiaries of the reform before the constitutional changes of 1988; 2) the introduction of gender-equitable changes; 3) the rise of rural militancy in the 1980s and the birth of the rural women's movement; 4) the reasons why relatively little progress was made in terms of women's land rights; 5) women's property rights under Brazil's recent reform of its civil code; 6) agrarian reform efforts under the government of Fernando Henrique Cardoso; and 7) gender and property relations on the agrarian reform settlements. Finally, some thoughts on the direction of the agrarian reform and the rural women's movement are offered.
KIT Library code: 501841

043   Mujeres sin tierra: la situación en Bolivia
DEERE, CARMEN DIANA; LEÓN, MAGDALENA. Bolivia 16 p. ill., tabs. Offprint of: *Tinkazos: Revista Boliviana de Ciencias Sociales*; (1998)2, p. 47-76. Includes lit.refs
This article analyses women's participation in the Bolivian agrarian reform of 1953 and the prospect that women will be beneficiaries under Bolivia's new agrarian legislation, the INRA Law of 1996. The latter combines neoliberal principles with those of social justice, and states that land redistribution efforts are to continue. Moreover, the new law provides for women to be adjudicated land on the same terms as men, irrespective of their marital status. However, no specific mechanisms for inclusion of women – such as joint titling of land – are included in the law or its regulations. This may be detrimental to women, particularly in collective adjudications of land to communities, since in these, land rights are usually determined according to 'traditional customs and practices', which tend to discriminate against women. Traditional inheritance practices are reviewed and are shown to support this claim.
KIT Library code: 501842

044   Statement by the Director-General on the occasion of the celebration of World Food Day
DIOF, JACQUES. *Director General's speeches* Food and Agriculture Organisation (FAO) <http//www.fao.org/> FAO, Viale delle Terme di Caracalla, 00100 Rome, Italy. <fao@fao.org> 3 p. October 1998
In a speech to mark World Food Day 1998, the Director General of the FAO considers the enormous contribution made by women in agriculture, forestry and fisheries, their domestic labour, and their crucial role in food security. FAO studies document the limited rights of women and their lack of property rights over the land they cultivate in a number of societies. FAO is working to document the wealth of knowledge rural women possess. There is widespread ignorance of the actual division of labour by sex, with most countries adopting a gender-blind approach to agricultural planning and policymaking. Although many countries have legally affirmed women's basic right to own land, women rarely exercise actual control of land. When women are given opportunities and access to resources and services, they become dynamic partners in the development process.
URL: http://www.fao.org/DG/Wfd98-e.htm

045   The 'good wife': struggles over resources in the Kenyan horticultural sector
DOLAN, CATHERINE S. *Journal of Development Studies* 37(2001)3, p. 39-70, ill., tabs, 100 lit.refs, ISSN 0022-0388,
In Central Imenti Division of Meru District, Kenya, a study was conducted to examine how contract farming, in particular the cultivation of French beans as an export crop, has engendered conflict over rights, obligations and resources. Horticulture, the historical domain of women, has been rapidly intensified, commercialized and, in many cases, appropriated by men in response to pressure for agricultural diversification and the expanding European market for specialty vegetables. Women have responded to the erosion of their rights in ways that appear paradoxical, some undergoing Christian conversion while others poison their husbands. These responses simultaneously affirm and contest the prevailing norms of the 'good wife'. In Meru, gender relations are key to the negotiation of household resources and the potential for capital accumulation in the export horticultural sector.
KIT Library code: 430414

046   Women in agriculture in Ghana
DUNCAN, BEATRICE AKUA. Friedrich Ebert foundation, Accra, 208 p. 1997 ill., maps, tabs. Includes glossary. Includes lit.refs ISBN 9988-572-42-5
The position of Ghanaian women, both farmers and women employed within the Ministry of Food and Agriculture and other agro-related institutions, is examined. In Ghana's agricultural sector, women form 52% of the total labour force and produce 70% of the bulk of food crops. Women account for only 15% of the labour force within the Ministry, and are also vastly underrepresented in research and tertiary institutions. Women in agriculture face discrimination in varying forms. The term 'discrimination' is applied very generally to

absorb anything from human judgements about agriculture to basic gender inhibitions. This approach has helped demonstrate that women in agriculture have had to grapple with the low prestige level of agriculture as an occupation. Other differentials in rural and urban development, as well as sex-based inhibitions founded on customary law, also have a discriminatory impact on them as women farmers. The recommendations that follow seek to lay emphasis on measures to install confidence in the legal system among women farmers, and include a call for a unified and equitable law on distribution of property upon divorce; an increase in the occupational prestige level of agriculture; and more support to the various units within the Ministry that directly affect women in agriculture.
KIT Library code: 231874

047   The transformation of use-rights: a comparison of two Papua New Guinean societies
DWYER, PETER D.; MINNEGAL, MONICA. *Journal of Anthropological Research* 55(1999)3 p. 361-383 ill. 35 lit.refs ISSN 0091-7710

The use people make of land and resources has material, social and ideological implications for their lives. Patterns of land use inform understanding of systems of use-rights, property, ownership and tenure. These matters are explored with specific reference to two Papua New Guinean societies: the Kubo and the Bedamuni in the Western Province. The use that they make of land and resources is described, focusing particularly on residence, gender, marriage, kinship and local understandings of rights that are accorded by either conventions of practice or conventions of inheritance. It is demonstrated that prevailing patterns of use and, hence, local systems of resource management co-vary with social relationships. Among both Kubo and Bedamuni, there is a disjunction between stated ideals of ownership and use of resources and actual practice, but that disjunction takes different forms. There are, in addition, important differences concerning the rights of women. Kubo women are co-owners with men of clan land, whereas Bedamuni women are not considered to be co-owners with men and can neither inherit resources nor transfer them to their children. In the northern section of Kubo territory, changes in residential arrangements and patterns of land use were initiated in the 1980s with the establishment of a mission station and airstrip at Suabi. These changes also influenced the understandings and practice of people living in more remote settlements. The changes observed among the Kubo are

summarized and a model proposed under which there could be a transformation to a non-hierarchical and communally based system for use-rights. Finally, the implications of that model are outlined.
KIT Library code: 429553

048   What do men owe to women?: Islam and gender justice: beyond simplistic apologia
ESACK, FARID. *AFLA Quarterly* (1998)1 p. 30-33 lit.refs in notes ISSN 1384-282X

The author reflects on gender justice within the Muslim faith. He states that while the struggle for gender equality is about justice and human rights for women, it cannot be regarded as a women's struggle any more than, for example, the battle against anti-Semitism is a Jewish struggle. While violence against women may physically and legally be a women's problem, morally and religiously it very much concerns men. The use of religious scriptures in discrimination against women is examined, showing that within the scriptures, an array of different forms of discrimination against women is legitimated, such as discriminatory laws in divorce and marriage. Additionally, women seldom have an independent existence but feature as appendages of men. In the context of seventh-century Arabia, the personal example of Muhammad was exemplary in encouraging a sense of justice and compassion towards all victims of oppression, including women. Similarly, the Qur'an contains a number of exhortations that potentially have the same effect. Despite these, both the Islamic theological-cum-legal tradition as well as Muslim cultural life are deeply rooted in various forms of gender injustice ranging from explicit misogyny to paternalism under the guise of kindness. The author concludes that each adherent of a religious tradition is simultaneously a shaper of that tradition and that while one cannot assume personal responsibility for all the crimes or achievements of that tradition, each adherent nevertheless shares in the shame or glory, and in Islam, as in almost all other world religions, men are the key managers and interpreters of religion.
KIT Library code: 422720

049   Women's rights to land, housing and property in post-conflict situations and during reconstruction: a global overview
FARHA, LEILANA; TOOMEL, KATRIN. *Land Management Series* 9 UN Centre for Human Settlements (Habitat) <http:// www.unchs.org/> Land Management Programme, UNCHS, PO Box 30030, Nairobi, Kenya. 86 p. 1999 Centre on

Housing Rights and Evictions (COHRE), 83 Rue de Montbrillant, 1202 Geneva, Switzerland. <http://www.cohre.org/>

This report argues that restitution of land and property after conflict usually marginalizes women, leading to social and political instability. Without land, housing and property rights for women there can be no sustainable peace-building. It recommends that women and women's organizations be included in the negotiation of peace agreements and in the reconstruction process from the outset. New laws related to land, housing and property, drafted in the reconstruction period, must include specific provisions that recognize and protect independent rights to land, housing and property for all women. Accessible and independent enforcement mechanisms must be created. All sectors of society need human rights education with a focus on women's rights. National organizations must explore strategies for effecting cultural change. Women's organizations and others must monitor government compliance with international legal obligations. United Nations agencies and other international agencies must re-examine their programmes through a gender lens and then coordinate and restructure their efforts. Case studies are included from Eritrea, Guatemala and Liberia.
URL: http://www.unchs.org/tenure/Publication/Womrights/pub_1.htm

050   Women's rights to land, property and housing

FARHA, LEILANA. *FM Review* April 2000 6 p. Centre on Housing Rights and Evictions, 83 Rue de Montbrillant, 1202 Geneva, Switzerland. <http://www.cohre. org/> <sleckie@attglobal.net>

An Inter-regional Consultation on Women's Land and Property Rights During Situations of Conflict and Reconstruction was held by the Rwandan government in Kigali in February 1998. The Consultation was co-sponsored by a number of UN agencies and was attended by more than 100 participants. It was organized to augment and support the Women for Peace Network. Many participants in the Consultation felt that customary law is a barrier to land and property ownership by women in many parts of the world. Although women quite often experience extreme trauma and hardship both during and following armed conflict, such situations may also offer women new opportunities and roles in relation to land, property and housing.
URL: http://www.fmreview.org/ fmr077.htm

051   Law and gender inequality: the politics of women's rights in India

FLAVIA, AGNES. Law in India series. Oxford University press, New Delhi, 250 p. 1999 ill., tabs. Includes index. Includes lit.refs ISBN 0-19-564587-1

The issue of gender and law reform in India is discussed and strategies that could safeguard women's rights within a sphere of complex social and political boundaries are examined. The origin and development of family laws in India is outlined, and state interventions at various strategic points in history are explored. The study is divided into four parts, dealing respectively with: the pre-colonial and colonial legal systems; post-independence developments, such as the Constitution enacted in 1950 and the Hindu law reforms of the 1950s; the political questions that shroud reforms within non-Muslim minorities (the Parsis and the Christians); and current debates, such as the issue of the Uniform Civil Code, which has brought minority rights and gender equality into direct conflict, as well as proposals for alternative measures. The study reveals that the history of women's rights is not linear with the religious and customary laws forming one end of the scale and the statutory reforms steadily progressing towards the other end. Rather, the history is complex with various interactive forces constantly at play. Women's rights are not only constrained by a uniform set of patriarchal norms but are also shaped and moulded by several social, economic and political currents. Unless a theoretical framework is evolved that situates marriage centrally within the context of economic structures, women's right to economic security in matrimonial relationships will continue to be illusive. There is also a need to locate property at the centre of matrimonial law reform, if adequate solutions to women's increasing poverty and destitution are to be evolved. Since patriarchy is reinforced through economic structures, a solution to the oppression and destitution of women has to be found primarily within the context of these structures and state responsibility towards women.
KIT Library code: 242232

052   Why women's property rights matter

FORTMANN, LOUISE. *Proceedings of the International Conference on Land Tenure in the Developing World with a focus on Southern Africa, Capetown Conference on Land Tenure Issues* Paper 19 German Technical Co-operation (GTZ) <http://www.gtz.de/> GTZ, Dag-Hammarskjöld-Weg 1-5, 65760 Eschborn, Germany. 10 p. January 1998 Department of

Environmental Science, Policy and Management, 145 Mulford Hall, University of California at Berkeley, Berkeley, CA 94720-3114, USA. <fortmann@nature.berkely.edu>

The paper explores the consequences of gendered tenure and property systems for women in particular and for society more generally. Three facets of gendered tenure, namely terms of access, property size and security of tenure, are discussed. Property systems that discriminate against women are shown to have adverse consequences for women and their families by reducing women's ability to produce and retain enough to maintain an adequate livelihood for their family, due to lack of access to land or lack of access to sufficient land; reduced access to credit; lack of control of land use and management decisions; lack of control over produce; and insecure tenure in both the short and long term. Data from two villages in central Zimbabwe show that gender has adverse effects on tree planting where women's tenure is insecure and has no such effects where their tenure is secure, suggesting that discriminatory tenure systems might have damaging environmental effects. The right of women to the intellectual products of their labour on agricultural land in the form of plant variety protection is almost non-existent, and the loss of these intellectual property rights is detrimental to society more generally. Discriminatory property systems are incompatible with the principles of democracy.
URL: http://www.gtz.de/orboden/capetown/cape19.htm

053   Gender and law initiatives in Francophone sub-Saharan Africa
WORLD BANK *Africa Region Findings* 148 <http://www.worldbank.org> 1818 H Street N.W, Room J8-105, Washington DC 20433, USA. <emorrishughes@ worldbank.org> 7 p. June 1999

As the result of two years of constructive dialogue between the World Bank, government agencies and grassroots' associations involved in the advancement of women, a workshop on 'Promotion of the societal status of women in Francophone sub-Saharan Africa' was organized in March 1998 in Cotonou, Benin, by the Association of Women Jurists with technical and financial assistance from the World Bank. The workshop aimed to provide for an exchange of views between civil society and government agencies, as well as between countries, on the substance of law, law enforcement and legal literacy issues as these relate to women's experience of discrimination. A programme of technical assistance was designed to strengthen the institutional capacity of government units; to facilitate strategic alliances between government and NGOs involved in promoting the societal status of women; and to support legal literacy and legal technical assistance at the grassroots' level.
URL: http://www.worldbank.org/afr/findings/english/find148.htm

054   "Here it is our land, the two of us": women, men and land in Zimbabwean resettlement area
GOEBEL, ALLISON. *Journal of Contemporary African Studies* 17(1999)1 p. 75-96 ill., tabs 66 lit.refs

Gender aspects of the current resettlement policy in Zimbabwe are discussed. It is argued that women's perspectives and needs have been marginalized in the discourse shaping land reform in Zimbabwe's resettlement programme, but that the benefits women derive from arable land have improved in resettlement. While the overall structural conditions created by the permit system in resettlement reduce women's access to land, it cannot be assumed that they do not control any part of the product of their agricultural labour. By looking in detail at the gendered power relations, it is found that certain types of crops are respected as belonging to women, and finding ways to enhance women's production of such crops may be an important strategy. It is argued that only jointly issued permits, leases or title deeds will increase women's land security in resettlement areas. This would help divorced women as well as those who remain married. It is recognized that for widows, the innovation of resettlement policy in allowing widows to receive permits on the death of a husband, has clearly had profound material and social benefits. It is hoped that current changes to inheritance law that improve the rights of widows, will soon be expanded to include inheritance of rights to land.
KIT Library code: 429778

055   Gender and law: Eastern Africa speaks: proceedings of the conference
GOPAL, GITA; SALIM, MARYAM. Directions in Development. World Bank, Washington, DC, 229 p. 1998 ill., graphs, tabs. Includes lit.refs ISBN 0-8213-4206-1

A conference was held in 1997 in Ethiopia to discuss and exchange experiences on gender and law in Eastern Africa. Discussions centred on themes important to women: land-related issues, family law, violence against women, employment and labour, and implementation in decentralized governance frameworks. Six countries participated: Eritrea, Ethiopia, Kenya, Tanzania,

Uganda and Zimbabwe. Customary laws and their conflict with statutory laws were invariably found to be at the root of many of the substantive legal issues related to women's economic rights in all countries. The inadequacy of existing legal regimes governing women's socioeconomic rights was another prominent issue. The wide divergence between de jure laws and actual practice make implementation and related issues a matter of concern. Despite legal reform in all the countries, many of the statutory rights remain on paper because implementation is weak or ineffective, and women's social and economic status continues to be largely defined by customary rules that are deeply rooted in country-specific historical, economic and social factors. Low levels of education for women lead to legal illiteracy. Unaware of their rights, most women are unable to enjoy the benefits of legal reform. In countries with high levels of illiteracy, scarce resources and limited access to information, changing the law can only be a first step. Government policy should focus on increasing women's opportunities to access resources outside the home. Equitable land policy will also go a long way towards enhancing the economic status of women. Processes must be found to involve women in legal reform to ensure that their voices are heard and considered, and reform must be based on a clear understanding of customary practices.

KIT Library code: 223028

056   Government indifference as lawyers defending women's rights are threatened with death
AMNESTY INTERNATIONAL. *ai index: asa 33/06/99* Amnesty International (AI) <http://www.web.amnesty.org> 4 p. April 1999
On 6 April 1999, Samia Sarwar, a 29-year old woman with two small children, was shot dead in her lawyer's office in Lahore, Pakistan. She had been seeking a divorce from her husband after years of domestic abuse and her family felt that their honour had been tarnished. Members of the Peshawar Chamber of Commerce, of which the victim's father is chair, and local ulema (Islamic scholars) have publicly stated that the honour killing was in accordance with religious and tribal traditions. They have accused the human rights lawyers, Asma Jahangir and her sister Hina Jilani, in whose offices the murder took place, of 'misguiding women'. Local ulema have issued a religious edict (fatwa) calling on believers to kill the two women. In 1998 several hundred honour killings were reported in Pakistan but the true number is thought to be considerably higher. Most honour killings go

virtually unpunished as the police and judiciary usually side with offenders.
URL: http://www.web.amnesty.org/ai.nsf/index/ASA330061999

057   Land distribution in KwaZulu-Natal: an analysis of farmland transactions in 1997
GRAHAM, A.W.; LYNE, M.C. *Development Southern Africa* 16(1999)3 p. 435-445 ll., tabs 15 lit.refs
The results of a census survey of all land transactions in the South African province of KwaZulu-Natal during the calendar year 1997 are presented. Data recorded by the Deeds Registry were stratified and analysed by race, gender and mode of land acquisition. It was estimated that 372 995 ha (7%) of the area available for redistribution have been transferred to new owners; only 0.43% of the available area was redistributed to disadvantaged people. Although low, the rate of redistribution appears to have increased dramatically since 1995. The quality of land varied markedly across different modes of land redistribution. Land purchased with government grants was of a much lower agricultural quality than land purchased privately. Relative to government assisted transactions, private market transactions accounted for a slightly smaller share of the area transferred to disadvantaged people but for a much larger share of the value of land redistributed. Inheritance and land donations accounted for the remaining redistributed land. Women were well represented in land transactions involving inheritance but were underrepresented in transactions financed with mortgage loans. In general, they acquired farms of much smaller size and land of lower quality than men.
KIT Library code: 429776

058   Diminished access, diverted exclusion: women and land tenure in sub-Saharan Africa
GRAY, LESLIE; KEVANE, MICHAEL. *African Studies Review* 42(1999)2, p. 15-39, Bibliogr. p. 34-38
Increasing commercialization, population growth and concurrent increases in land value have affected women's land rights in Africa. Most of the literature concentrates on how these changes have led to an erosion of women's rights. Some of the processes by which women's rights to land are diminishing are examined. Cases are presented to demonstrate how rights previously utilized have become less important. Furthermore, women's rights to land can be decreased by changing public meanings underlying the social interpretation and enforcement of rights, and women's access to land can diminish when the

actual rules of access change. Women have responded in different ways to reductions in access to land. They have mounted both legal and customary challenges to inheritance laws, made use of anonymous land markets, organized formal, cooperative groups to gain tenure rights, and manipulated customary rules using personal relationships. Through these means, women have created new routes of access to land and, in some cases, new rights.
KIT Library code: 429709

059   In the shadow of marriage: gender and justice in an African community
GRIFFITHS, ANNE M.O. University of Chicago press, Chicago, IL, 310 p. 1997 ill. Includes index. Includes lit.refs ISBN 0-226-30875-8
   Women's access to family law in Botswana is discussed. The role that marriage plays in the social construction of procreative relationships and the ways in which marital status affects the kinds of claims that women pursue with respect to their male partners are examined. Such claims, which include compensation for pregnancy, maintenance and rights to property, operate at both social and legal levels. The impact that these social contexts have on an individual's ability to access and manipulate a legal system that incorporates Tswana customary law and European law is analysed. The analysis is based on an ethnographic study carried out in Kweneng District over a number of years (1982-1989) and is based on everyday life and ordinary people's perceptions and experiences of their social and legal universe. Using detailed life histories and extended case studies, the gendered world in which women and men live is highlighted, as well as how this affects women's access to law. Access to resources plays a key role in constructing different forms of power that affect individuals' abilities to negotiate with one another and the types of discourse they employ. The results of the ethnographic study are presented and analysed within the framework of a number of more general theoretical questions concerning the relationship between gender and power and how this relates to law and legal pluralism.
KIT Library code: 221553

060   Women, descent, and tenure succession among the Bambara of West Africa: a changing landscape
GRIGSBY, W.J. *Human Organization* 55(1996)1 p. 93-98
   This article describes the impact of land tenure changes that negatively effect women's access to land for subsistence farming. The framework for describing changes in Mali has emphasized shifts from communal to more individualized tenure and commercialized agricultural practices. It is argued that this emphasis obscures the displacement of 'bush fallow' farming and the loss of greater access to a broad range of resources for women. Data are obtained from interviews collected over a six-month period during the early 1990s in rural Mali. It is posited that women's limited access to land hinders their potential to contribute to development. Patrilineal descent and patrilocal residence patterns limit women's access to land. The land constraints of women are viewed as only partially related to gender-biased development interventions and the closing of traditional land tenure arrangements. This study focuses on the Bambara, a Mande speaking ethnic group that is dependent on cereal crop production. Women share cooking and fuelwood responsibilities and thus have more time for small-scale market activity or work related to land-based resources. One manifestation of the changes is the decline in patrilineal control over land use and access, but little change is evident in transfers of land. The shift to commercialization and individualization and the reduction in bush fallow land means increased open access and increased competition for alternative sources of fuelwood and income-producing forest products. It is suggested that planning must identify spatial and organizational openings that accommodate women and increase their potential to contribute to development. Women in Bambara villages have successfully exploited social groups as the locus for gaining access to land for collective crop and garden production. It is suggested that future studies examine stratification of land based on gender and class factors.
KIT Library code: 429837

061   The effects of women's land tenure security on agricultural output among the Maragoli of western Kenya
GWAKO, EDWINS LABAN MOOGI. UMI, Ann Arbor, MI, 246 p. 1999 ill., graphs, maps, tabs. Doctoral diss. Washington University, 1997. Bibliogr.: p. 223-246
   The effects of women's land tenure security on agricultural output is explored, based on data collected from 120 households among the densely populated Maragoli of western Kenya. The main hypothesis tested is that women's agricultural output increases when they have tenure security. The study confirms the proposed hypothesis and thereby contradicts the World Bank's findings from eight African studies that tenure security

has no statistically significant effect on yields. It is demonstrated that women strategically bargain and invest more of their productive responses on the plots where they anticipate the greatest individual gains. The results of linear regression analyses reveal that tenure security significantly predicts about 45% of women farmers' agricultural output. This is achieved by women's selective use of extension services, fertilizer, and hybrid seeds, and greater agricultural labour input on the plots where they have greater tenure security. The results are corroborated by the results of both multiple linear regression and partial correlation analyses; they underscore women farmers' ability to boost agricultural output when there are appropriate incentives for them to do so.

KIT Library code: 238855

062   Widow inheritance among the Maragoli of western Kenya
GWAKO, EDWINS LABAN MOOGI. *Journal of Anthropological Research* 54(1998)2 p. 173-198 ill. 56 lit.refs ISSN 0091-7710

Continuity and change in the practice of widow inheritance or levirate marriage among the Maragoli of western Kenya are discussed. The perspectives of widows are examined to illustrate how levirate marriage affects them. It is argued that the practice benefits and serves different and sometimes conflicting interests for various groups of men and women, and the experiences and perspectives of Maragoli widows with regard to this practice are not homogenous. Some existing incentives favour the continuation of levirate marriage. For example, financial constraints and other continued strains on their households' limited resources may influence some widows' stand vis-à-vis this practice. The results of this study show that although levirate marriage still obtains among the Maragoli, signs of an impending change are appearing as more economically secure and resource-owning widows become increasingly assertive of their right to make independent decisions about what to do with their lives.

KIT Library code: 425057

063   Intrahousehold resource allocation in developing countries: models, methods, and policy
HADDAD, LAWRENCE; HODDINOTT, JOHN; ALDERMAN, HAROLD. Johns Hopkins university press, Baltimore, 341 p. 1997 ill., graphs, tabs. Includes index. Bibliogr.: p. 293-323 ISBN 0-8018-5572-1

This book considers how rights, responsibilities and resources are allocated among household and family members. Surveying a diverse body of theory and evidence, it examines the many social and cultural factors that influence decisions at the family and household level about the allocation of time, incomes, assets and other resources. Current theory as it has developed over the 1970-1997 period is reviewed. The process by which household allocations occur is important for policy and project design. It is sometimes claimed that models in which the household is posited to act as a single decision-maker, namely the unitary model, are silent on the issue of intrahousehold distribution. It is demonstrated that this claim is wrong. In addition, the suggestion that an alternative to the unitary model is a bargaining model neglects the important fact that there are at least four variants of these collective models. Although substantial progress has been made on the theoretical front, a number of major measurement and econometric issues are not being addressed. Further work on intrahousehold allocation will benefit substantially from interaction among researchers across a number of disciplines. Economics and anthropology appear to be heading towards a new convergence of concern around the nature and use of assets. The measurement of intrahousehold allocations can be enhanced by drawing on techniques from anthropology and nutrition.

KIT Library code: 230027

064   The impact of Mozambique's land tenure policy on refugees and internally displaced persons
HANCHINAMANI, BINA. *Human Rights Brief* 7(2000)2 Washington College of Law <http://www. wcl.american.edu> 4801 Massachusetts Ave NW, Washington DC 20016, USA. <web-admin@wcl. american.edu> 6 p. 2000

Although Mozambique's implementation of the July 1997 Land Law generally serves as a model example of compliance with international legal protection for returning refugees and displaced persons, some land tenure problems for returning refugees persist. It continues to be difficult for peasants to enforce their rights in the midst of competing large landholders and outside investors. Although the Land Law did much to protect the interests of the small farmers against the interests of large landholders, it did not contain enough provisions for addressing the competing land claims among peasants. In addition, enforcing the land rights of women remains challenging due to the history of discrimination against women who, in customary

practices, lacked land use, development and inheritance rights.
URL: http://www.wcl.american.edu/pub/humright/brief/v7i2/mozambique.htm

065   Gender politics, legal reform, and the Muslim community in India
HASAN, ZOYA In: *Appropriating gender: women's activism and politicized religion in South Asia* ed. by Patricia Jeffery and Amrita Basu. Zones of Religion. Routledge, New York, p. 71-88 1998 lit.refs in notes

This chapter addresses recent events in India and the various ways that Muslim women's rights have been debated and refracted through contests over secularism, community rights and gender issues. The debate about legal reforms that arose from the controversy over the Muslim Women (Protection of Rights on Divorce) Bill 1986 is considered. The arguments of defenders of the status quo and of those who advocated changes in personal laws are explored. The Congress Party converted women's rights into an issue of minority rights and secularism. The Hindu Right built its attack on Muslims by focusing on their treatment of women and completely ignoring the identity concerns of Muslims. In a discussion supposedly about women's rights, the most notable feature was the marginalization of Muslim women and the trivialization of their rights.
KIT Library code: 422650

066   The rights of women in Muslim societies
HILMY, NABIL A. *AFLA Quarterly* (1998)1 p. 6-25 1998 lit.refs in notes ISSN 1384-282X

An account is provided of women's rights in the Arab region in terms of their social roles, employment and education within the traditional Arab family. Much of the modern Muslim world has experienced significant changes with respect to the lives of women. These changes are discussed with particular reference to women's political and legal rights, participation in national development, and property and inheritance rights. The role of the state and the social construction of gender identity are also considered. The Convention on the Elimination of All Forms of Discrimination against Women (CEDAW) was adopted by the United Nations general assembly in 1979, but was not accepted by all the Islamic countries unconditionally. The reservations made by Egypt, Tunisia, Iraq, Democratic Yemen, Bangladesh and Jordan are outlined. The author concludes that major advances in women's rights in Islam have been achieved in recent years. These advances represent a radical departure from traditional Islamic doctrine. However, while reforms reflect the ideals and aspirations of the educated, West-oriented urban elite, they may be met with hostility and suspicion in the more conservative rural areas. Moreover, the vast majority of the Muslim judiciary remains loyal to the traditional doctrines and values that formed the basis of their education in the law. Thus, the legislation does not always reflect social reality and although the legal machinery for women's advancement exists, it does not function effectively everywhere.
KIT Library code: 422718

067   Gender and changing property rights in Laos
IRESON-DOOLITTLE, CAROL In: *Women's rights to house and land: China, Laos, Vietnam* ed. by Irene Tinker, Gale Summerfield. Rienner, Boulder, CO p. 145-152 1999 lit.refs in notes

Male-dominated political and economic systems may be subverting women's traditional and constitutional rights in Laos as land is formally registered in the name of the 'head of the household'. Land allocation and titling processes are part of broader social and economic change aiming to integrate Laos into regional and global capitalist economies. Laos has experienced dramatic social and economic changes since 1975, which have had various impacts on the people of Laos. Lowland Lao women will be particularly affected if traditional matrilineal rights are eroded by the introduction of a single set of laws for the country. Current land allocation and titling processes are occurring in response to pressure and funding from multilateral lending agencies and bilateral Western aid donors. The author states, however, that the governmental departments allocating land and creating model land-titling pilot projects are among the most sexist of the departments in a widely male-dominated government. All household land, including the land inherited by the wife from her parents, is registered in the name of the 'head of the household', who is always understood to be male. Women's customary and constitutional rights are therefore at risk. Formalizing property rights has a variety of implications for Laotian society in the future. The form and process of creating a 'modern' type of ownership currently being undertaken in Laos may institutionalize marked gender inequality despite constitutional guarantees for equality. Furthermore, these overall changes in the structure of the agricultural system may have a variety of other negative consequences.
KIT Library code: 427154

068   Liberalisation, gender, and the land question in sub-Saharan Africa
IZUMI, KAORI In: *Women, land and agriculture* ed. by Caroline Sweetman. Focus on gender. Oxfam, Oxford p. 9-18 1999 40 lit.refs

This paper focuses on land reform initiatives undertaken in a number of African countries since the late 1980s. Many African societies have experienced substantial changes in their formal and informal land tenure systems as part of a wider process of socioeconomic and political change, and land policy has become increasingly concerned with economic efficiency and investment rather than poverty alleviation, equity and livelihoods. Gender analysis of debates over land is therefore one of the most neglected issues in research and policy debates. The mainstream theories regarding land issues in Africa are gender-blind resulting in the formulation of land policies and land laws that ignore the interests and needs of women. Focusing on Tanzania and Zimbabwe, the article explores how economic and political liberalization have affected women's access and rights to land. Since the 1980s, traditional institutions governing land tenure and use in Tanzania and Zimbabwe have been affected and transformed in different ways according to their different past and present political and economic contexts. Women's access and rights to land are shaped by gender-determined power relations that exist across a range of institutions. Analyses of gender and land needs must go beyond the current common focus of weighing up the pros and cons of individual or indigenous land tenure. Research is urgently required into the ways in which land access and rights among women have been affected, negotiated and contested by and within the institutions of the state and the market, and the social institutions of the community, the family and the household. Several levels of analysis are necessary; particular areas for attention are the gaps between statutory institutional reforms at national level, informal institutional changes, and actual practice at local level.
KIT Library code: 429050

069   Past wrongs and gender rights: issues and conflicts in South Africa's land reform
JACOBS, SUSIE. *European Journal of Development Research* 10(1998)2 p. 70-87 bibliogr. p. 85-87

South Africa's agrarian situation presents a range of daunting issues, including extreme rural poverty and a government hindered by severe financial constraints. At the same time, the country's attempts to incorporate gender issues into land reform are virtually unique. Several major issues confronting the present pilot land reform programme and any future reform are discussed: demand for land; demand for services; the continued use of 'the household' as the unit of registration for subsidy; traditional authorities; forms of land tenure; and the nature of public participation. The analysis stresses that all of these are gender issues, as is the extent of conflict raised through overt discussion of gender processes. None of these questions has a straightforward 'answer' but their consideration is likely instead to raise additional questions.
KIT Library code: 429809

070   Structures and processes: land, families, and gender relations
JACOBS, SUSIE. *Gender and Development* 4(1996)2 p. 35-42 1996 lit.refs in notes

The author points to the existence of a striking similarity in some of the effects of land reform upon gender relations and women's family positions. This is the case despite the variation in land reform processes and in the cultures in which they occur. Family and kinship patterns both affect, and are affected by, land reform. This two-way relationship is examined, with particular attention given to the author's study of northeastern Zimbabwean Resettlement Areas, conducted during the mid-1980s, and Agarwal's 1994 study of women and land rights in South Asia. Sections discuss the effects of land reform; family formation, family relationships and land; family and land in South Asia; reforms that disadvantage women; benefits for women of land reform; and the Zimbabwean case study.
KIT Library code: 429839

071   Law for Pacific women: a legal rights handbook
JALAL, PATRICIA IMRANA. Fiji women's rights movement, Suva, 674 p. 1998 ill., tabs. Includes index. Includes glossary. Includes lit.refs ISBN 982-9000-00-1

This book emphasizes that women's rights are human rights and that to deny women's rights to equality is to deny that they are human beings. It provides information about existing laws from which women may benefit, makes the content and structures of the law more generally accessible in non-legal language, and initiates the process of legal literacy for women. The book has been written for human and legal rights teachers. A detailed study is presented of the laws affecting women in Fiji, as well as some analysis of how laws affect women in the Cook Islands, Kiribati, Nauru, Solomon Islands, Tonga, Tuvalu, Vanuatu and Western Samoa. Data were collected over the 1992-97 period. The information on all countries

listed aims to be a comprehensive starting point for national training on legal literacy. The types of laws that affect the human rights of women are considered: those that discriminate against women, those that disadvantage women in their application or effect; and those that have a powerful influence on women's lives or affect their overall status. Each chapter contains tables and discussions of the relevant legislation, as well as short reports of true cases that illustrate how the legislation is applied. Illustrations are also used to provoke group discussions. Limited access to land has severe consequences not only for the general human need for shelter but also for the ability of women to obtain money without reference to men. There is a very close relationship between power, land and wealth. A strategy for gaining more power would be to search for more positive interpretations of customary law and political struggle for a more just solution to the problem of the distribution of land. Finally, strategies for change are reviewed.
KIT Library code: 234021

072   Land rights
JALAL, PATRICIA IMRANA. In: *Law for Pacific women: a legal rights handbook* ed. by P. Imrana Jalal. Fiji women's rights movement, Suva p. 51-68 1998 ill.

The ways in which land may be owned and access to land is governed, as well as the ways in which ownership and access to land affect both indigenous and non-indigenous women in the Pacific, are addressed. The three basic ways in which land may be owned are by custom, by the state and by freehold. Land rights in the region appear to be affected both by gender and by social class. Legislation itself may not discriminate against women, but the current interpretation of customary law governing the control and management of custom land (land owned by groups of indigenous people) gives power over land mainly to men, particularly men of high rank. Women's limited access to land limits their ability to acquire money without reference to men and to obtain economic power. Without land as security, there is very limited access to credit or loans from commercial banks. This ultimately reinforces women's dependence on men. It is suggested that more positive interpretations of customary law be sought and that land courts be used to get legal recognition of these interpretations.
KIT Library code: 426063

073   Matrimonial property
JALAL, PATRICIA IMRANA. In: *Law for Pacific women: a legal rights handbook* Suva: Fiji women's rights movement, 1998, p. 400-448, ill.

A description is given of what is meant by matrimonial property, property owned by husband and wife together in legal and customary marriages. Legislation relating to matrimonial property in the Pacific region and the problems associated with court powers and procedures are subsequently discussed. A particular problem is the meaning of contribution when applied to the unpaid work women do, and the article examines how courts have approached this problem. Case studies from the region illustrate how matrimonial property is shared, with particular focus on women's share. The article concludes with discussions of legislation designed as a result of the United Nations Women's Convention requirement that member states 'eliminate discrimination against women in all matters relating to marriage' and ensure 'the same rights for both spouses in respect of the ownership, management, administration, enjoyment and disposition of property'.
KIT Library code: 426064

074   Effects of gendered land rights on urban housing by women in Botswana
KALABAMU, FAUSTIN. *Proceedings of the International Conference on Land Tenure in the Developing World with a focus on Southern Africa, Capetown Conference on Land Tenure Issues* Paper 34 German Technical Co-operation (GTZ) <http://www.gtz.de/> GTZ, Dag-Hammarskjöld-Weg 1-5, 65760 Eschborn, Germany. 8 p. January 1998 Department of Environmental Science, University of Botswana, Private Bag 00704, Gaborone, Botswana. <kalabamu@noka.ub.bw>

Analysis of the housing conditions of female- and male-headed households in Lobatse, Botswana, during 1981-91 indicate that more female-headed households live in owner-occupied houses on land held under 'Certificate of Rights' titles, while more male-headed households live in houses rented from companies and generally live in better quality housing. Although the Botswana Government has, since independence, instituted land and property rights initiatives targeted at the urban poor, the majority of whom are women, there have not been specific efforts to address women's disadvantaged position. The initiatives taken to date only meet women's practical needs in that they accept patriarchy and seek to solve women's problems within existing structures, legal frameworks and institutions, which are, in the first instance, responsible for the current gender inequalities and subordination of women. To empower women in land related matters, there is a need to rewrite the Deeds Registry Act so as to provide for joint registration of titles for couples married in 'community of property'. There is also a need to integrate gender, and women's perspectives in particular, in all land tenure and housing policies and programmes.

URL: http://www.gtz.de/orboden/capetown/cape34.htm

075   Subversive sites: feminist engagements with law in India
KAPUR, RATNA; COSSMAN, BRENDA. Sage, New Delhi 352 p. 1996. Includes index ISBN 81-7036-552-X

Drawing on recent developments in feminist legal studies, post-structuralist theory and cultural studies, this book explores the complex relationship between women and the legal apparatus. It seeks both to define the limits of the law and to explore its possibilities for bringing about progressive change in women's social status. The extent to which assumptions about women's identities as wives and mothers limit the promise of legal equality is examined. Among the issues discussed are: the various approaches to law that have been developed in the literature on women and law in India; familial ideology and the sexual division of labour in the legal regulation of women; the relationship between the discourse of equality and familial ideology in the context of constitutional sex discrimination challenges; the ways in which legal discourse is being used to advance the political agendas of the Hindu Right; and the role law can play in women's struggles for empowerment. The book explores alternative strategies for using law as a subversive site in feminist struggles and suggests ways of strengthening the strategies of women's movements for engaging with litigation, law reform and legal literacy. New insights are offered into the way in which the law can serve as a site for discursive struggle, rather than simply as a tool for social change.

KIT Library code: 215461

076   Women's land ownership rights in Kenya
KARANJA, PERPETUA WAMBUI. In: *Realizing the rights of women in development processes: women's legal entitlements to agricultural development and financial assistance* ed. Samuel O. Gyandoh et al.; contrib. by Jane B. Knowles.et al. Third World legal studies. International Third World legal studies association (INTWORLSA), New York, NY p. 109-135 1991 lit.refs in notes ISSN 0895-5018

Kenyan women have made tremendous contributions to the overall economic growth of the country through their almost exclusive participation in the agricultural sector in particular, as well as their employment in other sectors of the economy. However, an examination of the operation of the country's laws, government policies and directives reveals a high degree of marginalization, neglect and discrimination of women in the distribution of economic resources. Government intervention through land legislation and the formulation of policies intended to protect women's access to land have not been successful in correcting the existing sexual inequalities in access to and ownership of land, and women's economic wellbeing has continued to depend largely on their rights in marriage, divorce and inheritance. While customary land tenure was exclusive of women, the reforms instituted by the colonial administration and adopted by the independent government continued to undermine the land rights of women. The introduction of a monetary economy with land as the chief economic resource and the accompanying exclusion of women from ownership of land undermined and continue to undermine women's economic wellbeing. It is imperative that land policies be designed to enable women to own land or to have clearly stipulated rights over land that are commensurate with their producer roles. There is also a need to address their limited access to secondary factors of production, such as education, employment and credit.

KIT Library code: 426445

077   Women and common property resources in the management and health of livestock in Thai villages
KEHREN, TATJANA; TISDELL, CLEM. In: *Good governance issues and sustainable development: the Indian Ocean region* ed. Robin Ghosh, Rony Gabbay, Abu Siddique. Atlantic, New Delhi p. 149-167 1999 30 lit.refs

The importance of livestock industries for small farmers in Thailand and the use of common property resources in their development have increased in recent years, as some of these industries have experienced growing competition from the commercial sector. Private property rights in Thailand have evolved gradually in response to the increased benefits of defining property rights in land, induced by the commercialization of agriculture. However, in many areas, the degree of documentation of land rights is insufficient to be used legally as collateral on loans, which means that farmers in these areas have restricted access to credit. The article first provides an overview of the livestock industries in Thailand: pig, poultry and dairy. The role of women in the village livestock economy is then explored. While there has been some progress with respect to women's status in Thailand and their access to various professions

in recent years, their important contribution on farms in rural areas is still denied. Women play a significant but undervalued role in animal husbandry, and their impact on the health of livestock, as well as their potential contribution to an improvement of the present situation, needs to be considered. The Muak-Lek Dairy Project has shown that women in rural areas can contribute in terms of earning additional income, provided they are given the opportunity and have access to credit. For a healthier and sustainable development of the livestock industry in Thailand, more resources need to be directed towards the training of rural women in animal husbandry, as well as towards an improvement in their access to credit.
KIT Library code: 429062

078   The failure of popular justice in Uganda: local councils and women's property rights
KHADIAGALA, LYNN S. Development and Change 32(2001)1 p. 55-76 51 lit.refs ISSN 0012-155X
In 1987, as part of a decentralization scheme, Uganda granted judicial capacity to local councils at the village, parish and sub-country levels. In promoting local councils as tribunals of 'popular justice', the government argued that they would provide Ugandans with expedient, inexpensive and culturally appropriate justice. Women should have been the greatest beneficiaries of the local council courts. However, experiences of women in Kabale District in south-western Uganda show that popular justice has failed to provide a more accessible system of justice to the less powerful and to protect women's customary rights to land. The courts failed in three ways: (1) local councils turned out to be more expensive mechanisms for litigating property disputes; (2) women perceive local council courts to be biased against them: a woman who takes a marital land dispute to the male-dominated local council courts is likely to confront a council filled with her husband's relatives and social companions; and (3) local councils have at their disposal a set of gatekeeping mechanisms preventing women's access to the magistrates' courts.
KIT Library code: 430170

079   Law and the status of women in Kenya
KIBWANA, KIVUTHA. Claripress, Nairobi, 221 p. 1996. Includes index. Includes lit.refs ISBN 9966-9602-4-4
This book questions whether Kenya puts into practice the protection of women's rights as enshrined in the African Charter for Human and People's Rights and the UN Convention on the Elimination of All Forms of Discrimination against Women. It finds that the Constitution is not only silent on the question of gender discrimination against women but also allows discrimination of women in certain areas, especially those sanctioned by culturally determined personal laws. The first legal battle for the women's movement must be for them to obtain constitutional recognition and protection of the female gender. Field data gathered from Laikipia District demonstrates that discrimination is more rife among the pastoral community and in rural areas. All classes of women are discriminated against by men generally and by male government officials. Women most often have no land rights and no access to credit, employment or business opportunities. Women, contrary to popular myth, do not accept this discrimination and do in fact make efforts to assert themselves. Future land reform should address women's access to land. Such land tenure must give women secure land rights in equality with men because they are the tillers of land. There should be two categories of land registration: individualized land and family land. Family land would be equally owned by spouses and would include land for food production purposes and land acquired during the currency of any marriage. Disposal of family land would be conditional upon the existence of alternative income-generating sources for the family and willing spousal consent.
KIT Library code: 235471

080   Women in the Third World: a reference handbook
KINNEAR, KAREN L. Contemporary World Issues. ABC-CLIO, Santa Barbara, CA, 348 p. 1997. Includes index. Includes lit.refs ISBN 0-87436-922-3
A survey of the available literature and other resources on women in the Third World is presented. The vast range of literature and resources available offers many opportunities to learn more about women in the Third World, their lives and the challenges many of them face. The literature review covers family relations, violence, health care, work and politics. A detailed chronology of significant events and statutes relevant to women in the Third World is provided. Biographical sketches of the women who have played key roles in politics, social activism, education and other important areas are included. Facts and statistics concerning women's lives and status in developing countries are presented, as well as international agreements; a directory of representative private and public organizations, associations and

government agencies involved in working with women; and a detailed list of resources, including books, films, videocassettes, and Internet sites.
KIT Library code: 223784

081   Changing land tenure systems in the contemporary matrilineal social system: the gendered dimension

KODA, B. Seminar proceedings. Nordic Africa Institute (1998)32 p. 195-221 1998 22 lit.refs

An attempt is made to explore socioeconomic and political dimensions of land tenure systems from a feminist point of view. The southeastern part of Tanzania, particularly the Mtwara region, is selected to assist in contextualizing a matrilineal social system. Faced with the great importance attached to the agrarian sector in Tanzania, one would have believed that issues of concern in land tenure are gender neutral. However, available data points to the contrary. Women and men tend to be affected differently by land tenurial matters. While the root cause of this gender imbalance is essentially the traditional/cultural norms (ideologies and practices), nevertheless, influences from both foreign religions (Islam and Christianity), and the concepts of so-called 'modern governance' and 'modern economy' have persistently ensured the prevalence of gender imbalances.
KIT Library code: 429790

082   Demanding a place under the Kgotla tree: women's rural access to land and power

KOMPE, LYDIA; SMALL, JANET. In: *Realizing the rights of women in development processes: women's legal entitlements to agricultural development and financial assistance* ed. Samuel O. Gyandoh et al.; contrib. by Jane B. Knowles.et al.
Third World legal studies. International Third World legal studies association (INTWORLSA), New York, NY p. 137-156 1991 8 lit.refs ISSN 0895-5018

Based on fieldwork conducted in 1990 by the Transvaal Rural Action Committee (TRAC), a South African NGO, the position of women in Transvaal rural societies is explored with a particular focus on their status, access to decision-making and their rights to land and property. Twenty individual interviews were carried out with women from ten communities in the western, northern and southeastern parts of the Transvaal province. It is clear that there is a complex interrelationship between access to land, political and domestic power, and women's own self-esteem. Women who have legally inalienable rights to land have a greater chance of asserting some power on a local political level

as well as on a domestic level. However, access to land is not the only factor at play in women's powerlessness. Traditional value systems still dictate both men's and women's consciousness about themselves and their roles. In the context of land and power, women have very clear demands about the changes needed in the future. Many of the demands are related to the general improvement of the quality of their lives, such as better facilities in rural areas. While policymakers may acknowledge the importance of involving women, until the burden of manual domestic work is lightened, the women themselves may not have the time or energy to use the opportunities afforded them. The document reveals certain clear areas where policy change is urgently needed, such as securing women's independent access to land and housing, but there are many questions about how best to do this. The only real way to guarantee a gender-sensitive policy that includes the actual needs of rural women is to help construct channels that allow them to voice their concerns.
KIT Library code: 426447

083   The emergence of an Afro-Caribbean legal tradition: gender relations and family courts in Kingston, Jamaica

LAFONT, SUZANNE. Austin & Winfield, San Fransisco, 222 p. 1996 ill., tabs. Includes lit.refs. Includes index ISBN 1-880921-91-X

The Western-based cultural assumptions that have influenced much of the research and many of the social policies and legal systems in the Caribbean are examined, focusing on gender negotiations and conflict among low-income Jamaican family court clients. Background information is provided on the family structure of low-income Jamaicans, the family laws and family courts. Male and female relationships are discussed, focusing on sex-specific responsibilities and transgressions. A variety of intake reports and case studies from family court counselling sessions are presented and used to demonstrate the ways in which the family laws and family court are being used as weapons of redress and retaliation in Jamaica. Recent Jamaican State policy concerning social relations hoped to close the discrepancies between social legislation, informed predominately by the British legal code, and the needs of its culturally distinct population. However, social policies and family laws still do not conform to the low-income family structure in Jamaica but rather support the nuclear family. In many ways, the state has undermined women's power in Jamaica by promoting the nuclear family and its ideals of male dominance. Further consideration needs to be given to the family laws in Jamaica. The dynamics between the lower income gender ideology and the family laws must be understood before policymakers can formulate culturally relevant family legislation.

KIT Library code: 225994

084   Land policy issues

DEPARTMENT OF LAND AFFAIRS In: *White Paper on South African land policy.* <http://land.pwv.gov.za/> 184 Jacob Mare Street, Pretoria 0802, South Africa. 21 p. 1997

This chapter of the White Paper on land outlines the main policy issues that must be addressed if the land reform in South Africa is to achieve its aims. Constitutional, institutional, environmental and budgetary issues are examined, as well as the land market; institutional issues; environmental issues; land redistribution; restitution; and land tenure. Discrimination in women's access to land and the elimination of this discrimination are considered. South Africa

URL: http://land.pwv.gov.za/White%20Paper/ white5.htm

085   Land rights research programmes

Centre For Applied Legal Studies, University of the Witwatersrand <http://www.wits.ac.za/> DJ Du Plessis Building, West Campus, University of the Witwatersrand, P Bag 3, PO WITS 2050, South Africa <125ta2ti@solon.law.wits.ac.za> 6 p. 1999

The Land Rights Research Programme has five main projects: communal property associations (CPAs); equity, women's empowerment and land reform; tenure security and evictions; changes in property relations in the context of land reform; and negotiated rule making in the context of social reform legislation. South Africa

URL: http://www.wits.ac.za/cals/land.html

086   Human rights and property: a bill of rights in a constitution for a new South Africa

LANGE, ROEL DE; MAANEN, GERRIT VAN; WALT, JOHAN VAN DER. *Recht en Kritiek* vol. 19, no. 3. Stichting Ars Aequi, Nijmegen p. 225-354 1993. Includes lit.refs ISSN 0165-7607 ISBN 90-6916-142-7

Constitutional arrangements in South Africa formed a central part of the heated debate between the government, the African National Congress (ANC) and other groups involved in the struggle to end apartheid. However, outside South Africa, little attention is paid to discussions about a future Bill of Rights as a part of the South African constitution. This publication therefore aims to document and contribute to these discussions. Two points are highlighted: the general human rights debate and the issue of property. The four articles deal specifically with: majority rule and minority rights, which is the main agenda of the human rights debate; a historical perspective of the human rights debate in South Africa; constitutional property arrangements in various countries; and ownership as a constitutional right in South Africa, based on the experience of Germany. Several texts that play an important part in the present constitutional debate in South Africa are also provided: the ANC Freedom Charter (1955) and three recent proposals for a Bill of Rights – the ANC proposal (1993), the Government's proposal, and the proposal made by the South African Law Commission. These documents allow a comparison to be made of their different approaches and priorities.

KIT Library code: 167759

087   Impact of privatization on gender and property rights in Africa

LASTARRIA-CORNHIEL, SUSANA. *World Development* 25(1997)8 p. 1317-1333 bibliogr. p. 1330-1333 ISSN 0305-750X

This document explores the transformation of customary tenure systems and their impact on women's rights to land in Africa. The focus is on the diversity of land rights within customary tenure systems, the different institutions and structures (for example, inheritance and marriage) that influence rights to land, and the trend towards uniformity and increasing patrilineal control. With privatization, rights to land have become concentrated in the hands of those people (for example, community leaders, male household heads) who are able to successfully claim their ownership rights to land, while others, such as poor rural women, ethnic minorities lose the few rights they had and generally are not able to participate fully in the land market.

KIT Library code: 420256

088   Land management

LEE-SMITH, DIANA; TRUJILLO, CATALINA. *Caucus Position Papers, CSD NGO Women's Caucus, Caucus of Non-Government Organisations of the NGO Steering Committee to the United Nations Commission on Sustainable Development (CSD) concerned with gender & sustainable development issues* Earth Summit <http:// www.earthsummit2002.org/> 6 p. October 1999. Gender Unit, United Nations Centre for Human Settlements: Habitat (UNCHS), P. O. Box 30030 Nairobi, Kenya. URL: <http://www.unchs.org> <diana.leesmith@unchs.org>

The work of UNCHS (Habitat) on women's access and rights to land and housing shows that women are disadvantaged in societies where male inheritance customs are strong. This becomes particularly severe in situations of conflict and reconstruction. In such situations, the position of widows and single women may be extremely serious. Without husbands, the majority of women survivors may be unable to have their own place to live and may be condemned to life in refugee camps. The international pressure for women's equal rights to land originated with a number of grassroots meetings, particularly in Africa, supported by the Women and Shelter Network of the Habitat International Coalition. During the preparations for the Beijing Conference in 1995, four global women's networks formed a Super-Coalition on Women, Homes and Community to lobby on women's issues of homes and housing. Women's movements and public agencies need to further coordinate their efforts in campaigning for women's rights to land. This paper is also available in Spanish at: <http://www.earthsummit2002.org/wcaucus/Caucus%20Position%20Papers/land/land%20spanish.htm>
URL: http://www.earthsummit2002.org/wcaucus/caucus%20Position%20Papers/land/land.htm

089   La mujer rural y la reforma agraria en Colombia
LEÓN, MAGDALENA; DEERE, CARMEN DIANA. *Cuadernos de Desarrollo Rural* (1997)38/39 p. 7-23 ill., tabs 26 lit.refs. With English summary

The situation in Colombia with respect to the legal dispositions governing women's access to land and land rights is described. Colombia's recent agrarian legislation and the process that led to its adoption are reviewed. The activities of Antmucic, the national association of peasant and indigenous women, were critical in establishing the priority that the legislation gives to female heads of household and the joint titling of land by couples. The 1994 agrarian law has resulted in an important increase in the number of women beneficiaries of Incora (Colombia's agrarian reform agency). However, much remains to be done to achieve gender equity.
KIT Library code: 429781

090   Southern Africa's land dilemma: balancing resource inequities
MALUWA, TIYANJANA In: *Sacred spaces and public quarrels: African cultural and economic landscapes* ed. by Paul Tiyambe Zeleza & Ezekiel Kalipeni. Africa World Press, Trenton, NJ p. 301-321 1999 46 lit.refs

A general overview is provided of the land question in Southern Africa with the objective of presenting a survey of some of the conceptual and common policy issues and dilemmas that constitute the land problem in the region. A number of critical issues are addressed: land privatization; the challenges of counterbalancing customary and statutory land rights; the struggles over land restitution and land restoration following the end of colonial rule, particularly the demise of apartheid in South Africa; the persistence of women's inequitable access to land and other property rights, despite formal equality guaranteed by the constitutions of all the Southern African countries; and the question of ethnicity and indigenous people's claims to land. So many years after independence, the land question remains as hotly contested in all Southern African countries as it was during the years of struggle for political liberation. A number of issues still lie at the heart of this question, for example: the quality and quantity of land available, the procedures and financial costs of land acquisition and redistribution; the efficiency of land use; and the economic and social impact of land reform. There is now an increasing acceptance of the centrality of land allocation in schemes designed to combat poverty and socioeconomic deprivations in general, and also a recognition that the land interest is deeply interwoven with both the public interest and the common interest of the nation as a whole. State intervention is needed to resolve the dilemmas and problems identified. Without it, the imbalances in access to and control over land and related resources will persist. Such imbalances represent a denial of social justice and equity, especially for the millions of rural poor spread around the Southern African sub-continent.
KIT Library code: 426534

091   Gender and the politics of the land reform process in Tanzania
MANJI, AMBREENA. *Journal of Modern African Studies* 32(1998)4 p. 645-667

The course of the land tenure reform debate in Tanzania over the last seven years is explored to show that the issue of women's unequal rights to land has received inadequate attention. Within what can be characterized as the mainstream of the debate, the boundaries of which have been set by those engaged in research and the drafting of reports and legislation, there has been an almost complete neglect of gender issues. The tendency has been to subsume women's access to land under that of men rather than to address it in its own right. This marginalization of gender issues

has not been challenged by gender progressive groups in Tanzania, who have proved incapable of launching a critique of the reforms or proposing a manifesto of their demands. Rather than setting the policy agenda, they have simply reacted to proposals; rather than presenting detailed analyses of the issues at stake, they have limited themselves to an instrumental approach to draft legislation. Whilst Tanzania has shown itself relatively ready to adopt equality provisions in international conventions, and has incorporated a Bill of Rights into the constitution, it is clear that the state is not altogether progressive in implementing these objectives beyond the level of rhetoric. This obstacle will have to be considered in formulating a strategy for progress on women's rights to land.
KIT Library code: 429806

092   'Her name is Kkamundage': rethinking women and property among the Haya of Tanzania
MANJI, AMBREENA. *Africa* 70(2000)3, p. 482-500, 43 lit.refs ISSN 0001-9720,
With English and French summary
The shortcomings and strengths of several models for deepening our understanding of women's relation to land are demonstrated through a number of case studies of women and property among the Haya people in Kagera, northwestern Tanzania. None of the models taken alone is fully adequate to explain the range of ways in which women interact with property in Kagera or their experience of struggles over land. The entitlement model offers the greatest scope for understanding the norms that affect women's relation to property. However, the model must be adjusted in certain respects; there must be a better understanding of the effects of resistance and a conceptualization of how norms are generated. The implications of these modifications for entitlement analysis are considered. A modified entitlement model would enable an assessment of the diversity of social and legal influences on women's property relations.
KIT Library code: 429604

093   Gendered access to land and housing in Lesotho
MAPETLA, MATSELISO. *Agenda* (1999)42 p. 70-77 ill., photogr. 14 lit.refs ISSN 1013-0950
Based largely on data from six Lesotho-focused studies conducted in the last seven years, this assessment highlights the legal, structural and financial constraints that result in inequality between women and men and between women of different marital status in accessing property. It also examines different strategies used by various actors in the delivery of housing,

from state to individual levels. It is revealed that there is a shortage of land and housing in Lesotho and that delivery systems of these resources operate within a legal framework that is discriminatory towards married women in particular. The roles of the state, the private sector and individuals in working out strategies in order to access land and housing are considered. Women's access to housing appears to be constrained by factors embedded in the legal system and the patriarchal Basotho customs that entrust property rights in men; by discriminatory institutional policies; and by limited or no access to financial resources. Women themselves, individually and/or collectively, are adopting alternative strategies. In the process, they are bringing about changes in gender relations at various social levels.
KIT Library code: 430516

094   Property rights as a tool for desirable development
MARCUSE, PETER. In: *Sustainable development and the future of cities* ed. by Bernd Hamm, Pandurang K. Muttagi. Intermediate technology, London p. 121-131 1998 6 lit.refs
Property rights can be a very flexible instrument for many purposes: meeting basic human needs; distributing power democratically; achieving a desired level of equality; stimulating the accumulation of wealth; and providing for sound city planning. Property should be understood as being associated with various rights, of which 'owning' is just one. Different things – land, houses, factories, tools and consumer goods – can be owned in different ways, and there are many different kinds of owners: individuals, cooperatives, non-profit organizations, businesses and the state. A systematic approach that 'mixes and matches' different forms of property rights for different types of property and different owners must be used to achieve the best results. Property rights, imaginatively defined and implemented, could thus provide an effective and flexible means of achieving a wide range of public policy goals.
KIT Library code: 424821

095   Farming in the shadow of the city: changes in land rights and livelihoods in peri-urban Accra
MAXWELL, DANIEL; LARBI, WORDSWORTH O.; ZAKARIAH, SAWUDATU; ARMAR-KLEMESU, MARGARET. *Cities Feeding People* Report Series 3 International Development Research Council (IDRC), Canada, <http://www.idrc.ca> 30 p. February 1998. Food Consumption and Nutrition Division, International Food Policy

Research Institute, 1200 17th Street NW, Washington DC 20036-3006, USA.

This paper reviews the literature on peri-urban land use, changing property rights, and livelihoods, and then compares four case studies within the peri-urban periphery of Greater Accra, Ghana, to asses the impact of rapid urban sprawl on the area immediately surrounding the city. Cases examined include the loss of land to housing in Ngleshie-Amanfro village in Ga District; the protection of agricultural land from urban sprawl in Abakobi village; environmental degradation as a result of changing market demand in Nsakina village, Ga District; and the commercialization of smallholder agriculture in Samsam-Odumsai. Data were collected in 1996 and 1997. Tenure transformation that has arisen due to rapid urbanization has created more hardships, economically and socially, for the most vulnerable in society. While there appears to be no major difference between men and women in these communities regarding whose land is being lost, women clearly have fewer alternative livelihood options when faced with the loss of farming land. Cultural factors prevent Muslim women in Ngleshie-Amanfro from taking up other livelihoods. Women in Nsakina, are prevented by the distance that must be travelled to find new land for farming or new markets for trading.

URL: http:/www.idrc.ca/cfp/rep23_e.html

096   Reform of personal status laws in North Africa: a problem of Islamic or Mediterranean laws?

MAYER, ANN ELIZABETH. *Middle East Journal* 49(1995)3 p. 432-446 lit.refs in notes ISSN 0026-3141

Treatment of the marital relationship in contemporary personal status laws in North Africa over the 1950-95 period challenge stereotypical Western ideas about the problems of personal status law reform in Muslim countries. In their definitions of the roles of husband and wife, laws in the Maghreb countries resemble laws in European countries such as France before the dramatic reforms of the past few decades. More specifically, conceptions of marriage are not very different from those embodied in earlier European models. Faced with pressures for additional reforms, North African countries have adopted dissimilar strategies. Tunisia has adjusted its laws to approximate modern standards. These modern standards are not Western standards but aspects of a new, international norm of equality that goes against the grain of long-entrenched discriminatory features of Western law and culture, even as it conflicts with the inherited patriarchal traditions of Muslim countries. The Moroccan strategy has

been to make gradual and cautious modernizing reforms. Algeria has first temporized and then chosen the road of reaction, although without fully reviving a system based on Maliki law. Further progress towards adopting a modern model of family law seems likely in Tunisia and Morocco, but Algerian legal development is likely to be thrown off course by the explosive political situation there.

KIT Library code: 413186

097   Urban property ownership and the maintenance of communal land rights in Zimbabwe

MBIBA, BEACON. Land rights in Africa at Oxfam, UK. <http://www.oxfam.org.uk/landrights/> 2 p. September 1999 <mbibab@sbu.ac.uk>

The dominance of the white farm issue in Zimbabwe has delayed serious attention to more subtle land conflicts. The PhD thesis summarized here focuses on the continued maintenance of communal land rights by urban property owners and explores what would happen if these rights disappeared. It uses 'sensitizing devices' from structuration theory to reconcile insights from both modernization and dependency theories. Drawing on key institutional informant interviews, household interviews and grey literature, it integrates quantitative and qualitative materials, revealing that beyond the status quo argument, agents deploy a multiplicity of arguments that both reinforce and transform the meaning and maintenance of rights. In reality and in the absence of an explicit state policy on this issue, poor families and women are relinquishing their communal land rights and this has practical implications for urbanization.

URL: http://www.oxfam.org.uk/landrights/ zimurban.rtf

098   Women, land and authority: perspectives from South Africa

MEER, SHAMIM. Oxfam, Oxford x, 147 p. 1997 ill., maps, tabs. Includes index. Includes lit.refs ISBN 0-85598-375-2

Women's access to and control over land and related resources are examined in the papers in this book. The focus is on the present conditions, experiences and circumstances of women in a number of different localities within rural South Africa, and key policy considerations and debates are raised. It is argued that women's equal access to land is an issue that needs to be addressed within the broader discussion of land reform in South Africa. It is a controversial issue, since women's equal access will challenge many existing beliefs, practices and traditions. The papers are arranged in three sections:

1) traditional tenure and questions of women's access, control and authority; 2) the gendered nature of access to land and the gendered construction of priorities for land use in situations where rules of tenure are being changed; 3) gender relations on farms and among evicted farm workers. Together the papers highlight the complexity of gender relations in the household and the community, and point to the necessity for strategies to organize and empower women in order to address women's disadvantaged access to and control over resources, including land.
KIT Library code: 224066

099   Constraints to land reform and gender equity goals
MEER, SHAMIM. *Agenda* (1999)40 p. 71-88 ill., photogr. 41 lit.refs ISSN 1013-0950

The slow pace of land reform in South Africa and the marginalized status of gender equity goals within the programme are examined. The main policy goals of the land reform programme are set out and problems in institutionalizing gender equity concerns are discussed. Administrative and institutional weaknesses within the Department of Land Affairs and the failure of government departments to work together are identified as contributing factors to the poor performance within the programme. Constraints to land reform at macro level emerge from the nature of the transition to democracy and from the existing power balance within South African society wherein poor rural men and women do not constitute a social force able to advance their own interests. Redistributing land and rectifying gender imbalances are two potentially explosive issues since they challenge existing relations as well as the way in which social relations are constructed within the household, community and state. Advancing gender equity in land ownership thus presents enormous challenges to the status quo and is met by resistance from chiefs, white farmers and men in communities and households. Unless the intended beneficiaries of land reform become agents able to pursue and advance their own interests, the policy goals of social justice and gender equity will not be addressed. This suggests the need for a two-pronged strategy for NGOs and women's organizations: engaging the state and trying to get institutions and policies right in the interests of poor working class and marginalized women and men, while simultaneously supporting initiatives to build social movements.
KIT Library code: 430513

100   Gender, property rights, and natural resources
MEINZEN-DICK, RUTH SUSEELA; BROWN, LYNN R.; FELDSTEIN, HILARY SIMS; QUISUMBING, AGNES R. *World Development* 25(1997)8 p. 1303-1315 56 lit.refs ISSN 0305-750X

Attention to gender differences in property rights can improve the outcomes of natural resource management policies and projects in terms of efficiency, environmental sustainability, equity, and empowerment of resource users. While differences across cultures and resources must be recognized, it is important to identify the nature of rights to land, trees and water held by women and men, and how these rights are acquired and transmitted from one user to another. The focus here is on how the shift from customary tenure systems to private ownership – of land, trees and water – has affected women; the effect of gender differences in property on collective action; and the implications for project design.
KIT Library code: 420255

101   Gender, households, and markets: inherited land and labour force participation of rural household in the Cordillera Region, Philippines
MENDOZA, L.D. Global Development Network (GDN) <http://www.gdnet.org> 29 p. 2097

The unitary view of the household can easily overlook the importance of the household, the family or the domestic sphere as an arena where gender relations play a critical role. A collective approach to the household, on the other hand, enables gender relations to become a constituent part of household analysis. An account can be made of the differences and similarities between husbands and wives with special attention given to the resources that spouses have access to, control or own. This article analyses the unitary model in the context of a farm household in the Cordillera Region of the Philippines. Information is provided on how farm households in the region obtain access to land, showing how the customary land law defines land tenure and farm management practices. The key variable analysed is the amount of inherited land of husbands and wives. The evidence allows the rejection of the income-pooling hypothesis of a unitary model of the household. Through the collective approach, some of the links between social institutions, household relations, women's land rights, and married women's participation in the labour force are identified.
URL: http://www.gdnet.org/files.fcgi/843_LORELEI.pdf

annotated bibliography

102   South Asians and the dowry problem
MENSKI, WERNER F.; THAKUR, HIMENDRA.
Gems 6. Trentham, London, 262 p. 1998 Bibliogr.:
p. 245-259. Includes index ISBN 1-85856-141-8

The problem of dowry murders is examined
based on three international conferences held
between 1995 and 1997 with the aim of trying to
understand how dowry-related violence is
brought about and how such violence might be
restricted. Each year in India, thousands of
brides are burnt, killed or maimed due to
disputes over dowry. In some provinces it is
virtually unknown; in others it is endemic. Such
murders and other dowry-related violence have
been on the increase and now also occur among
South Asian communities in Britain and North
America. A legal, historical, cultural, economic
and social analysis of the dowry problem is
provided. The discussions and analyses highlight
the fact that one of the key problems in the
dowry debate continues to be that South Asian
women are in certain circumstances perceived as
property that is passed on and exchanged
between families. The dowry problem is an
immensely complex phenomenon and no quick-
fix solutions can be offered. The various legal
protection mechanisms developed by South Asian
legal systems have led to some prosecutions, but
these have not been sufficient to control or stop
dowry murders. North American legal systems
and English law have only just begun to take
notice of legal problems relating to dowry among
South Asians in England, the USA and Canada.
Long-term solutions to the problems of dowry
must be directed at changing attitudes towards
women in India. Key issues for further research
are identified and practical steps are proposed to
help brides in India who flee from domestic
violence, including the establishment of
professional institutes for training and
accommodation for victims; changes in the
Indian legal system; strengthening the Dowry
Prohibition Act of India; organizing mutual
support groups; and promoting research and
education programmes.
KIT Library code: 232923

**103   Local action, global change: learning
about the human rights of women and girls**
MERTUS, JULIE; FLOWERS, NANCY; DUTT,
MALLIKA; BUNCH, CHARLOTTE. United
Nations Development Fund for Women (UNIFEM),
New York, 254 p. 1999 ill., tabs. Includes index.
Includes lit.refs ISBN 0-912917-01-6

The future of human rights for all depends on
respect for women's human rights, for if their
human rights can be belittled, then the
universality of human rights for all is

undermined. This book seeks to demonstrate how
the language of human rights can help express,
examine and address the stories of women's and
girls' lives and put them into a larger framework.
Each section of the book provides ideas for
organizing for action at the community, state,
regional and international level, demonstrating
that through local action, we can bring global
change. It combines information on the principal
topics of women's human rights with exercises
for making them meaningful and strategies for
taking action to realize them, allowing for wide
differences in culture, age, religion, geography,
economics and politics. The book is intended for
a wide range of individuals and groups, including
literate people and those with little or no formal
education, rural women, governmental, non-
governmental and community organizations,
students and teachers. Factual information is
drawn from United Nations sources as well as
from the Beijing Platform for Action.
Introductory exercises link personal experience
to human rights concepts, introduce interactive
methodologies and start the process of critical
analysis for taking action. Topical chapters
address specific topics in women's human rights,
stating objectives, defining the topic area,
offering statistics and special information as well
as strategies and examples for taking action.
Tools for human rights education and advocacy
are provided in the appendices.
KIT Library code: 242035

104   Land and housing: women speak out
MJOLI-MNCUBE, NONHLANHLA. *Agenda*
(1999)42. Durban 110 p. ill., graphs, tabs. Includes
lit.refs ISSN 1013-0956

This publication aims to provide a forum for
discussion about women's relationship to the land
and shelter in South Africa, focusing on rural
gender relations. In the rural land sector, it
appears that issues of gender justice affecting
the majority of poor rural women are recognized
in policy but have yet to bear fruit in practice.
For many women, secure tenure and title are
illusory or conditional on social obligations.
Social relationships and women's status within
the household emerge as major determinants of
women's ability to command resources,
particularly land and shelter. Contributions cover
various aspects of land and housing, including:
the prejudice and harassment women face in
acquiring rights to land; rural women and the
land question; lobbying for women farmworkers'
rights; strategies adopted by gender activists to
put gender issues on the agenda of national land
and agrarian reform processes; and gendered
access to land and housing in Lesotho. New

gender perspectives

research and the concerns that women raise in these contributions suggest that there is a need for clarity on whether traditional authorities can in fact curtail and deny women's land rights. There is also a need to recognize the complexity of gender power relations in women's land rights. Women need to be able to exercise choices without conflict or penalization for advancing their gender interests, interests that often involve the community's wider welfare and wellbeing.
KIT Library code: 237465

105   From patriarchy to gender equity: family law and its impact on women in Bangladesh
MONSOOR, TASLIMA Dhaka: University press, 1999. 400 p. ill., tabs Bibliogr.: p. 341-382 ISBN 984-05-1455-5
Recent legal developments in Bangladesh are examined to assess their contribution in terms of an improvement in the overall situation of women in the country. Apart from the reforms concerning the family courts ordinance of 1985, the existing family law reforms are shown to be mainly procedural. In particular, they appear unable to protect women effectively from violence and economic deprivation. It is argued that despite some recent reforms purporting to improve women's status, there is no real change in the situation of patriarchal domination. The dominant patriarchal structures, with the interlinked forces of religion, tradition and seclusion, are sustained not only in family life but also in family law. It is suggested that gender equity in family law can be meaningfully developed by better implementation of existing family law, particularly by sensitizing the judiciary and society to the particular needs of women.
KIT Library code: 248176

106   Legal developments on women's rights to inherit land under customary law in Tanzania
MTENGETI-MIGIRO, ROSE. *Verfassung und Recht in Übersee* 24(1991)4 p. 362-371 18 lit.refs ISSN 0506-7826
This paper examines the question of land inheritance rights in Tanzania. Before the advent of colonial domination, social organization was based on clans comprising single families headed by a man. In this context, women were excluded from inheriting family or clan land. With the coming of colonialism, the socioeconomic set-up in the traditional society started to crumble, and after independence, new policies further affected both traditional land tenure and social organization. These changes, however, did not completely erode the customs and practices that regulated property relations, and the coexistence of the two has had a significant impact on

women's rights. Rules on inheritance are now to be found in the Local Customary Law Order (Declaration No. 4) 1963. The specific rules for daughters and widows for the inheritance of family and clan land are outlined. The rules discriminate against women and afford them only limited rights to inheritance. The first attempts to upset the Rules on the basis of equality began in 1968, and in 1984 the Bill of Rights was enacted, which precluded discrimination of any kind. The enactment of the Bill of Rights is an important step towards realizing equal rights for women, especially in matters of inheritance. Although legal reform has to go hand in hand with social and economic changes in other spheres of private and public life to ensure real equal opportunity for all citizens, the authors conclude that the elimination of discriminatory laws and the introduction of affirmative laws are nevertheless essential first steps.
KIT Library code: 403934

107   Legally dispossessed: gender, identity and the process of law
MUKHOPADHYAY, MAITRAYEE. *Gender Culture Politics*. Stree, Calcutta, 246 p. 1998. Includes index. Bibliogr.: p. 228-240 ISBN 81-85604-39-8
A study is presented of Hindu and Muslim women litigants and their experiences of the process of law, based on fieldwork undertaken in 1991 and 1992. The contexts of litigation are examined: the nature of disputes; the attitudes of lawyers; experiences in court; and the logic of judgements. Personal or family law in India has two salient features: it seeks to control and regulate social relations in the private sphere of the family, and it is specific to and separate for particular religious communities – Hindu, Muslim, Christian and Parsi. At present, the personal laws of all communities treat women as subordinate to and dependent on male kin. Thirty case studies are provided of Hindu and Muslim women litigating for property or maintenance as wives, daughters/sisters or widows. Through the depiction of these struggles for family property, the connection between the private and the public domains is revealed, as well as their role in maintaining gender asymmetry and patriarchal power. The relationship of women to the state is also considered. Women are implicated in the state's goal of modernization, progress and development. Exploring the woman-state relationship through the experiences of the women's movement in the 1970s and 1980s, the reasons given by the women involved in the study for appealing to the state are examined.

The significance of the Uniform Civil Code for equality between men and women is also discussed.
KIT Library code: 241211

108   Women's property rights in South India: a review

MUKUND, KANAKALATHA. *Economic and Political Weekly* 34(1999)22 p. 1352-1358 32 lit.refs ISSN 0012-9976

A synthesis is presented of the findings of ongoing research studies on women's property rights and customary practices in south India. These rights and practices are changing as traditional south Indian society is transformed in a process of broader socioeconomic change. The issues raised relate to customary rights – the property rights allowed to women under customary practices, as compared to the rights allowed under the traditional legal systems. The historical evolution of these rights and how interventions from the state and other agencies have redefined them at several points in time are examined. The historical evidence from south India, particularly the Tamil region, suggests that women had considerably stronger rights to property than is indicated in legal texts. Women owned property and had the authority to alienate this property through gifts or sales. One of the most pronounced changes that has taken place in social arrangements in the last few decades and that has had a profound impact on the status of women has been the spread of the practice of payment of a dowry to the bridegroom by the parents of the bride. The shift to dowry is accompanied by a loss of control by the woman over this property, which is now vested with the family of the husband, whereas traditionally this remained the bride's property. The factors that lie behind this shift, including changing occupational structures, access to education, and urbanization, are discussed. The author concludes that women's status in south India has in some ways regressed in the past thousand years. The value of women in the family and in broader social perception has been steadily eroded as women's property has been transferred to the husband through the payment of dowry.
KIT Library code: 426011

109   Enhancing land reforms in Southern Africa: reviews on land reform strategies and community based natural resources management

MUTEFPA, F.; DENGU, E.; CHENJE, M. ZERO, Harare 108 p. 1998 ill., graphs, tabs. Includes lit.refs ISBN 1-77917-004-1

Linkages between land reform and community-based natural resources management (CBNRM) in Botswana, Mozambique, South Africa, Zimbabwe and Zambia are explored, and ways to enhance this process are identified. Subjects include: (1) land tenure; (2) land policy and legal reforms; (3) land use planning; (4) the role of non-governmental organizations in land matters; and (5) equity, gender, sustainability, efficiency and food security aspects. With the exception of Botswana, land reform programmes aim to promote equity in access to land and democratization of the allocation process, usually by encouraging decentralization and subsidiarity. In Mozambique, the new Land Bill provides an opportunity for testing an interactive model of partnership between the private sector and the family sector. Policies and strategies to enhance CBNRMs are suggested. In the case of Zambia, the following measures are recommended: ploughing back leasehold tax benefits to rural communities; introducing a land development tax; enhancing the role of women in accessing and controlling land resources; creating awareness on land policy and legal reforms; establishing efficient land surveys and titling systems; and promoting participatory planning.
KIT Library code: 236878

110   Enhancing land reforms in Southern Africa: case studies on land reform strategies and community based natural resources management

MUTEFPA, F. ZERO, Harare 87 p. 1998 ill., tabs. Includes lit.refs ISBN 1-77917-005-X

Case studies from Botswana, Mozambique, South Africa, Zambia and Zimbabwe on land reform strategies and community-based natural resources management are presented. In Botswana, the main thrust of the land reform policy prior to 1994 was to look at the administrative mechanism. In Zambia, land tenure change was seen as the way forward. This involved the introduction of 99-year leasehold titles to land in former communal areas. In Zimbabwe, land redistribution was the cornerstone of the land policy. The current policy of compulsory acquisition is criticized for its slow pace, for being overambitious, and for being too politically motivated. In South Africa, the land policy has three components: land restitution, redistribution, and tenure reforms. Findings indicate the need to boost the communities' awareness of the land reform programmes across the region. Land policies have been lacking in gender sensitivity, while in most cases communities are not averse to women owning land.
KIT Library code: 236879

111   Women's land and property rights in conflict situations
MWAGIRU, MAKUMI; KARURU, NJERI. CCR-WLEA series 1. Centre for conflict research and women and law in East Africa, Nairobi 80 p. 1998. Includes lit.refs

Women's land and property rights during periods of conflict and reconstruction are examined. There has been an increase in the number of people forced out of their homes for political reasons. Women in particular face various obstacles in situations of conflict and reconstruction, particularly regarding access to and control of land and property, which they need in order to create sustainable livelihoods. Kenya has a large population of refugees, in addition to internally displaced people. Solutions should therefore be approached progressively from the international, national and the local level. This book is the result of collaboration between three organizations: the Gender Equity Support Programme (GESP), the Centre for Conflict Research (CCR) and Women and Law in East Africa – Kenya (WLEA-K). The four chapters discuss women's rights in situations of conflict in Kenya; their basic human rights; international legal and diplomatic postures; women's right to land and property; and rights to survival. Finally, an overview is provided of efforts that have been made, both in terms of legislation and programmes, to assist the internally displaced and more specifically women, and strategies are proposed that can be used to improve future programmes. There is an urgent need for the government to seek ways of making international conventions such as the Convention on the Elimination of All Forms of Discrimination against Women (CEDAW) enforceable in Kenya, and to change existing legislation to enable displaced women to repossess property left behind.
KIT Library code: 241355

112   Why men come out ahead: the legal regime and the protection and realization of women's rights in Uganda
NAGGITA, ESTHER DAMALIE *East African Journal of Peace and Human Rights* 6(2000)1, p. 34-61, lit.refs in notes ISSN 1021-8858

A brief review is provided of the international legal regime for the protection of women's rights and legal provisions in Uganda relating to marriage and divorce, succession, and inheritance of property. At present, Uganda's domestic law and women's rights, particularly those relating to family and property, either directly or indirectly discriminate against women. An assessment of the limitations of the law and the legal regime in the protection of women's rights shows the many factors that work together to entrench and strengthen women's subordination and enhance existing inequalities against them. The need to reformulate the Ugandan legal regime is stressed and suggestions towards this end are made.
KIT Library code: 429694

113   The status of women under Islamic law and under modern Islamic legislation
NASIR, JAMAL JAMIL. Arab and Islamic Laws Series. Graham & Trotman, London, 159 p. 1994. 1st ed.: 1990. Includes index. Includes lit.refs ISBN 1-85966-084-3

The rights and status of women living under Islamic law are examined. It is argued that many misconceptions and illusions surround the legal rights and obligations of women in Islam. This book therefore aims to correct some of these misconceptions and to demonstrate that women under Islam are far from being subordinate and powerless followers of men. Women enjoy full autonomy as far as their property is concerned and receive many benefits in terms of respect, marital rights, maintenance, guardianship and custody of minors. The book is divided into seven sections, covering: rights, formalities and conditions of marriage; entitlement to and disputes over dower; entitlement to maintenance; dissolution of marriage; the duration and requirements of the Iddat (period after the dissolution of a marriage during which the woman must remain unmarried); parentage and the establishment of paternity; and fosterage and custody.
KIT Library code: 185473

114   Women farmers and economic change in northern Ghana
NAYLOR, RACHEL In: *Women, land and agriculture* ed. by Caroline Sweetman. Focus on Gender. Oxfam, Oxford p. 39-48 1999 23 lit.refs

There is no doubt that structural adjustment can have negative consequences, especially for the poorest people. But the economic language used in discussions of this topic, such as 'impact', 'vulnerability' and the 'rural poor' can be simplistic and can mask the diversity and complexity of rural life and the resourcefulness and power of rural dwellers, particularly women. This article looks at the consequences of the liberalization of cotton production in communities in Langbensi, northern Ghana, in terms of gender relations in the household and the community, drawing on research carried out over an 18-month period during 1995-6. While both men and women seem to benefit, women are also taking on new burdens. To ensure a better future for all, men and women farmers need to cooperate within the household. Without negotiating rights to land, labour and decision-making, it is difficult for women to do more than satisfy basic needs. It is by working with other agencies on the scene, such as Langbensi Agricultural Station, a non-governmental organization, that women have begun to address strategic gender needs. By drawing on the expertise and the lending power of the Station, the women's groups have increased not only their material status but also their capacities to organize and their level of confidence. These slow, empowering changes have the potential to increase the ability of women in communities to engage with and profit from the many 'external' agricultural agencies they interact with in the development process, many of whom continue to show biases based on misunderstandings of household dynamics and the agricultural system.

115   Title to the land?

NGUBANE, SIZANI. *Agenda* (1999)42 p. 7-11 ill., photogr. ISSN 1013-0950

This article reports the findings of a discussion on land issues affecting women in the KwaZulu-Natal midlands in South Africa, where the Association for Rural Advancement (AFRA) is organizing a rural women's movement. For all the women interviewed, land offers a means of alleviating poverty and generating income. The women discussed the problems they have in relation to gaining access to land. Women have no independent rights to land, and inheritance laws give unequal succession rights to girl and boy children. In addition, women are not aware of their own rights and are thus open to abuse. Through their stories, women identified a need to lobby for women's equal and secure land rights. Although no longer constitutionally defined as minors in the law of the country, the women's experiences reported in the discussions show that women continue to be treated as subordinate to men. As a result of the gendered division of labour in the communities, women carry much of the responsibility for the labour associated with food production, as well as the burden of responsibility for maintaining the household, energy and water collection, and childcare. The prime constraint women face is the absence of a strong lobby campaigning for women's land rights in rural areas. Recommendations include: programmes that enhance the status of women in rural areas; adult and basic education and training; rural women's empowerment and inclusion in all government and private sector

structures; setting aside land for women's projects; and ensuring that girl children have the same inheritance rights as boys.

116   The scramble for women's land rights in Tanzania

ODGAARD, RIE. *Researching Development* Centre for Development Research (CDR), Denmark, <http:// www.cdr.dk> CDR, Gammel Kongevej 5, DK – 1610 Copenhagen V, Denmark. <cdr@cdr.dk> 2 p. June 1999 <rie@cdr.dk>

It is often assumed that women in patrilineal communities have no access to land in their own right. Research from Iringa and Mbarali Districts, Tanzania, shows that such rights for women were provided for in the customary rules. According to the customary rules of the Hehe and the Sangu peoples, both males and females were entitled to a share of their father's property. The rights to inherit were tied to the responsibility for children, old and sick people. Sons and brothers of deceased persons were expected to carry the bulk of responsibility for children, the old and the sick, and were therefore entitled to larger shares of the deceased person's estate than daughters and sisters.

URL: http://www.cdr.dk/newsletter/nw299-4.htm

117   Reconfiguring tradition: women's rights and social status in contemporary Nigeria

OKEKE, PHIL E. *Africa Today* 47(2000)1 p. 49-63 49 lit.refs ISSN 0001-9887

A review of the place of tradition in restructuring women's social status and rights in contemporary Africa is provided. Using Nigeria as a case study, the analysis traces women's progression from the pre-colonial era, examining their absorption into the colonial society and their progress in the post-independence era. Their legal status over this entire period is outlined as a crucial basis for initiating the struggle to improve their social position. The final section makes a case for reconfiguring the cultural basis to advance their social status and rights. It is argued that any attempt to re-examine Nigerian women's place as citizens and a valid social group must begin with recognizing the historical passage that has placed them in a subordinate position to men and with reconfiguring those patterns of inequality that the current social arrangement clings to as 'tradition'. The author concludes by drawing attention to certain developments on the international scene that could boost women's struggle to improve their lot across the continent.

118   The status of widows in 10 countries: seclusion and exclusion
OWEN, MARGARET. Empowering Widows in Development <http:// www.oneworld.org/ empoweringwidows> 36 Faroe Road, London W14 0EP, UK. <margaretowen@compuservecom> 60 p. undated

This report reviews the status of widows in ten developing countries. Widows are the poorest, most wretched, most discriminated against and most isolated women in the developing world. In most situations, the idealized extended family has broken up, offering no support to widows. Poverty, land shortage, migration, urbanization, AIDS and conflict have destroyed their traditional means of support. Increasing numbers of women experience widowhood early in their lives, sometimes when they are as young as seven or eight. They rarely remarry and many millions are left as sole supporters of minor children without any education or training for work, restricted by cultural limitations on their lifestyle. Having rarely any rights of inheritance or access to resources left by their husbands, widows are hounded from their homes, robbed of their possessions and left destitute. In addition, they are often the victims of life-threatening mourning and burial rites. Children of widows, especially daughters, suffer huge disadvantages. Of all the countries reviewed in this report (Ghana, Malawi, Mozambique, Nigeria, Tanzania, Uganda, Zambia, Zimbabwe, Bangladesh and India), only certain states in India have any system of social security and pensions, although the value of such pensions is often derisory and they are difficult to obtain. The main hope for widows in these countries is that they band together, organize themselves and collectively work to gain their rights. Legislative reform is important but it alone cannot bring about necessary changes. Literacy, education and access to justice systems are equally important. Widows' groups and contacts in each of the countries are listed.
URL: http://www.oneworld.org/empoweringwidows/ 10countries/index.html

119   Women and land tenure dynamics in pre-colonial, colonial and post-colonial Zimbabwe
PETERS, BEVERLY L.; PETERS, JOHN E. *Journal of Public and International Affairs* 10 Princeton University, USA <http://www. princeton.edu/> Woodrow Wilson School of Public and International Affairs, Princeton University, Robertson Hall, Princeton, NJ 08544-1013, USA. <jpia@princeton.edu> 27 p. 1998

In sub-Saharan Africa, women produce 60-80% of agricultural food crops and cash crops.

Despite this, they often lack legal access to land and support services for production and distribution. As a result, women often have to support their dependants without adequate agricultural, educational, institutional and financial support. Based on an analysis of the historical development of women's access to land within the Shona and Ndebele ethnic groups in Zimbabwe, the paper argues that action should be taken in three broad areas. First, legal barriers to women's land rights should be challenged. Second, women have to be provided with full extension and support services, tailored to their needs. Third, support must be given to NGOs and movements that actively support women's land rights.
URL: http://www.wws.princeton.edu/~jpia/10.html

120   The generation and use of information on women's land rights in the design of sustainable agriculture projects
QUISUMBING, AGNES, R. In: *High-level consultation on rural women and information.* Rome, 4-6 October 1999. Proceedings. Document Repository, Food and Agriculture Organisation (FAO) <http://www.fao.org/> FAO, Viale delle Terme di Caracalla, 00100 Rome, Italy. <fao@fao.org> 4 p. 1999

The absence of gender-disaggregated data on land rights has often been used as an excuse for not formulating gender-specific interventions. Many policymakers are now convinced that policy and legal reforms to strengthen women's access to land are essential ingredients for their empowerment. The effectiveness of such reforms will depend on an understanding of women's and men's existing rights to land, and how these rights affect access to other natural resources. This is where the generation and use of new information on women's land rights is essential.
URL: http://www.fao.org/docrep/X3803E/ x3803e14.htm

121   Intergenerational transfers in Philippine rice villages: gender differences in traditional inheritance customs
QUISUMBING, AGNES R. *Journal of Development Economics* 43(1994)2 p. 167-195 ill., tabs 70 lit.refs ISSN 0304-3878

This paper provides econometric evidence of gender differences in education, land and non-land asset transfers from parents to children in five rice villages in the Philippines. A distinct feature of this study is that it analyses different forms of parent-child transfers and thus allows for the possibility that unequal transfers of one type may be compensated for by transfers of another type. Data is used from a retrospective survey conducted by the author specifically to analyse intrahousehold differences in transfers in the five villages. The results suggest that wealth constraints, indicated by differential ability to bestow land, lead to differences in educational investment in children, with poorer families tending to concentrate educational investment in the eldest child. In a sub-sample, daughters appeared to be disadvantaged in education and to receive significantly less land and total inheritance. They may be partially compensated with non-land assets. Daughters of better-educated mothers receive more land, non-land assets and total inheritance, while better-educated fathers tend to give land to sons, but favour daughters in education.

122   Intrahousehold allocation and gender relations: new empirical evidence
QUISUMBING, AGNES R.; MALUCCIO, JOHN A. *Discussion Paper 84* International Food Policy Research Institute (IFPRI) <http://www.ifpri.cgiar.org/> IFPRI, 2033 K Street NW, Washington DC 21176, USA. 31 p. September 1999 <a.quisumbing@cgiar. org> <j.maluccio@cgiar.org>

The paper reviews recent theory and empirical evidence testing unitary versus collective models of the household. In contrast to the unitary model, the collective model posits that individuals within households have different preferences and do not pool their income. Moreover, the collective model predicts that intrahousehold allocations reflect differences in preferences and 'bargaining power' of individuals within the household. Using new household datasets from Bangladesh, Indonesia, Ethiopia and South Africa, measures are presented of individual characteristics that are highly correlated with bargaining power, namely human capital and individually controlled assets, evaluated at the time of marriage. In all case studies the unitary model is rejected as a description of household behaviour but to different degrees. Results suggest that assets controlled by women have a positive and significant effect on expenditure allocations for the next generation, such as education and children's clothing. The individual level education outcomes are examined, concluding that parents do not have identical preferences for sons and daughters within or across countries.

URL: http://www.ifpri.cgiar.org/divs/fcnd/dp.htm

123   Women's land rights in the transition to individualized ownership: implications for the management of tree resources in western Ghana
QUISUMBING, AGNES R.; PAYONGAYONG, ELLEN; AIDOO, J.B.; OTSUKA, KEIJIRO. FCND Discussion Papers, no. 58. Food Consumption and Nutrition Division, International Food Policy Research Institute. 47 p. 1999

The impact of changes in land tenure institutions on women's land rights and the efficiency of tree resource management in western Ghana, where cocoa is the dominant crop, are examined. A brief background is given on prevailing land tenure institutions, land use and the distribution of land between women and men in the study sites. The study shows that customary land tenure institutions have evolved toward individualized systems to provide incentives to invest in tree planting. However, contrary to the common belief that individualization of land tenure is detrimental to women's land rights, it is found that these have been strengthened through gift transactions and the practice of the Intestate Succession Law. Investment in tree planting is affected not simply by the level of land tenure security, but also by its expected changes, as tree planting strengthens land tenure security. Cocoa yields are lower on allocated family land and rented land under share tenancy due to distorted work incentives. While men and women are equally likely to plant trees, women obtain lower yields on their cocoa plots, suggesting the presence of gender-specific constraints such as credit. This suggests that attempts to equalize land rights of women and men are unlikely to lead to gender equity and improved efficiency and productivity of women farmers unless constraints faced by women are addressed.

URL:http://www.ifpri.org/divs/fcnd/fcnpubs.htm#dp

124   Women's access, control and tenure of land, property and settlement
QVIST, EWA. Department of Geomatics, University of Melbourne, Australia <http://www.geom.unimelb.edu.au> 9 p. 1998

Women face various constraints around the world related to access to land and property. There are cultural, economic and social barriers preventing women owning, inheriting and using land. Case studies from Egypt, Uganda, India, the Ukraine and Sweden demonstrate that women have less access, control and tenure of land, property and settlement and that these obstacles are different in different cultures. Many governments at all levels have failed to adopt appropriate rural and urban policies, which is the primary cause of inequity. The existence of two sets of laws related to land and property leads to frequent ownership and inheritance disputes where women are usually the losers. Women's and men's unequal conditions in society, in working life and in the family must be made visible before they can be taken into account in policymaking. Women have largely been excluded from participating in decisions concerning the development of human settlements. They have also practically no access to shelter credit. Land delivery and land information systems should be examined from a gender point of view. Women often do not have awareness of their legal rights. NGOs and women's groups can be important actors at community level to increase this awareness and facilitate joint action.

URL: http://www.geom.unimelb.edu.au/fig7/
Brighton98/Comm7Papers/TS26-Qvist.html

125   Nepal: the movement for equal property rights for women

RANA, BANDANA. *Women in Action* (1999)1, p. 58-61, ill., photogr. ISSN 0101-5048

One of the biggest hindrances to women's economic development and empowerment in Nepal is the absence of a legal provision that grants women equal property rights. An overview is given of women's current status concerning property rights and the activities undertaken in the 1990s to promote equality in legal provisions relating to the inheritance of parental property, divorce, citizenship, and tenancy rights. Some of the problems encountered in the movement for equal property rights for women are highlighted.

KIT Library code: 426818

126   Land rights for poor women in India

RAO, NITYA; RANA, KUMAR. *Connections* (1998)12 p. 15-18 10 lit.refs

An account is provided of the struggles of women in India for land. Land rights for women as a necessary precondition for their empowerment has gradually been gaining visibility in the women's movement, based on the principles of social equity and justice. To understand the value of land rights for rural women, it is important to understand the social character of land and property relations, and the legal and ideological practices related to it, which are often located within the kinship and family structures. To rural women, land rights do not only imply control over an object, but bring social, cultural and economic benefits, such as higher status, security against absolute poverty, the capacity to challenge male oppression and domestic violence, and access to credit, information and other services. The situation of the Santhali women of South Bihar is used as a case study. The Santhalis perceive women as objects or property to be transferred from the father to the husband. Thus women have no claim over the property of either the father or the

husband, which leaves older widowed women who are unable to work barely able to survive. The powerlessness and suppression of the Santhalis in the context of the larger society has led their men to give vent to their own feelings of power on their women. NGOs in the area have been highlighting these issues for the past few years, and several ways of tackling these problems have been discussed and are outlined here. The experience of other countries demonstrates that women's participation in organized resistance and struggles is crucial. With some support from men emerging within their own society, Santhali women are now no longer prepared to bear gross injustices, and a small group of Santhali women has emerged to fight for an equal place in society for Santhali women.

KIT Library code: 425718

127   Land rights and women: case of Santhals

RAO, NITYA; RANA, KUMAR. *Economic and Political Weekly* 32(1997)23 p. 1307-1309 1997 11 lit.refs

The Santhals in south Bihar, India, perceive women as 'objects' or 'property', *'jinis kanako'*, to be transferred from the father to the husband. Hence women do not have any claim over the property of either the father or the husband, whether movable or immovable. This custom, codified in 1922-1923 during British rule, has been interpreted mechanically by the Santhal Pargana Tenancy Act, formulated after independence in 1949. This Act does not provide any room for the woman to inherit land, on the grounds that 'Santhal tribal law is quite definite in not allowing women to inherit'. Santhali women oppose the implementation of the Act and are prepared to go up to the Supreme Court to fight for an equal place in society.

KIT Library code: 429831

128   Women's health and human rights in Afghanistan

RASEKH, ZOHRA; BAUER, HEIDI M.; MANOS, M. MICHELE; IACOPINO, VINCENT. *Journal of the American Medical Association* 280 (1998) p. 449-455. American Medical Association <http://www.ama-assn.org/> 14 p. August 1998 Physicians for Human Rights, 100 Boylston St, Suite 702, Boston, MA 02116, USA. <phrusa@phrusa.org>

A cross-sectional survey is presented of women who lived in Kabul, Afghanistan, prior to September 1998 when the Taliban regime took control. Self-reported changes in physical and mental health, access to health care, war-related trauma, human rights abuses, and attitudes

annotated bibliography

towards women's human rights were examined for 160 women. These women were resident either in Kabul or in refugee camps and residences in Pakistan. Data were collected in 1998. It was established that the combined effects of war-related trauma and human rights abuses by Taliban officials have had a profound impact on Afghan women's health. Moreover, support for women's human rights by Afghan women suggests that Taliban policies regarding women are incommensurate with the interests, needs and health of Afghan women.

URL: http://www.ama-assn.org/special/womh/library/readroom/vol_280/jsc80298.htm

129   Initiatives to help widows in the struggle for property and inheritance rights in Tanzania
REHMTULLA, SHAMSHAD. Author, The Hague 18 p. 1999. Includes lit.refs
AIDS, livelihood and social change in Africa, Wageningen, 1999

Most African states have a dual legal system consisting of the western-based statutory law and customary laws. In many of the African customary laws, the right to own or inherit land and immovable property is denied to women. AIDS has reinforced the problems that women face with regard to property and inheritance rights and is also responsible for the increase in young widows. This paper examines the problems that women face with regard to their property and inheritance rights and discusses the initiatives being taken to help them. Tanzania is used as a case study, as the position of women there may be comparable to that of women in other African countries, particularly the neighbouring states of Kenya, Uganda, Zambia and Zimbabwe. The socioeconomic situation of women in Tanzania is briefly discussed and the relevant laws applicable to land tenure and inheritance are reviewed. Initiatives undertaken by NGOs, the government and the donor community to fight for women's rights are outlined, and the constraints they face in achieving their goals are addressed. The Kilimanjaro Women Information Exchange and Consultancy Organization (KWIECO) runs a programme that aims to educate women and disseminate information on women and development issues. A detailed discussion of this programme is provided as an example of the initiatives being undertaken in Tanzania. Finally, actions that could be taken by civil society, the government and the donor community are proposed, and research needs are outlined.

KIT Library code: 237975

130   Women, men and trees: gender, power and property in forest and agrarian landscapes
ROCHELEAU, DIANNE; EDMUNDS, DAVID. *World Development* 25(1997)8 p. 1351-1371 1997 ill., graphs 75 lit.refs. ISSN 0305-750X

This publication presents a methodological approach for determining gender differences in tree tenure that distinguishes the legal and theoretical perspectives of how men and women view property and emphasizes the complexity and diversity of rural landscapes. A review of the relevant literature on African landscapes reveals that forests and trees are generally controlled by men under customary or statutory law; consequently, gender is viewed as a complicating factor in tree tenure, due to unequal power relationships between men and women. However, these power relationships are mutable, rendering gender domains in tree tenure complementary and debatable. Therefore, this mutability of power relationships gives policymakers greater leverage in promoting a more gender- and class-equitable distribution of rights to natural resource management and use.

KIT Library code: 420258

131   Disjunctions and continuities: dowry and the position of single women in Bangladesh
ROZARIO, SANTI In: *Negotiation and social space: a gendered analysis of changing kin and security networks in South Asia and sub-Saharan Africa* ed. Carla Risseeuw, Kamala Ganesh. Sage, New Delhi p. 259-276 1998 36 lit.refs

The practice of parda in Bangladesh controls the spatial mobility of women and is integrally related to the traditional ideological principles of purity/pollution and honour/shame. While parda effects all women, the degree observed is determined by a woman's age, class and religious background. Although very poor women had always been employed outside the home, the post-war period saw a sudden and huge increase in their numbers. Over the past decade there has been an influx of a large number of lower middle class women into jobs involving regular work outside the home, most notably in the garment industry. To take into account more women working outside the home, parda is increasingly becoming defined in moral rather than spatial terms. In this new situation, women are eager to be seen as respectable and 'good' in the eyes of the community, and the ideologies of parda and purity have become more important as a means of regulating one's own individual behaviour. The shift from bride wealth to dowry in the Bangladeshi context is a consequence of women's devalorization, which is justified through the ideology of purity. Although economic changes

have made women more economically viable, their status continues to be defined in terms of marriage and motherhood. Women's increased physical mobility, the surplus of unmarried women, and the demands for dowry are all interrelated and are linked to major political and socioeconomic changes that have occurred in Bangladesh since 1971. There is a disjunction between women's new economic role and traditional gender ideology.
KIT Library code: 424714

132   Land reform: the Ugandan experience
RUGADYA, MARGARET. Land rights in Africa at Oxfam, UK, <http://www.oxfam.org.uk/landrights/> 12 p. September 1999, Uganda Land Alliance

The paper considers the historical perspective to land reform in Uganda, salient features of the 1995 constitution, and challenges and constraints to implementing the 1998 Land Act. In implementing the Land Act, the Ministry of Water, Lands and Environment, which is the line ministry, has adopted a participatory and consultative approach to the planning as well as the actual execution of the implementation by involving all key stakeholders. The main thrust of this strategy is a creative 'bottom up' approach to the implementation by involving a range of stakeholders from the outset and by building capacity at the centre, in local institutions, and at the grass-roots. This is not going to be easy given Uganda's tradition of top-down administration. However, Uganda has already made several strides in its decentralization programme. The main challenge is to balance the need for strong co-ordination at the centre with effective mobilization of district-based institutions to use the powers devolved to them by the Land Act. It is proposed that the Government work with committed NGOs concerned with land, agriculture, food security and women to promote partnership in implementing the Act.
URL: http://www.oxfam.org.uk/landrights/Ugaexp.rtf

133   Legal literacy: a tool for women's empowerment
SCHULER, MARGARET; KADIRGAMAR-RAJASINGHAM, SAKUNTALA. Women, Law & Development. PACT communications, New York, 346 p. 1992 ill. Includes lit.refs. Includes index

Strategies for women's empowerment are discussed with the aim of contributing to conceptual and methodological clarity about legal literacy and the issues surrounding it. The book is primarily concerned with how women develop the knowledge and the cognitive, social and political skills related to rights awareness and

action and how lawyers and other advocates can foster their formation. It is also concerned with how legal literacy, as a component of a strategy, fits into a broader political struggle for justice. The book is divided into five parts, the first of which contains an introduction to and a theoretical critique of legal literacy as a tool for women's empowerment. The other papers – from Bangladesh, the Caribbean, Ghana, India, Mexico, Peru, the Philippines, Sri Lanka, Uganda and Zimbabwe – are grouped according to strategic themes highlighting the role of lawyers as agents of legal literacy, non-professional community-based organizers as agents of legal literacy, and legal literacy and political organizing. They reveal gender-based inequities in the legal and political systems, as well as pervasive social oppression, and also offer evidence of unequal outcomes for women in the distribution of economic resources and in the delivery of justice, even where the laws themselves are neutral and non-discriminatory. The conditions of poverty, ignorance, violence and isolation in which many women live are described, as well as the lack of control and direction in their lives. Besides providing primary sources for identifying the issues facing women, the case studies also provide a sample of strategies used to empower women.
KIT Library code: 171880

134   Women's human rights step by step: a practical guide to using international human rights law and mechanisms to defend women's human rights
SCHULER, MARGARET A.; THOMAS, DOROTHY Q. Women, Law & Development International, Washington DC, 197 p. 1997 ill. Includes lit.refs. Includes index ISBN 1-890832-00-6

During the past decade, women from all over the world have launched an unprecedented international movement for women's human rights. Yet despite promising changes in international law and policy, women still face denial of their fundamental rights. Moreover, they often lack the tools and training needed to shape and use the human rights system to combat abuse and advance their rights. Designed as a basic guide to the operation of human rights mechanisms and strategies at national, regional and international levels, this manual explains why and how to use these strategies and mechanisms to promote and protect women's human rights. Various aspects of women's human rights advocacy are discussed, including key human rights concepts and their relevance to women's rights, mechanisms and strategies for

enforcing women's human rights, and the challenges still facing women's human rights advocates. The manual offers a framework for building strategies, as well as concrete suggestions for initiating women's human rights advocacy, and demonstrates, through cases and experiences, how women's human rights advocates are already using the human rights system to enforce their rights.
KIT Library code: 219380

135   The legal status of married women in Lebanon

SHEHADEH, LAMIA RUSTUM. *International Journal of Middle East Studies* 30(1998)4 p. 501-519 lit.refs in notes ISSN 0020-7438

The status of married women in the Lebanon is examined both in the Personal Status Code and in secular and civil law. Although the Lebanese constitution does not discriminate between the sexes, the law does at different levels. What stands out, however, is that this discrimination is aimed mainly at married women, giving the impression that a woman forfeits most of her rights as an individual and a citizen upon marriage. The legislation governing the status of women does not necessarily reflect their actual condition in society. Should they have recourse to the law, however, they then discover it to be highly discriminatory. This is made clearer by some public officials who take action against women by unilaterally denying them rights to act as witnesses or to renew their passports without their husband's permission. In recent years, social pressure has resulted in the repeal of two discriminatory laws, but there are still a number of laws and statutes that are flagrantly discriminatory and even categorize women in the same legal class as the mentally retarded, senile and legally under age. The personal status codes of some religious sects also allow husbands to subjugate their wives and deprive them of their young children in cases of divorce or widowhood.
KIT Library code: 424261

136   Not yet democracy: reforming land tenure in Tanzania

SHIVJI, ISSA G. London: IIED, 1998., 132 p.: ill., tabs Includes index
Includes lit.refs ISBN 1-899825-90-8

In 1991, a Commission of Inquiry into Land Matters was formed in Tanzania and a report produced in 1992. The work of the Commission is here placed within its broader context and its findings set within the current democracy debate all over Africa. The main problems of land tenure in Tanzania are analysed, as well as the alternative processes and structures of land tenure reform recommended by the Commission, and the critiques of its Report. The government's response and the Bill for a new Land Act are also discussed against the wider background of the interplay of political, social and economic forces.
KIT Library code: 233061

137   The struggle for equal inheritance rights in Nepal

SHRESTHA, RAJSHREE. *Connections* (1998)12 p. 20-24

After the restoration of the monarchy in Nepal, the Constitution of the Kingdom of Nepal 2047 (1990) was declared and promulgated. The Constitution has provisions of freedom and equality for all citizens of the country. Although the Constitution guarantees equality of community, caste and gender, the customary practices and statutory implementation through the Civil Code of the Country 2020 (1963) is biased and discriminates against women. Realizing this, two young lawyers registered a writ petition in 1993 that demanded the dismissal of gender discriminatory provisions within the Civil Code. Following consideration of this petition, in 1995 the Supreme Court directed the Government to bring forth a bill on pro-women legislation that was just and equitable. In order to include the views of many different people and professionals, the Legal Aid and Consultancy Centre (LACC) undertook the challenge of assisting the government in the drafting process of this legislation concerning property rights of women from an NGO perspective. The final bill included more than 80% of the proposals made by the NGOs. Lobbying for the bill has been one of the most difficult parts of the process and has been met with threats and intimidation. The lobbying process continues, as the bill has not been passed in the X-XIII sessions of the House of Parliament.
KIT Library code: 424510

138   Arab women: unequal partners in development

SHUKRI, SHIRIN J.A. Avebury, Aldershot, 214 p. 1996 ill., tabs. Bibliogr.: p. 193-210. Includes index
ISBN 1-85972-165-6

A case study conducted in a rural village in Jordan's Shayfoun district revealed that Arab women are unequal partners in the development process. Economic development in the region over the last 15 years has worsened the relative position of women and led to more poverty and social problems. A patriarchal system of property and inheritance continues to affect both interpersonal relationships and interactions between people and resources. Many marriages are arranged, reinforcing female passivity.

gender perspectives

Moreover, dowry provision is regarded as termination of a father's responsibility to support his daughter – a custom that jeopardizes the wellbeing of divorced and widowed women. Central to gender inequities in the Arab region is the concept of honour (sharaf), which limits women's visibility around unrelated men and restricts their mobility in public places. Under this system, women lose status if they work outside the home, forcing them to remain marginalized in low-productivity, home-based economic activities and reinforcing male control over productive resources. Even within the home, women depend on men to manage their income and the budgeting of monthly expenses. These cultural patterns have undermined the effectiveness of legislation aimed at raising Arab women's status. If gender inequities in the Arab region are to be removed, women must be integrated into the development process from the beginning, given access to land, training, and credit, and provided with domestic technology to lessen the burden of household chores.

KIT Library code: 200068

139 Property, power, and the political economy of farming households in Costa Rica
SICK, D. *Human Ecology* 26(1998)2 p. 189-212 ill., tabs 44 lit.refs

The relationship between size of landholdings and household economic status is fairly clear, particularly in societies where agricultural exports dominate the economy. Less clear is the effect of differential access to and control of productive property within households and the ways in which it affects the economic opportunities of individual household members. Property holdings and inheritance patterns among coffee-producing households in two small rural communities in Perez Zeledon, Costa Rica, were examined. The results show that while cultural norms regulating labour contributions do affect the balance of authority within households, de facto property rights can significantly enhance an individual's decision-making power both within households and between generationally-related households. Unless new opportunities arise as population increases, coffee production expands and land becomes increasingly scarce, we shall likely see increased stratification both within households (as women inherit less land) and among households, as some sons inherit at the expense of other sons and daughters.

KIT Library code: 429811

140 Peasant women and access to land: customary law, state law and gender-based ideology: the case of the Toba-Batak (North Sumatra)
SIMBOLON, INDIRA JUDITKA. Author, Wageningen, 324 p. 1998 ill., maps. Doctoral diss. Wageningen. With Dutch summary. Bibliogr.: p. 303-320. Includes glossary ISBN 90-5485-887-7

This study discusses the opportunities, constraints and strategies relating to access to land of peasant women who live in the changing Toba-Batak patrilineal community of North Sumatra, Indonesia. Fieldwork was undertaken in North Tapanuli District during 1993-94. Peasant women's access to land is seen in the wider context of the pressure of land scarcity due to the individualization, 'statization' (increasing state control and allocation) and privatization of communal land. Access to land is gained, prevented and diminished through the three processes of adat (customary law), privatization and statization. Toba-Batak women mainly gain access to land through adat, namely through social identity based on descent and residence in interfamilial relations. Under the pressure of the ongoing processes of statization and privatization, peasant women see that it is not the local men, their husbands or male relatives, who ultimately deny their rights to land. Both men and women see the state's enormous authority and private investors' privileges as the real threat to their communal identity, and it is their communal identity that guarantees their social and economic security as a whole. Therefore, the struggle for peasant women's rights to land should be seen in a wider context, and placing emphasis solely on women's individual rights is not always appropriate. State hegemony over land is not only achieved through imposing state or state-derived land rights on the local people or their land. The state expands its hegemony by establishing administrative and political institutions down to the village level. The implementation of often contradictory state programmes and policies is equally detrimental to the majority of the local people.

KIT Library code: 231666

141 Women's land rights: a case study from the northern Transvaal
SMALL, JANET. In: *Women, land and authority: perspectives from South Africa* ed. by Shamim Meer. Oxfam, Oxford p. 45-52 1997 lit.refs in notes

A case study is presented of women's land rights and authority structures based on interviews conducted in 1994 in three villages in the Northern Transvaal. In this area, men control the affairs of the communities, including land

tenure, and women's access to land has been weakened by the fragmentation of households in response to economic forces. The chapter describes the socioeconomic context of the study area and discusses how women's lands rights have been based on their relationships with men. Customary marriage and divorce laws compel women to reconcile with husbands who abandoned them even if the husbands have another wife. The local government structure also affords the highest status and decision-making power to married men. Only one village has adopted major changes that give women power to participate in decision-making due to the desire of migrant men to have their views represented by their wives. Consideration of natural resource allocation reveals that women who collect natural resources are excluded from decision-making. Policy changes to foster sustainability must involve women or they will fail. It is concluded that women are highly aware of the problems they face; that infrastructure development is urgently needed to improve women's lives; that local governments must ensure the participation of women; and that giving independent residential land rights to women will increase their independence from men and their ability to resist discrimination.
KIT Library code: 429833

142   The status of women is the major causative factor in the persistence of hunger
HUNGER PROJECT <http://www.thp. org> Global Office, East 26th Street, New York, NY 10010, USA. <info@thp.org> 8 p. September 2000

Some 80% of food for subsistence and sale is grown by Africa's 100 million rural women. On a daily basis, women's work includes multiple chores both within and outside the household. However, women are frequently malnourished, illiterate, overworked, underskilled, mistreated and powerless. They own only 1% of the land and have restricted access to credit. They have a low social and economic status, are dependent on their husbands, and may even have an 'inherent inferiority complex'. In addition, they are poorly represented in government.
URL: http://www.thp.org/prize/99/status_women.htm

143   Standing at the crossroads: WLSA and the rights dilemma: which way do we go?
STEWART, J.E.; NCUBE, W.; DENGU-ZVOBGO, K.C. WLSA, Harare 48 p. ca. 1998. Includes lit.refs

Women and Law in South Africa (WLSA) has been undertaking research into issues affecting women and the family for nearly a decade. During this period, a considerable body of data has been built up by the six countries in the

network: Botswana, Lesotho, Mozambique, Swaziland, Zambia and Zimbabwe. WLSA has come to profoundly question the way in which rights are conceptualized, administered and delivered. Persistently, WLSA research has revealed that although women have clearly exercisable rights at law, for a variety of reasons they do not pursue them, thereby perpetuating their exclusion from participation, often because of the dominant male ideologies and perceptions that will affect them in other areas of their lives. They thus opt out of their legal entitlements or they bargain away these rights to secure a place within their families, communities and society. A fundamental tenet of WLSA's approach to solving these problems is that it must start from the revaluing of women's roles and women's realms whilst at the same time pursuing the inclusion of women in the public sphere as full and equal partners to men. This work describes not only the realities of women's lives but also explores women's expectations and women's values. Guaranteeing women's right to participate in the full spectrum of economic spheres in every society, as well as providing the mechanisms to take up such guarantees, must be a primary concern of every government.
KIT Library code: 241001

144   Democratization and women's rights in the South African constitution: the challenge of African customary law
THANDABANTU NHLAPO, RONALD. *World Culture Report. Highlights.* Sector for Culture, United Nations Educational, Scientific and Cultural Organisation (UNESCO) <http://www. unesco.org/ culture/> UNESCO, 7 place de Fontenoy, 75352 Paris 07 SP, France. 3 p. 2000

A fundamental question is to know how notions of culture and cultural diversity should be accommodated in constitutional structures that actively seek to promote the values of democracy and fundamental rights. Tracing a link between culture and African customary law, especially African family law, and the provisions of the South African constitution relating to African customary law and fundamental rights, some inevitable tensions are identified between the different set of provisions, centred primarily around the question of women's rights and gender equality. The major point of friction between customary laws and practices, on the one hand, and individuals rights, on the other, is the matter of patriarchy. A list of cultural practices, related to marriage and supported by customary law, is compiled to demonstrate the sources of such tension. A two-pronged strategy is proposed to deal with these problems: the cultures themselves

gender perspectives

need to adapt to changing imperatives; and judicial and legislative methods should be designed to realize the goals of the constitution. Creativity is going to be required on the part of both the courts and the legislators. It is possible to accommodate culture and cultural arrangements in the context of a modern constitution without sacrificing fundamental rights, even in the sensitive area of women's human rights.
URL: http://www.unesco.org/culture/worldreport/html_eng/wcrb24.htm

145   Access to land: a rural perspective on tradition and resources
THORP, L. In: *Women, land and authority: perspectives from South Africa* ed. by Shamim Meer. Oxfam, Oxford p. 35-34 1997 lit.refs in notes
An outline is provided of initial findings and tentative policy recommendations arising from the African Jurisprudence Law Survey pilot project that sought to determine prevailing conditions in customary law governing land access and tenure, especially as they affect rural women. Data for this qualitative evaluation were collected through interviews with 28 men and 26 women of varying socioeconomic backgrounds living in various parts of the country. The survey results are presented in terms of the home/kraal ownership; the customary land-tenure system; land 'ownership' and security of tenure; women's role in the land tenure system; hopes for land distribution; and how land should be redistributed. Another perspective is provided by describing the community of Cornfields, a land tenure system that mixes title deeds and traditional land-holding practices. Policy issues and recommendations arising from this pilot study are that 1) customary tenure must be incorporated into any 'new' land tenure scheme; 2) the traditional system affords security because land can be assigned to people without money; 3) the customary system is marked by constantly changing rules and norms, so land reform efforts should identify and move with these reforms; 4) policymakers must consult the intended beneficiaries of the policies and listen to previously disadvantaged members of the community; and 5) information about reforms should be widely disseminated.
KIT Library code: 429834

146   Women's empowerment through rights to house and land
TINKER, IRENE In: *Women's rights to house and land: China, Laos, Vietnam* ed. by Irene Tinker, Gale Summerfield. Rienner, Boulder, CO p. 9-26 1999
Women's rights to house and land in rural and urban situations have not, until recently, been

deemed a critical problem by scholars or practitioners concerned with development issues. Development projects focused on rural areas and sought to relieve the drudgery of subsistence living, improve income, provide credit, and increase agricultural production within families. As families everywhere disintegrate, cultural traditions that protected women are collapsing. To survive, women need the security of land and house to provide income and shelter for their children, and they need the power to control who shares the house. Pressures from population growth on agricultural land, together with land consolidation by wealthy landowners and agribusinesses are causing land shortages and increasing landlessness. Women are particularly vulnerable because land they farm is seldom regarded as their own either under customary or civil law. The current state of women's rights to land and housing in developing countries is here surveyed. Efforts to recognize women's economic rights through development programmes are reviewed, and the issues of poverty and female-headed households are discussed, as well as the factors that empower women in household bargaining. A geographical examination of land and housing problems and possible solutions is provided. Finally, an analysis is presented of suggested laws and practices that could provide women with some claim to land and housing, as well as existing laws that could be enforced to protect women's rights. A growing number of NGOs are working with poor women in both rural and urban areas to help them defend their access to land and housing, understand their legal rights and organize for self-protection.
KIT Library code: 427153

147   Women and rural land in Vietnam
TRAN THI VAN ANH. In: *Women's rights to house and land: China, Laos, Vietnam* ed. by Irene Tinker, Gale Summerfield. Rienner, Boulder, CO p. 95-114 1999 ill. lit.refs in notes
Following a review of land use in Vietnam, women's access to and use of land in the periods before and after 'doi moi' are addressed, highlighting the discrepancies between women's rights to land in theory and the diverse realities in the rural areas of Vietnam. The impact of the shift from farming on collective land to farming on land controlled by the household or an individual is examined. The effects of the land laws of 1988 and 1993 on land allocation and the land use rights of the farmer families and women in particular, are discussed in terms of the actual process of land division and allocation; the quality of allocated land; the status of landless and land-poor farmers; and land use registration.

It is shown that under the law, women farmers were given the same opportunities for access to land as men. In practice, however, women were hardly ever involved in the implementation process. In addition, there are many gaps in the legislation pertaining to land division in marriage and after divorce that adversely affect women. Disputes are arising between family members, which are not covered by the land law or the family and marriage law.

148   Meret shehena, 'brothers' land': S.F. Nadel's land tenure on the Eritrean plateau revisited
TRONVOLL, KJETIL. *Africa* 70(2000)4 p. 595-613
29 lit.refs. With English and French summary
ISSN 0001-9720

The contemporary practice in the Eritrean highlands of the communal land tenure system called 'meret shehena' is described. Following a brief history of land reforms in Eritrea, the ethnography of the system is explained, in terms of the rules defining rights of habitation and access to land, and the process of land rotation and management. Attention is also given to women's right of access to land. Comparisons with observations reported by Nadel, an anthropologist, in his 1950s publication 'Land tenure on the Eritrean Plateau', are drawn throughout the ethnographic presentation to identify aspects of continuity and change. It appears that the customary operational guidelines of the system have been virtually unaffected by the wars and political turbulence that have taken place during the last 50 years. By way of conclusion, the new land tenure law is discussed and some points of concern are raised about how the new system will affect the Eritrean highland peasantry.

149   Gender and land rights in Mexico: a case study from southern Veracruz
VÁZQUEZ GARCÍA, VERÓNICA. *Journal of Iberian and Latin American Studies* 3(1997)1, <http://www.his.latrobe. edu.au/> Department of History, La Trobe University, Bundoora, Victoria, Australia 3083. <s.niblo@latrobe.edu.au> 15 p. Colegio de Postgraduados en Ciencias Agrícolas, Texcoco, Mexico.

This article examines the mechanisms that exclude women from land distribution processes in rural Mexico and the strategies used by some of them to obtain land. Data were collected during fieldwork in 1993 and 1994. A Nahua-speaking community of southern Veracruz is used as a case study. First, work and property relations in

Pajapan households and the increasing separation of women from land during the cattle-raising period (1950–1980) placed them in a disadvantaged position when the land was distributed in 1981. Women were also at a disadvantage regarding the organizations through which the land rights were delivered. The legal criteria defining beneficiary status also contributed to the exclusion of women. Despite this, women in Pajapan employed the most effective discourses available to them to articulate their land claims. These discourses were based on kinship or on state-defined forms of land tenure.

150   Reforming property rights in Laos
VIRAVONG, MANIVONE. In: *Women's rights to house and land: China, Laos, Vietnam* ed. by Irene Tinker, Gale Summerfield. Rienner, Boulder, CO p. 153-162 1999

Lowland Lao women's power and decision-making ability in the home contrast strongly with their lack of power outside the home. This contrast has set the stage for their loss of traditional property rights as male-dominated governmental agencies formally allocate and register land use rights, possibly reducing women's decision-making power in the home and community. Strategies to avoid these negative effects are outlined. Some strategies have already been attempted to include women's legal rights in the land allocation and titling process, but these have so far been insufficient. Continued training and monitoring of allocation and titling teams, gender awareness, and constitutional rights for women seem essential. Greater effort must also be made to ensure that information about the land allocation and registration processes is made available to all affected women. It remains a challenge to implement constitutionally mandated gender equality for Laotian women during Laos's economic transition. More information, education, institutional change and community development are needed to enable women to have equal access to all opportunities and resources so that they can contribute to the sustainable development of their country.

151   Land reform and gender in post-apartheid South Africa
WALKER, CHERRYL. *UNRISD discussion paper 98*. UNRISD, Geneva, 21 p. 1998. Includes lit.refs
ISSN 1012-6511

Post-apartheid South Africa has embarked on a market-driven programme of land reform that aims to redress the injustices of the land

distribution system, reduce poverty, contribute to sustainable land use and economic development, and establish tenure security for all. The programme also includes a policy commitment to gender equality as a long-term goal. Gender issues are addressed in the three components of the programme: land redistribution, land restitution, and tenure reform. Designing and implementing the land reform strategy remains a difficult task for a number of reasons, the greatest constraint being the lack of capacity on the part of the government. Government employees are often not trained to engage in awareness raising and organizational development, and there are no detailed guidelines on how to ensure that women are not marginalized in land reform processes. There may also be hostility towards interventions. A second constraint is associated with the strength of patriarchal attitudes and the government's reluctance to intervene to curb the powers of traditional authorities at local level. A further constraint is created by the absence of a strong lobby campaigning for women's land rights in rural areas. The extent to which women can benefit from land reform is limited by their lack of knowledge of the formal structures and legal opportunities being put in place. The NGO sector has a major responsibility to raise rural women's awareness of the opportunities arising for them and to help build women's organizations at local level. While there have been some encouraging initiatives, the overall level of organization is weak. There is also a real disjuncture between the demand for rapid land reform and the time needed to build women's capacity to maximize the opportunities that land reform holds for them.
KIT Library code: 228948

152   Cornfields, gender and land

WALKER, CHERRYL. In: *Women, land and authority: perspectives from South Africa* ed. by Shamim Meer. Oxfam, Oxford p. 55-73 1997 lit.refs in notes

A case study is presented based on a 1994 assessment of Cornfields, a pioneering land redistribution scheme on a freehold farm owned by a Trust in KwaZulu-Natal. Although the Trust's legal framework for acquisition has been established, questions remain about participation eligibility, determination of land use, and management. This chapter considers the categories of residents (landlords and tenants) involved in the Trust in order to identify barriers to membership, and also explores the gender issues that govern women's access to land, property, inheritance, and community decision-making. Data for this study were gathered

through household surveys, focus group discussions, interviews with key informants, and a literature survey. The analysis sketches the history of Cornfields and considers Trust membership in terms of gender and tenure; employment; cattle ownership; reasons for not joining; and ways of dealing with those who lack the funds to join. The next section looks at the expectations for Trust land; infrastructure developments needed; the significance of agriculture; and controls on access and use. The chapter then analyses the Trust Committee, the role of the Chief and the role of women. Further consideration of women's status at Cornfields centres on changing family forms; the power, status, and authority of the household head; women's access to land, property, and inheritance; and women's representation on community structures. While women are disadvantaged in other ways, there is no pattern of gross inequality with regard to Trust membership or ownership of cattle. The author ends by considering the implications of these findings for development of gender-sensitive land reform policies.
KIT Library code: 429832

153   Land tenure and institutional capacity

WOLDEGIORGIS, ORIGINAL. NOVIB partners forum on sustainable land use, Addis Ababa 26 p. 1999. Includes lit.refs

The recent history of land tenure in Ethiopia is reviewed and the deficiencies of the current landholding system are identified. The advent of the Ethiopian Peoples Revolutionary Democratic Front as state power in May 1991 saw the dissolution of many institutions established by the Derg administration. In 1994, the Kebele Administration (KA) was established as the lowest tier of the administrative system and as a replacement for the peasant associations. The KA is the key factor in land issues. It is shown that the KA reiterates traditional gender biases in the allocation of land and land-related resources. The Amhara and Tigray regional states have distributed land to the peasants and each has issued a proclamation about land rights. The approach to land distribution in Amhara is described and the role of indigenous institutions is discussed.
KIT Library code: 234100

154   Land tenure and gender

WOLDEGIORGIS, ORIGINAL. NOVIB partners forum on sustainable land use, Addis Ababa 21 p. 1999. Includes lit.refs National workshop on "Food security through sustainable land use: policy and implementation issues on institution, land tenure and extension", Addis Ababa, 1999

annotated bibliography

127

Recent land laws and proclamations in Ethiopia are reviewed and the land rights of women in female-headed households, as widows, divorcees, daughters and wives in polygamous marriages are discussed. The question of sustainability with respect to recent land distribution in the Amhara and Tigray Regions is examined. It is argued that land is the source of political, economic and social power. The need to improve the land rights of women is emphasized.
KIT Library code: 234103

155   Women and land rights in Kenya
Kenya Human Rights Commission, Nairobi 38 p. 1998 ill., tabs. Includes lit.refs
The problems women in Kenya face with regard to land rights are assessed. Women's access to and control over land and related resources are examined, focusing on the present conditions, experience and circumstances of women within different tenure regimes. Key policy considerations and debates are also raised. It is argued that women's equal access to land is an issue that needs to be addressed within a broader discussion of land reform in Kenya. This is a controversial issue since women's equal access to land will challenge many existing beliefs, practices and traditions. Policy recommendations intended to ensure that women enjoy the benefits of land ownership without discrimination include: (1) promotion of joint registration of land titles by husbands and wives; (2) constitutional reform; (3) equal representation of men and women on Land Boards; (4) legislative reform; (5) establishment of the Land Use Commission to look into the issue of land reform; and (6) adoption of an affirmative action policy to involve more women in the political process.
KIT Library code: 234562

156   Women and land tenure
FAO Focus: Women and food security
Food and Agriculture Organisation (FAO) <http://www.fao.org> FAO, Viale delle Terme di Caracalla, 00100 Rome, Italy. 4 p. March 1997
One of the most serious obstacles to increasing the agricultural productivity and income of rural women is their lack of security of tenure. Historically, women's access to land was based on status within the family and involved right of use, not ownership. Land reform, legislative reform and the forces of modernization have had a mixed effect on women's access to land. Ways of overcoming barriers to women's ownership of land are proposed. Finally, limitations on married women's property ownership in a number of Latin American countries is reviewed.
URL: http://www.fao.org/focus/e/women/tenure-e.htm

157   The women's handbook
CENTRE FOR ADULT EDUCATION, University of Natal-Pietermaritzburg; Midland's Women Group; Commission on Gender Equality (CGE) <http://www.cge. org.za> CGE, 10th Floor, Braamfontein Centre, Braamfontein 2017. <cgeinfo@cge. org.za> 405 p. undated.
This is a comprehensive handbook on women's rights for women living in the Ndlovu Regional Council, also known as the KwaZulu-Natal Midlands, although much would be relevant to all South African women. It is written so that women with a few years of schooling (standard five or grade seven) can read it and it is available free of charge in English, Zulu, Afrikaans and Xhosa. The book tells of the rights that all South Africans should have, referring to the Women's Charter and explaining how the laws are made. The powers and responsibilities of different parts of the Government are reviewed, as well as groups that are supposed to protect these rights such as the Commission on Gender Equality. There is detailed information on many different subjects, namely marriage and divorce; homosexuality; government help and grants for the aged and disabled; police, courts and legal help; death; violence; women's health and health services; children and youth; services; work; transport; land and housing; self-employment; and working together and lobbying. The information covers women's rights, what the law says, how to deal with problems and contact details of local organizations that can help. Workshops were held throughout the region to consult women on their opinion of important issues that should be covered in the handbook and to provide feedback on the draft versions. Although this handbook covers one region in South Africa, it is a model of its kind and is therefore of interest to a far wider audience both within and outside South Africa.
URL: http://www.cge.org.za/publication.htm

158   De-intensification and the feminization of farming in China
YUNXIAN, W. *Gender Technology and Development* 3(1999)2 p. 189-214 ill., tabs 14 lit.refs
Economic policy reform in China initiated in 1978, and in particular the implementation of the 'household responsibility system', have brought about profound changes in gender roles and relations in agriculture. The impact of land management patterns on women's conditions and position and the consequent changes in gender relations are examined, using data from fieldwork in two villages in Zhejiang province as well as secondary information and data from farm surveys covering more than ten years. The collective farming facilities of earlier times are

now in disarray. Farming has become the primary occupation for many rural women, particularly married women, while men look for better-paid, off-farm employment opportunities. The deteriorating conditions in Chinese agriculture therefore affect mainly women, who are obliged to look after the land for family subsistence and food security though there is little earning from it. Patriarchal norms are gaining a firm foothold. The preference for male children is becoming stronger as the rural system disintegrates and there are increasing intrahousehold conflicts. Women's status is increasingly becoming incumbent on the husband's property while women, in their own right, have little or no control over land.

KIT Library code: 429775

159   Zimbabwe's Supreme Court decision denying women's inheritance rights violates international human rights treaties

URGENT ACTION ALERT, Sisterhood is Global Institute (SIGI) at: <http://www.sigi.org> SIGI, 1200 Atwater, Suite 2, Montreal, QC, Canada H3Z 1X4. <sigi@qc.aibn.com> 5 p. June 1999

In a case involving inheritance rights, the Supreme Court of Zimbabwe made a unanimous decision in April 1999 that gave precedence to customary law over the Constitution. The ruling that women cannot be considered equal to men before the law because of African cultural norms and the nature of African society violates several human rights treaties to which Zimbabwe is party. In the facts of the case, Venia Magaya, sued her half-brother for ownership of her deceased father's land after her brother evicted her from the home. Under the Constitution and international treaties, Magaya has the right to land. However, the Court ruled that women should not inherit land because women were not able to look after their original (birth) family because of their commitment to their new family due to marriage. The Musasa Project and several other women's rights organizations presented a petition protesting against the Magaya decision to the Supreme Court and the Parliament. The Courts response, reproduced in full, is unsatisfactory. Urgent action is needed to prevent this case from being used as a precedent for further degradation of women's rights. Readers are requested to write to the relevant authorities in Zimbabwe, details of which are provided.

URL: http://www.sigi.org/alert/ zimb0699.htm

160   Zimbabwe women's fight to put gender on the land agenda

NEW AFRICA *Guardian* <http://www.newafrica. com> Mikocheni Light Industry Area, P. O. Box 1287, Dar es Salaam, Tanzania. <webmaster@ newafrica.com> 2 p. January 1999

Some 70% of the agricultural labour force in Zimbabwe are women but they are unable to own land in their own right. Critics charge that the beneficiaries of the government's controversial land redistribution scheme will only benefit the black middle class and not women who are legally landless. As women do not have independent rights to land, they are completely dependent on their husbands for land, sometimes putting up with abuse for this reason. There is much resistance to women's land rights due to fear that it will lead to the break-up of families and divorce. Many NGOs are campaigning for women's land rights.

URL: http://www.newafrica.com/gender/articles/ land_agenda.htm

161   Current land policy in Latin America: regulating land tenure under neo-liberalism

ZOOMERS, ELISABETH BERNHARDINE; HAAR, GEMMA VAN DER. Royal Tropical Institute, Amsterdam 333 p. 2000 ill., maps, tabs. Bibliogr.: p. 311-327 ISBN 90-6832-137-4

A workshop on land in Latin America was held in Amsterdam, the Netherlands, in 1999. The aim of the conference was to collect experiences with land policy in Latin America, make a critical assessment of land tenure reform under neo-liberalism and contribute to the debate on how land policy could be used as an instrument for sustainable development. The results of the workshop and a selection of the papers are published in two volumes. The objective of this first volume is to present an overview of experiences with the privatization and individualization of land rights in different countries; to analyse the implications for different groups; and to assess the contribution to sustainable development. It includes case studies from Costa Rica, Mexico, Bolivia and Honduras. The chapters address a wide range of contemporary research issues, such as the consequences of privatization policies for agricultural production and environmental conservation; the struggle for land within the framework of new social movements and democratization; the precariousness of ownership arrangements with respect to environmental behaviour and nature conservation strategies; and the existence of a plurality of legal and normative systems with regard to land and natural resources. It is concluded that state policy should create flexible legal frameworks and be differentiated in order to respect the diversity of local situations as well as the wishes of the majority of the rural

population. Land policy should stimulate private investment in land and natural resource management and increase security over land, whilst maintaining cultural and spiritual values. Governments have an important task in making land legislation compatible with other laws, social goals and other fields of action.
KIT Library code: 247535

162   Land and sustainable livelihood in Latin America
ZOOMERS, ELISABETH BERNHARDINE. Royal Tropical Institute, Amsterdam 257 p. 2001 ill., maps, tabs. Includes lit.refs ISBN 90-6832-141-2 Land in Latin America: new context, new claims, new concepts, Amsterdam, 1999

This publication is based on the findings of a workshop on land in Latin America, held in Amsterdam, the Netherlands, in 1999. The results of the workshop and a selection of the papers are published in two volumes. This second volume focuses on the role of land in the livelihood strategies of farmers. It analyses the implications of changing land tenure regimes for land use and the income-generating capacity of farmers, as well as the consequences for the non-material aspects of life, such as prestige, identity and social relations. An attempt is made to provide an insider's view of rural life. Case studies are provided from Mexico, Nicaragua, Chile, Bolivia and Peru. Topics covered include: social and environmental interdependency in Bolivia; land reform and technology in Peru; conflict over natural resources and conservation in Mexico; income generation strategies among Nicaraguan agricultural producers; and land tenure and social change in Chile. It is concluded that man-land relationships need a conceptual update. The role of land in the livelihood strategies of farmers cannot be described in general or static terms; attention must be paid to the diversity and dynamics of livelihood strategies, the multidimensionality of land, and the institutional setting. Even though there is an important link between access to land and livelihood strategies, giving access to land will often not be sufficient to alleviate poverty or solve the problems of rural development.
KIT Library code: 248912

163   Audit of legislation that discrimination [sic] on the basis of sex/gender
ZYLICH, LANA; ALBERTYN, CATHI. Commission on Gender Equality (CGE) <http://www.cge.org.za> CGE, 10th Floor, Braamfontein Centre, Braamfontein 2017, South Africa. <cgeinfo@cge.org.za> 62 p. August 1998 Gender Research Project, Centre for Applied Legal Studies, University of Witwatersrand, Private Bag 3, Wits 2050, South Africa. <125je3wa@solon.law.wits.ac.za>

This is a comprehensive attempt to identify inequality and discrimination in the law of South Africa on the basis of sex and gender. Legislative discrimination is found to be both direct and indirect or systemic. South Africa has made progress in the elimination of direct discrimination in the law. Certain key areas of law still require immediate attention: the inequalities of the customary law of succession and inheritance; domestic and farm workers remain excluded from the benefits of the Unemployment Insurance Fund Act and the Compensation for Occupational Injuries and Diseases Act; gay and lesbian couples and families remain the subject of overt discrimination in the Marriages Act and other laws; and different sexual rights still exist in the Sexual Offences Act. The audit reveals that most of the inequality and discrimination experienced by women lies not in the letter of the law but in its impact. Discrimination lies in the absence of policies and programmes or in the existence of gender-biased or insensitive policies and programmes. Hence, a seemingly neutral law may adversely affect women or a good law may be poorly implemented or administered in a discriminatory manner. Such hidden and often systematic discrimination is difficult to identify. In the area of housing, the application of certain legal provisions does not go far enough in ensuring gender equality in the housing sphere. The regulations surrounding the implementation of the Births and Deaths Registration Act mean that women lose their name upon marriage and can only retain it with 'a good and sufficient reason'. Control, access and quality of water inequitably reside with those enjoying riparian rights and land ownership. This means that rural women, who historically do not own land and whose traditional duty is to ensure that the household is supplied with water, have to travel long distances carrying heavy loads of water. The unequal value attached to women's work means that they receive unequal pay: the law has been unable to deal with this inequality. In addition, the treatment of women in the Courts is often based on myths and stereotypes that result in discrimination and inequality.
URL: http://ww.cge.org.za/docs/contents11.htm

gender perspectives

Author Index

(numbers refer to abstract numbers)

Achieng', Judith, 001
Adams, M., 002
Adoko, Judy, 003, 004
Afkhami, Mahnaz, 005
Agarwal, Bina, 006, 007, 008
Ahmad, Anis, 009
Aidoo, J.B., 123
Albertyn, Cathi, 163
Alden, Wily Liz, 010
Alderman, Harold, 063
Al-Hibri, Azizah Y., 011
Allen, Jennifer, 012
Andrew, Nancy, 013
Armar-Klemesu, Margaret, 095
Armstrong, Alice K., 014
Asiama, Seth Opuni, 015

Basu, Srimati, 016, 017, 018, 019
Bauer, Heidi M., 128
Benda-Beckmann, Keebet von, 020
Berg, Adri van den, 021
Beydoun, Rana, 012
Bhaskar, Manu, 022
Blackwood, E., 023
Brown, Lynn R., 100
Bunch, Charlotte, 103

Cavin, Anne-Claude, 024
Cawthorne, Maya, 025
Chekir, Hafidha, 026
Chen, Martha Alter, 027, 028
Chenaux-Repond, M., 029
Chenje, M., 109
Cleaver, Frances, 030
Cole, Josette, 029, 031
Combrinck, Helene, 032
Córdova Plaza, Rosío, 034
Cossman, Brenda, 075
Cross, Catherine, 035, 036
Crowley, Eve, 037

Deere, Carmen Diana, 038, 039, 040, 041, 042, 043, 089
Dengu, E., 109
Dengu-Zvobgo, K.C., 143
Diof, Jacques, 044
Dolan, Catherine S., 045
Duncan, Beatrice Akua, 046
Dutt, Mallika, 103
Dwyer, Peter D., 047

Edmunds, David, 130
Esack, Farid, 048

Farha, Leilana, 049, 050
Feldstein, Hilary Sims, 100
Flavia, Agnes, 051
Flowers, Nancy, 103
Fortmann, Louise, 052
Friedman, Michelle, 035

Goebel, Allison, 054
Gopal, Gita, 055
Graham, A.W., 057
Gray, Leslie, 058
Griffiths, Anne M.O., 059
Grigsby, W.J., 060
Gwako, Edwins Laban Moogi, 061, 062

Haar, Gemma van der, 161
Haddad, Lawrence, 063
Hanchinamani, Bina, 064
Hasan, Zoya, 065
Hilmy, Nabil A., 066
Hoddinott, John, 063

Iacopino, Vincent, 128
Ireson-Doolittle, Carol, 067
Izumi, Kaori, 068

Jacobs, Susie, 069, 070
Jalal, Patricia Imrana, 071, 072, 073

Kadirgamar-Rajasingham, Sakuntala, 133
Kalabamu, Faustin, 074
Kapur, Ratna, 075
Karanja, Perpetua Wambui, 076
Karuru, Njeri, 111
Kevane, Michael, 058
Kehren, Tatjana, 077
Khadiagala, Lynn S., 078
Kibwana, Kivutha, 079
Kinnear, Karen L., 080
Knowles, Jane B., 076
Koda, B., 081
Kompe, Lydia, 082

LaFont, Suzanne, 083
Lange, Roel de, 086
Larbi, Wordsworth O., 095
Lastarria-Cornhiel, Susana, 087
Lee-Smith, Diana, 088
León, Magdalena, 038, 039, 040, 041, 042, 043, 089
Lyne, M.C., 057

Maanen, Gerrit van, 086
Maluccio, John A., 122
Maluwa, Tiyanjana, 090
Manji, Ambreena, 091, 092
Manos, M. Michele, 128
Mapetla, Matseliso, 093
Marcuse, Peter, 094

Maxwell, Daniel, 095
Mayer, Ann Elizabeth, 096
Mbiba, Beacon, 097
Meer, Shamim 035, 098, 099, 141, 145, 152
Meinzen-Dick, Ruth Suseela, 100
Mendoza, L.D., 101
Menski, Werner F., 102
Mertus, Julie, 103
Minnegal, Monica, 047
Mjoli-Mncube, Nonhlanhla, 104
Monsoor, Taslima, 105
Mtengeti-Migiro, Rose, 106
Mukhopadhyay, Maitrayee, 107
Mukund, Kanakalatha, 108
Mutefpa, F., 109, 110
Mwagiru, Makumi, 111

Nadeau, Marc, 012
Naggita, Esther Damalie, 112
Nasir, Jamal Jamil, 113
Naylor, Rachel, 114
Ncube, W., 143
Ngubane, Sizani, 115

Odgaard, Rie, 116
Okeke, Phil E., 117
Otsuka, Keijiro, 123
Owen, Margaret, 118

Payongayong, Ellen, 123
Peters, Beverly L., 119
Peters, John E., 119
Phipps, Nicole, 012

Quisumbing, Agnes R., 100, 120, 121, 122, 123
Qvist, Ewa, 124

Rana, Bandana, 125
Rana, Kumar, 126, 127
Rao, Nitya, 126, 127
Rasekh, Zohra, 128
Rehmtulla, Shamshad, 129
Rocheleau, Dianne, 130
Rozario, Santi, 131
Rugadya, Margaret, 132

Salim, Myriam, 055
Schuler, Margaret A., 133, 134
Shehadeh, Lamia Rustum, 135
Shivji, Issa G., 136
Shrestha, Rajshree, 137
Shukri, Shirin J.A., 138
Sick, D., 139
Simbolon, Indira Juditka, 140
Small, Janet, 082, 141
Stewart, J.E., 143
Summerfield, Gale, 067, 146, 150
Sweetman, Caroline, 068, 114

Thakur, Himendra, 102
Thandabantu Nhlapo, Ronald, 144
Thomas, Dorothy Q., 134
Thorp, L., 145
Tinker, Irene, 146, 147
Tisdell, Clem, 077
Toomel, Katrin, 049
Tran Thi Van Anh, 147
Tronvoll, Kjetil, 148
Trujillo, Catalina, 088

Vaziri, Haleh, 005
Vázquez García, Verónica, 149
Viravong, Manivone, 150

Walker, Cherryl, 151,152
Walt, Johan van der 086
Woldegiorgis, Original, 153, 154

Yunxian, W., 158

Zakariah, Sawudatu, 095
Zoomers, Elisabeth Bernhardine, 161, 162
Zylich, Lana, 163

Geographical index

(numbers refer to abstract numbers)

Afghanistan, 128
Australia, 073

Bangladesh, 066, 105, 118, 122, 131, 133
Bolivia, 043, 161, 162
Botswana, 014, 025, 059, 074, 109, 110, 143
Brazil, 042
Burkina Faso, 024

Cameroon, 021
Caribbean region, 083, 133
Chile, 038, 040, 162
China, 146, 158
Colombia, 038, 040, 089
Cook islands, 071, 072, 073
Costa Rica, 038, 040, 139, 161

Egypt, 066, 124
El Salvador, 038, 040
Eritrea, 049, 055, 148
Ethiopia, 055, 122, 153, 154

Gambia, 030
Ghana, 015, 046, 095, 114, 118, 123, 133
Guatemala, 041, 049

Honduras, 038, 040, 161

India, 006, 007, 008, 016, 017, 018, 019, 022, 027,
    028, 051, 065, 075, 102, 107, 108, 118, 124, 126,
    127, 133
Indonesia, 023, 122, 140
Iraq, 066
Islamic countries, 005, 011, 048, 065, 113

Jamaica, 083
Jordan, 066, 138

Kenya, 045, 055, 061, 062, 076, 079, 111, 129, 155
Kiribati, 071, 072

Laos, 067, 146, 150
Latin America, 030, 031, 038, 039, 040, 042, 156,
    161, 162
Lebanon, 135
Lesotho, 014, 093, 143
Liberia, 049

Malawi, 118
Mexico, 034, 038, 040, 133, 149, 161, 162
Mozambique, 014, 025, 031, 064, 109, 110, 118, 143

Nauru, 071, 072
Nepal, 125, 137

New Zealand, 073
Nicaragua, 038, 040, 162
Nigeria, 117, 118
North Africa, 096

Pakistan, 009, 056, 128
Papua New Guinea, 047
Peru, 038, 040, 133, 162
Philippines, 101, 121, 133

Rwanda, 050

Solomon Islands, 071, 072
South Africa, 001, 013, 014, 032, 035, 036, 057, 069,
    084, 085, 086, 096, 098, 099, 104, 109, 110, 115,
    122, 141, 143, 144, 145, 151, 152, 157, 163
South Asia, 070, 102
Southern Africa, 002, 014, 025, 031, 035, 052, 090,
    109, 110
Sri Lanka, 133
Sub-Saharan Africa, 001, 010, 053, 058, 068, 087,
    142, 144
Swaziland, 014, 025, 143
Sweden, 124

Tanzania, 024, 031, 055, 068, 081, 091, 092, 106,
    116, 118, 129, 136
Thailand, 077
Tonga, 071, 072
Tunisia, 026, 066, 096
Tuvalu, 071, 072

Uganda, 001, 003, 004, 010, 055, 078, 112, 118, 124,
    129, 132, 133
Ukraine, 124

Vanuatu, 071, 072
Vietnam, 146, 147

West Africa, 024, 060
Western Samoa, 071, 072

Yemen, 066

Zambia, 014, 025, 109, 110, 118, 143
Zimbabwe, 001, 014, 025, 029, 031, 052, 054, 055,
    068, 070, 097, 109, 110, 118, 119, 129, 133, 143,
    159, 160

geographical index

Web resources

Websites

Http://allafrica.com/women
Women's section of the AllAfrica news website. News articles can be searched by subject, country and region.

Http://www.apwld.org/
The Asia Pacific Forum on Women, Law and Development (APWLD) is an independent NGO committed to enabling women to use law as an instrument of social change. Their site offers a calendar of events, Forum news, publications, and access to their e-mail newsletter.

Http://www.arabwomencourt.org/womenscourt
Women's Court, the Permanent Arab Court to Resist Violence Against Women, aims to fight all forms of violence practised against women in Arab societies.

Http://www.cge.org.za/
The Commission on Gender Equality (CGE) is one of the six state institutions supporting constitutional democracy in South Africa. The aim of the Commission is to promote gender equality and to advise and make recommendations to parliament or any other legislature with regard to any laws or proposed legislation affecting gender equality and the status of women. Its site includes press releases, full-text publications of the Commission, and an online form for complaints.

Http://www.cospe.it/retedonne/Associazioni/col_rabat.htm
Collectif Maghreb Egalité '95, a network of women's associations, intellectuals and researchers, acting within the dynamic of the movement of defence of women's fundamental rights in the Maghreb (Algeria, Morocco, Tunisia). The site introduces the Collectif and presents a list of their publications.

Http://www.fao.org/Gender/en/agri-e.htm
The Agriculture section on FAO's Gender and Food Security site includes information and documents on land tenure and land management.

Http://www.hrlawgroup.org/site/overview/ourwork.htm
Site of the International Human Rights Law Group, a US-based non-profit organization of human rights and legal professionals engaged in human rights advocacy, litigation and training around the world. Their work includes the areas of women's rights advocacy and rule of law programmes. The site presents information on their programmes in the various countries, reports and press releases.

Http://www.hrw.org/women
Women's Rights section of the Human Rights Watch website. Site includes news releases, current events, and publications on women's rights all over the world.

Http://www.igc.org/iwraw/
Site of the International Women's Rights Action Watch (IWRAW), a global network that monitors the implementation of the Convention on the Elimination of All Forms of Discrimination against Women (CEDAW). The site offers access to past and current IWRAW publications, including country reports, and provides instructions and sample documents for NGOs participating in the CEDAW reporting mechanism.

Http://mwengo.org/land/features.htm
LandWeb presents news and information on NGOs and land advocacy in eastern and southern Africa. Also included are country reports and a land directory.

Http://www.muslimtents.com/sistersinislam/
Sisters in Islam (SIS) is a group of Muslim professional women committed to promoting the rights of women within the framework of Islam. The site offers discussions of issues and themes, including equality and domestic violence, presents publications, letters to the editor and reports on events.

Http://www.nlc.co.za/landrigh.htm
The National Land Committee (NLC) in South Africa has been carrying out the Land Rights and Access Programme since 1985. The programme's goal is to reverse the racially skewed land ownership patterns and to defend the rights of the rural poor, especially women and other vulnerable groups.

Http://www.nwjc.org.au/
The National Women's Justice Coalition (NWJC) promotes women's equality before the law in Australia by raising awareness, networking, lobbying and advocating. The site contains links to and information on current issues, a reading room, and access to the Australian Virtual Centre for Women & the Law.

web resources

Http://www.oneworld.org/empoweringwidows
This is the website of Empowering Widows in
Development, a small UK-based NGO founded in
1996. It aims to: raise awareness and
understanding of the problems encountered by
widows in developing countries; promote the
status of widows' rights on the international
human rights agenda; and assist developing
country organizations that support widows in
fighting for their rights. The website contains
international news, resources and a law file.

Http://www.oxfam.org.uk/landrights/eafrica/
index.html
The Oxfam Land Rights Resource Bank for East
Africa (Burundi, Kenya, Rwanda, Tanzania,
Uganda) offers summaries of Oxfam papers on
land tenure and rights in East Africa. The papers
can be downloaded as full-text documents.

Http://www.pgaction.org/will/index.htm
The Women in Legislation League (WILL) is a
subsection of the Parliamentarians for Global
Action website, which was added during the
Beijing Plus Special Session in New York in 2001.
WILL functions as an online legislative resource
centre to disseminate gender-related legislation
and monitor country commitments to the 12
critical areas identified in the Beijing Platform
for Action.

Http://www.un.org/womenwatch/daw/cedaw
Convention on the Elimination of All Forms of
Discrimination against Women (CEDAW)
website. The site presents the text of the
Convention, general recommendations, country
reports, optional protocol, and reports on the
sessions of the UN Committee on the Elimination
of Discrimination against Women.

Http://www.unifem.undp.org/hrights.htm
Women's' Human Rights section of the UNIFEM
website.

Http://wbln0018.worldbank.org/essd/essd.nsf/
ruraldevelopment/portal
The World Bank's Rural Development and
Agriculture portal offers access to the Land
Policy Network (LPN), an information resource
for researchers, policymakers and practitioners
involved in land policy in developing countries.
Click on Land Policy in the list of Key Issues. The
LPN site includes a question and answer service,
papers and tools, conference reports, and a
newsletter.

Http://www.wld.org/
Women, Law and Development International is a
human rights organization. Their site offers
news, information on their programmes and
other work, and access to their full-text online
newsletters.

Http://www.wlsa.co.zw
Women and Law in Southern Africa (WLSA)
Research Trust is a research organization in
seven countries of southern Africa: Botswana,
Lesotho, Malawi, Mozambique, Swaziland,
Zambia and Zimbabwe. Their site includes a list
of publications, information on their
programmes, and offers access to their online
newsletter.

Http://www.wits.ac.za/cals/cals.html
The Centre for Applied Legal Studies (CALS) of
the University of Witwatersrand, South Africa,
works on human rights issues. Its research
programme includes the Land Rights Research
Programme with a project on women and land,
and the Gender Research Project.

Articles and short papers

Http://africaonline.com/site/Articles/1,3,21642.jsp
'African women's inheritance rights initiative' by
the Integrated Regional Information Network
(IRIN). 15 August 2001. 1 p.

Http://www.ahrchk.net/solidarity/199811/
v811_13.htm
'Land, property and adequate housing: women's
human rights' by Leilani Farha. In: Human
Rights Solidarity, 8 (1998)11, 3 p. A publication of
the Asian Human Rights Commission.

Http://www.earthsummit2002.org/wcaucus/
Caucus%20Position%20Papers/land/land.htm
'Land management' by Diana Lee-Smith and
Catalina Trujillo. 1999. 5 p. Position paper on land
resources on behalf of the UN Commission on
Sustainable Development (CSD) NGO Women's
Caucus, Earth Summit.

Http://www.epw.org.in/34-21/sa3.htm
'Property rights for women: case for joint titles
to agricultural land and urban housing' by Jeemol
Unni. 11 p. Economic and Political Weekly, May
22–28, 1999

Http://www.equalitynow.org/action_eng_17_1.html
'Uganda: exclusion of women from land ownership' is a brief review of the current situation of women's land rights in Uganda and recommended actions to promote land rights for women. 2 p.

Http://www.fao.org/waicent/faoinfo/sustdev.wpdirect/wpan0001.htm
'Gender, land and fertility: women's access to land and security of tenure' by Jacques du Guerny. FAO, March 1996. 5 p.

Http://www.hri.ca/fortherecord2000/documnetation/commission/2000-13.htm
'Women's equal ownership of, access to and control over land and the equal rights to own property and to adequate housing.' Commission on Human Rights, resolution 2000/13. 3 p.

Http://www.ifpri.cgiar.org/2020/focus/focus06/focus06_02.htm
'Land rights' by Eve Crowley. In: Empowering women to achieve food security.
Focus 6, Brief 2 of 12, August 2001. 3 p.

Http://www.nepalnews.com.np/contents/englishdaily/ktmpost/2001/jul/jul18/index1.htm
'Women to get parental property even after marriage' by Binaj Gurubacharya. The Kathmandu Post, July 18, 2001. 2 p.

Http://news.bbc.co.uk/hi/english/world/south_asia/newsid_1175000/1175614.stm
'Nepali women fight for their share', Daniel Lak. BBC News, 17 February, 2001. 4 p.

Http://www.oneworld.org/ips2/june99/15_20_055.html
'Rights–Bangladesh: women demand equality, Government cites religious bar' by Tabibul Islam. IPS World News, June 1999. 2 p.

Http://www.oneworld.org/ips2/may98/13_38_045.html
'Culture and religion limit women's access to land' by Nana Rosine Ngangoue. Rights-Africa section, World News of IPS (Inter Press Service), 1998. 2p.

Http://unesco-nairobi.unon.org/eamwa/issuesburundi.html
'Burundi: Bridging the gap in the struggle for land rights in Burundi' by Jocelyne Sambira. East Africa Media Women Association, 27 April 2001. 2 p.

Http://www.womenenews.com
'Ugandan women seek right to own land' by Jennifer Bakyawa. Women's E-News, 4 September 2001. 3 p.

Http://www.worldbank.org/afr/findings/english/find126.htm
'Gender and Law: Eastern Africa speaks': a brief report on the progress achieved with the Gender and Law Programme carried out in Ethiopia, Kenya, Tanzania, Uganda, Zimbabwe. Briefings, no. 126, January 1999. 5 p.

About the authors

Lina Abou-Habib currently works as project coordinator of the Machreq Maghreb Gender Linking Information Project (MACMAG-GLIP). She previously worked as Programme Coordinator in the Lebanon for Oxfam UK/Ireland, serving as the lead reference person on gender in the Middle East. Before this, she was seconded to the gender team at Oxfam UK/Ireland head office in Oxford where she concentrated on the Middle East with a particular focus on the Beijing preparations and programme research on disability, gender policy implementation and strategic planning.
Contact address:
Machreq Maghreb Gender Linking Information Project (MACMAG GLIP),
POB 165302, Achrafieh 11 00 2030, Beirut, Lebanon.
Tel: +961 1-611079
Fax: +961 1-612924
E-mail: labouhabib@macmag-glip.org
Website: www.women-machreq-maghreb.com

Fiona Archer works as a consultant in rural development in South Africa and supports a number of small projects on a voluntary basis. She gained a Masters in Archaeology and a teaching diploma from the Universities of Stellenbosch and Cape Town. She became involved in land issues through ethnobotanical studies, showing the importance of land and resources to the people of Namaqualand in the Northern Cape, South Africa. She subsequently became an activist in this sector from 1984 to 1994 and supported the development of women's organizations in the area for a number of years. From 1995–1999, she specialized in participatory processes that relate to community-based natural resource management, focusing on energy issues, integration of development and conservation and community based tourism. She also worked as an advisor on San land issues in the Ministry of Land Affairs while managing a national natural resource management programme and became Director of the South African San Institute in 1999.
Contact address:
8 Highstead Flats, 3 Highstead Road, Rondebosch, 7700, South Africa.
E-mail: archer@iafrica.com

Shoba Arun is a lecturer at the Women's Opportunities Unit, University of Ulster, and is the course director of the Masters Programme in Management and Professional Development for Women. Having obtained a PhD in sociology from the University of Manchester, the United Kingdom, she worked primarily in the area of gender and economic reforms, and on the role of ICTs in development.
Contact address:
Women's Opportunities Unit, School of Social and Community Sciences,
Dalriada Building, University of Ulster, Newtownabbey, N.Ireland, BT37 OQB.
Tel: +44 28-90366899
Fax: +44 28-90368201
Email: sv.arun@ulst.ac.uk

Rebecca Cook is Professor of Law at the University of Toronto, Canada, and a member of the Washington D.C. Bar.
Contact address:
Rebecca J. Cook, JD, JSD
Professor, Faculty of Law, University of Toronto,
78 Queen's Park Crescent, Toronto, Ontario, Canada M5S 2C5.
Tel: +416 978-4446
Fax: +416 978-7899
E-mail: rebecca.cook@utoronto.ca
Website: www.law-lib.utoronto.ca/diana

Sarah Cummings, **Henk van Dam**, **Angela Khadar** and **Minke Valk** are information specialists within the Gender Resource Unit, which forms part of the Information Services Department of KIT (Royal Tropical Institute) in the Netherlands. They are editors of the Gender, Society & Development series.
Contact address:
Gender Resource Unit, Information Services, KIT (Royal Tropical Institute),
P.O. Box 95001, 1090 HA, Amsterdam, the Netherlands.
Tel: +31 20-568 8594/ 8573/ 8347/ 8344
E-mail: s.cummings@kit.nl; h.v.dam@kit.nl; a.khadar@kit.nl; m.valk@kit.nl

Carmen Diana Deere is Professor of Economics and Director of the Center for Latin American, Caribbean and Latino Studies at the University of Massachusetts-Amherst, USA. During 2000 she held a Fulbright-Hays Faculty Research Fellowship at the Federal University of Rio de Janeiro. She has written extensively on Latin American agrarian reform processes, peasant household economics and rural women in Latin America. She is co-author (with Magdalena León) of 'Empowering women: land and property rights in Latin America', and 'Women in Andean agriculture: peasant production and rural wage employment in Colombia and Peru'. She is also co-editor (with León) of 'Rural women and state policy: feminist perspectives on Latin American agricultural development'.
Contact address:
Economics Dept., Univ. of Massachusetts, Amherst, MA 01003 USA.
E-mail: deere@econs.umass.edu

gender perspectives

Magdalena León, a sociologist, was previously Professor in the Faculty of Humanities and Social Sciences and Director of the Women and Gender Documentation Center at the National University of Colombia, Bogotá, Colombia. Currently, she is a visiting scholar at FLACSO-Quito, Ecuador. She is the editor of *Poder y empoderamiento de las mujeres and Mujeres y participación política: avances y desafíos en América Latina* and is also co-author of various books with Deere (see above).
E-mail: Leon@flacso.org.ec

Shamim Meer has worked as a consultant in the area of development since 1994. Her work has involved conducting evaluations, gender training, and facilitating processes for gender mainstreaming within organizations. She has worked with NGOs in rural development, urban development and human rights; with women's organizations; and with the trade union movement. Previously, she worked as a women's rights, community, media and political activist and was a co-founder of the publications SPEAK and Agenda, both of which focus on women's and gender issues. Her academic qualifications are in sociology and development studies. Her Masters thesis was on women's land rights in South Africa's Bantustans.
Contact address:
P.O. Box 45213, Mayfair 2108, Johannesburg, South Africa.
Tel: +27 11-8373239
E-mail: shamim@iafrica.com

Maitrayee Mukhopadhyay is a senior gender advisor to the Women and Development Programme at KIT (Royal Tropical Institute). She was previously a policy advisor for gender at Oxfam UK/Ireland where she was responsible for training and research related to the implementation of Oxfam gender policy with a specific geographic responsibility for South Asia and the Middle East. Maitrayee also has extensive experience as an international consultant and was course director and tutor for the Gender Planning and Training Programme at the Institute of Development Studies, UK. She has a PhD in Social Anthropology from the School of African and Asian Studies, University of Sussex, UK.
Contact address:
KIT Gender / IC, Royal Tropical Institute,
P.O. Box 95001, 1090 HA, Amsterdam, the Netherlands.
Tel: +31 20-568 8271
E-mail: m.mukhopadhyay@kit.nl

Jeanne Maddox Toungara is Associate Professor of History at Howard University in Washington, D.C. She received her doctorate in history from the University of California, Los Angeles, in 1980. Born in California, she has lived and worked for many years in Côte d'Ivoire, where she taught at the Université Nationale de Côte d'Ivoire. She regularly conducts field research on Ivorian traditions relating to the state and women, and she is a consultant and lecturer for non-governmental organizations on issues of development and Ivorian politics. She is also the executive secretary of the West African Research Association based in Washington, D.C. Her articles have appeared in the Journal of Modern African Studies, African History, and African Studies Review, and she is currently writing a book-length manuscript on traditions of the Malinke state of Kabasarama.

Contact address:
History Department, Howard University
2441 Sixth Street NW, Washington, D.C. 20059.
Tel: +202 806-6815
Fax: +202 806-4471
E-mail: jtoungara@howard.edu

gender perspectives